AQA

information &

communication

technology

for A2 Level

THIRD EDITION

Julian **Mott** ◀
Anne **Leeming** ◀

Edited by a Chief Examiner:
Helen Williams ◀

HODDER
EDUCATION
AN HACHETTE UK COMPANY

The Publishers would like to thank the following for permission to reproduce copyright material:

Photo credits:
p.1 © Palindra – Fotolia.com; **p.5** © mihaicalin/iStockphoto.com; **p.7** and **27** PhotoBox; **p.8** © D. Hurst/Alamy; **p.14** © Kuttig – People/Alamy; **p.40** *t* © PhotoAlto *b* Paxton Charities; **p.42** ©Photodisc/Getty Images; **p.44** ©Martin Firus/istockphoto.com; **p.54** *t* TV Licensing website, *b* DVLA website; **p.59** © PhotoAlto; **p.68** ©Photodisc/Getty Images; **p.71** © benjamin py – Fotolia.com; **p.73** © ManicBlu – Fotolia.com; **p.76** © deanm1974 – Fotolia.com; **p.93** © imagestopshop/Alamy; **p.103** Royal Borough of Windsor and Maidenhead's website; **p.111** Natural History Museum website; **p.117** ©Seapix/Alamy; **p.121** © PhotoAlto; **p.148** NHS Choose and Book website; **p.152** Acutest website; **p.188** Pass website; **p.190** Freeskills website; **p.200** and **201** dbapool; **p.212** © Simon Stacpoole/Rex Features; **p.214** © T.M.O.Buildings/Alamy; **p.218** Freelancers network website; **p.219** Regus website.

Acknowledgements:
p.12 Andrew Clark, *Guardian*, 27 April 2007; **p.14** Patrick Wintour, *Guardian*, 9 February 2008; **p.98** Brian Clegg, *PC Week*; **p.139** © APM Group Ltd 2002. Reproduced with permission; **p.198** Angelique Chrisafis, *Guardian*, 20 March 2003.

All exam questions reproduced with permission of the Assessment and Qualifications Alliance.

t = top, *b* = bottom, *l* = left, *r* = right, *c* = centre

Although every effort has been made to ensure that website addresses are correct at time of going to press, Hodder Education cannot be held responsible for the content of any website mentioned in this book. It is sometimes possible to find a relocated web page by typing in the address of the home page for a website in the URL window of your browser.

Hachette's policy is to use papers that are natural, renewable and recyclable products and made from wood grown in sustainable forests. The logging and manufacturing processes are expected to conform to the environmental regulations of the country of origin.

Orders: please contact Bookpoint Ltd, 130 Milton Park, Abingdon, Oxon OX14 4SB. Telephone: (44) 01235 827720. Fax: (44) 01235 400454. Lines are open 9.00 – 5.00, Monday to Saturday, with a 24-hour message answering service. Visit our website at www.hoddereducation.co.uk

© Julian Mott and Anne Leeming 2009
First published in 2009 by
Hodder Education
an Hachette UK Company
338 Euston Road
London NW1 3BH

Impression number   5 4 3 2 1
Year   2013 2012 2011 2010 2009

Cover photo TEK Image/Science Photo Library
Typeset in Stone Informal 11pt by DC Graphic Design Limited, Swanley Village, Kent
Printed in Italy

A catalogue record for this title is available from the British Library

ISBN-13: 978 0340 958 292

Contents

Emerging technologies

▶ Enabling devices for remote and mobile working

There have been great developments in devices that enable a user to carry out his work and keep in touch when away from the office. The now nearly universal mobile phone allows contact to be maintained almost anywhere. On virtually every train journey, you will find people carrying out work-related conversations using a mobile phone.

A **personal digital assistant (PDA)** is a device that acts as an electronic organiser. It is easy to use, fits in a pocket or handbag, is portable and can share information with a PC. A PDA can be used for **Personal Information Management (PIM)** (keeping notes, maintaining a calendar and "to-do" lists), to manage contacts and appointments. Many PDA devices can also connect to the Internet and act as **global-positioning system (GPS)** devices.

A **smartphone** is a small device that combines the functions provided by a mobile phone and a PDA. It is an advanced form of mobile phone. A user of a smartphone can choose to install, configure and run applications; in this way a smartphone can be made to meet the individual needs of the user. A smartphone allows a user to:

- send and receive mobile phone calls
- use PIM features
- send and receive email
- send and receive instant messages
- communicate with remote computers
- use applications such as a word processor
- access the World Wide Web.

Some smartphones (see Figure 1.1) are also WiFi capable. Such devices allow people to carry on with many work functions while on the move. They can be contacted wherever they are and are able to keep up to date with all kinds of messages. Many business people travel with a mobile phone and a PDA, or a smart phone. They may also carry around a laptop computer. If the laptop is wireless enabled, they will be able to access the Internet wherever they can find a WiFi hotspot – for

Figure 1.1 A smartphone interface

example, in cafes, airports or on trains. Many laptop users now access the Internet with mobile broadband using a **mobile dongle** – a small device that plugs into a USB port. This method of access uses mobile phone technology to access the Internet. Performance varies in different parts of the country and access costs start at around £10 a month.

New devices, called **portable Internet devices**, combine the portability of a smartphone with the greater functionality of a PC. These devices include **ultra-mobile PCs (UMPCs)** and **mobile Internet devices (MIDs)**. They are lighter than a laptop and have more functions than a smartphone. Internet access is faster, easier and cheaper using a portable Internet device. UMPCs are designed for business users; they run Windows and so provide a familiar interface that allows the same applications to run as those used in the office. They also offer web applications such as browsing, email and GPS navigation.

case study 1
▶ Gas boiler repair man

Mrs Williams had a problem with her gas boiler. She phoned for a repair man who arrived the next day. Along with his toolkit, the repair man, Bob, brought in a laptop computer.

Bob used his laptop during his time with Mrs Williams. After inspecting the boiler, he logged onto his wireless-enabled laptop and accessed a central database to check whether the parts that he needed to do work on the boiler at a later date were in stock. When the day's job was complete, he logged details of his work on an online job sheet and produced an invoice which he printed out for Mrs Williams.

Whilst online, Bob made a booking for Mrs Williams with a salesman to discuss the options for a replacement boiler. To do this Bob was able to access the salesman's diary. Before logging off, Bob checked the address of his next appointment.

1. What hardware would Bob need to access the central database from Mrs Williams' house?

2. In what ways does access to new technology make Bob's job easier?

3. Can you think of any drawbacks for Bob?

Current technology also allows individuals to work from home. An increasing number of office-based employees are working from home occasionally, or regularly for one or two days a week. Modern telephone technology allows for **conference calls**, where more than one person can join in a conversation. With the use of **voice over Internet Protocol (VoIP)** and a webcam, such a conference call can be undertaken with a visual component as well.

case study 2
▶ John's conference call

John is a worker in an Australian church. He is based in a city and works with churches in remote towns spread over a huge geographic area. Every few weeks, he has a virtual meeting with the leaders of churches in four remote towns.

A few days before the meeting, John circulates an agenda together with the date and time of the meeting. He will attach any documents that are relevant to the discussions. All the other participants confirm that they are available at the time.

The group have agreed a protocol of speaking at the meeting – each person identifies themselves before they start talking – to avoid confusion.

1. What alternatives are there for John to setting up this virtual meeting?

2. Discuss the benefits and drawbacks of the virtual meeting and each of the other alternatives.

The speed of access to networks together with the growth in wireless technology has made collaborative working a reality for many people. For example, a team can share access to, and add data to, a spreadsheet that may contain information relating to the progress of a project. One member of a committee may produce a report of the committee's findings in draft form. Other members of the committee may review the report, adding their comments as they do so. Each person would be able to see the comments of all previous reviewers.

▶ Benefits to business from advances in technology

The advances made have brought many benefits to business. The wide range of devices discussed earlier has enabled workers to keep in touch with all aspects of their work when away from the office. Important messages can be answered immediately and documents examined.

Travel arrangements can be made easily at the last minute; for example, a car rental can be booked using a portable device and time spent at an airport can be reduced by checking in online.

Video conferencing allows meetings to take place between people located around the world without the time or cost needed to travel.

The ability to sell goods online through a website means that a greater market can be accessed for goods and services. As more and more people use the Internet to buy goods, some companies have closed expensive stores, saving money in rental, staffing and other overhead costs.

Many organisations are no longer limited to employing local people. As much work can be done away from an office, an organisation can employ workers located at a distance. Employees can work from home as technology allows them to keep in touch and work collaboratively.

Advanced technology allows for faster data collection as much data can be collected directly rather than having to be collected on paper and then keyed in. Meter readings can be made using a hand-held device, written documents can be scanned and converted to text, and Point of Sale terminals allow details of products sold to be read using a bar-code scanner.

As processing speeds increase and online access to databases is established, systems become more efficient and a company is able to respond more quickly to customers. When a customer phones up her local garage with a query about the latest service to her car, the person answering the phone can provide the answer straightaway by accessing her record on the database using the computer on the desk.

Many utility companies are increasingly able to bill customers online, thus doing away with the need to print and post paper bills.

Information systems can provide managers at all levels with specific information that they need in a form that is most appropriate. This information can be available as needed and provides a basis for more speedy and accurate decision making.

case study 3
▶ Changes in a small business selling T-shirts

A small business that designs, makes and sells T-shirts was set up in 1994 by a couple, Ted and Irana. They had a small shop where they sold the T-shirts, with a workshop at the back. After a few years, they produced a small catalogue and took orders for products by post. By 2005, the business had grown considerably. A website was set up and a year later the business started selling goods online. They have just implemented a system that integrates sales, stock control and ordering.

Ted and Irana now have two small children. Irana, who deals with all the bookkeeping for the business, is able to carry out most of her work at home.

1. In what ways would the new integrated sales system be of benefit to the business?

2. What other types of ICT system could benefit the business?

3. What other uses could the business make of the Internet other than online sales?

▶ Benefits to leisure from advances in technology

Changing leisure habits have had an impact on business as some markets have shrunk whilst others have grown.

The faster processor speeds and greater memory capacity of modern computers has led to a huge growth in the gaming industry as the quality of graphics and video has improved.

The way in which television is viewed is also changing. The move to digital TV has brought a growth in TV channels and ways of accessing them. Pay-to-view services can be used to access a wide range of channels showing different kinds of programmes, such as specialist film, sport or nature channels.

Digital photography

Photographs taken using digital cameras are stored and printed using a home computer system. Digital cameras can take movies or still photographs. Many photographs and video clips are now taken on mobile phones. The move from film to digital cameras has been very rapid. The quality of images that can be produced has increased rapidly over the last few years; it is measured in **mega pixels**.

Figure 1.2 Transferring photos from a digital camera to a computer

To transfer image data from camera to computer, a digital camera can be connected to a computer via a USB port, or the memory card can be removed from the camera and inserted into a card reader connected to the computer.

Image-processing software packages such as Adobe Photoshop, Windows Media Player or Windows Movie Maker can be used to modify an image, perhaps by cropping, altering the brightness or contrast, or removing the "red eye" effect caused by the use of a flash. Photographs can then be printed out to a particular size, kept on storage media (such as CD-R) or displayed as slideshows on the screen. There is no need to print out every photograph as they can be stored in an electronic album rather than a paper-based one. Printers that are of photographic quality allow the user to adjust the paper feed size and use high-quality printing onto photographic quality paper. Printers dedicated to printing photographs are also available.

The use of digital cameras has made it much cheaper to take photographs than by using a film camera. The photographer can take many photographs of a scene, delete some and only keep the most successful. This would have been very costly using film.

The change from film to digital photography has created a major change for companies that developed and printed photographs from film. A number have closed down their high-street shops and concentrated on online services. They have diversified into many new products as the demand for their old, core activities has reduced. Those that still provide a high-street service have installed special kiosks where the customer can insert a CD-ROM or camera memory card and select photographs for printing. The kiosk has a high-quality printer which produces copies of the chosen photographs in minutes.

These changes have had a major impact on the way that the companies run their businesses. Employees with different skills are required; ICT systems are now at the heart of the business. All the changes have come about as a result of the development of digital photography, which has made the film-based technology nearly obsolete.

case study 4
▶ Printing digital photographs

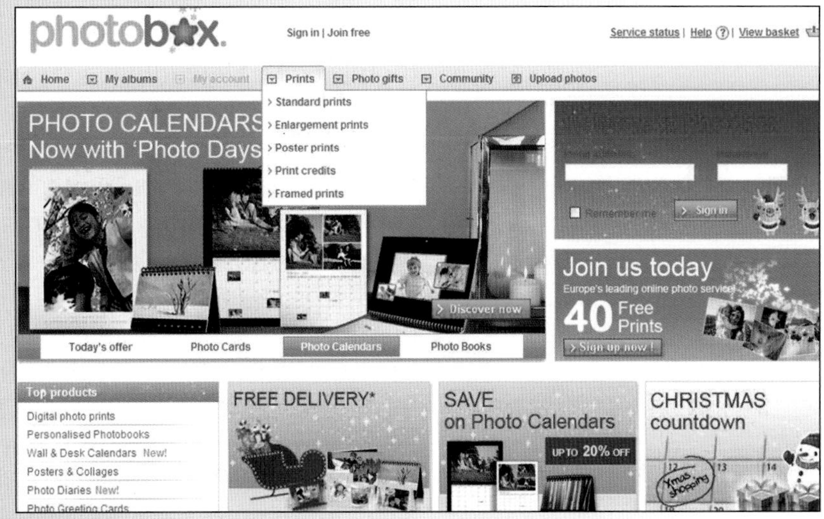

Figure 1.3 PhotoBox website

There are many companies that print digital photographs for a home user who does not wish to print them himself. One such company is PhotoBox. As well as offering standard photo printing services, PhotoBox offers an ever-increasing range of printed products, such as calendars made up of images of the customer's photographs and customised to include text for certain dates.

1. Go to PhotoBox's website at http://www.photobox.co.uk/shop/prints/standard-prints.

2. List six services offered by PhotoBox.

3. Why does a company such as PhotoBox need to offer such a wide range of services?

4. What are the benefits to the business of offering services in this way?

case study 5
▶ Showing photographs

Another service offered photographers is the ability to share photographs online with friends. Flickr is a website where a person can store his or her photographs, tag them and share them with others, either through a link to the site or by embedding them in his or her blog or web page.

1. Explain what is meant by tagging a photograph.

2. What are the benefits of tagging?

3. Uploading photographs can be time-consuming. The process can be speeded up if data compression is used. Describe what data compression is.

Music

For many years people bought records from a shop on vinyl, then on CD. Nowadays, more and more people are downloading music via the Internet. There are many sites where you can listen to samples of music of all types, including the latest releases, and then download those that you wish to purchase, paying by debit or credit card. Acquiring music in this way is much easier for an individual.

To reproduce music well, a high-quality **sound card** is required. Sound data, like all data, is stored within a computer in digital form. The sound we hear is in wave or analogue form; the digital data needs to be converted into analogue form, amplified and output via a loud speaker. The conversion from digital to analogue form (or from analogue to digital) is carried out by the sound card; the quality of the sound is determined by the sampling rate (the number of times a second that a measurement of the sound wave is made and stored as a number) – the higher the sampling rate the better the quality of the sound. The greater the resolution of the sound card, the greater the accuracy of the sound that is stored.

The ability to download music online is causing profound changes for the music industry. Sales of music online are growing rapidly but the income from these sales is not as much as the loss of income resulting from the downturn in CD sales. Some estimates suggest that there are 40 illegal downloads for every legal one. The growth in Internet technology and the ability for music and video to be downloaded easily has meant that companies have had to make substantial changes to the way in which they function.

case study 6
► **Tom's music**

Figure 1.4 Tom listening to music on his MP3 player

Tom enjoys listening to music both at home and on the move. He downloads the music of his favourite artists from the iTunes website –

often as soon as the album becomes available. He either pays using his credit card or with vouchers that he has received as a present. He stores all the tracks on his PC's hard drive.

Tom can listen to music in a number of different locations around his house and garden. He has several amplifier (speaker) systems that are connected wirelessly to his PC. He can play different music at different locations at the same time! He has a handheld remote controller that allows him to transfer music from his computer or direct from the Internet on to a device at any location.

When he is away from the house, he uses his iPod. This has its own hard disk which he can load with music from his computer.

1. Describe the advantages and disadvantages to Tom of having a computerised music system.

2. Explore what iTunes offers on http://www.apple.com/uk/itunes/.

3. Describe the type of interface that is provided on an iPod or similar device.

4. What problems might arise from buying music online using a credit card?

5. Discuss how the growth of acquiring music by downloading rather than by buying a CD in a shop has affected music publishers.

Potential future uses of ICT ◄

The move towards ICT-based techniques of identification is likely to grow in the future. Already, many passports contain encoded biometric data of facial characteristics. Fingertip identification is used to register pupils in some schools.

More and more services are provided online; an increasing percentage of the population makes use of these services as a matter of routine. The potential of the Internet provides a challenge to businesses large and small.

Portable Internet devices are still part of a developing technology. As they become smaller and cheaper with increased capacity, their use will become widespread; businesses will increasingly produce alternative versions of their websites that are suitable for these devices.

Implications of future developments of ICT ◀

▶ Impact on society

As greater and greater use is made of ICT, people who do not have access to the equipment and services will be at an increasing disadvantage. The **digital divide** was studied in the AS course.

As the growth in storage capacity and speed of processing continues, more data will be stored. The development of huge databases that can interact and access data from each other will mean that "joined-up" information can be produced – a central government bureau might have the technology to link together information on a specific individual's health, financial, educational and criminal records, together with details of mobile phone and Internet usage. Physical movement could be tracked too through the use of CCTV and sensors accessing signals from a GPS receiver in an individual's car. Many people fear that such a "Big Brother" state could become a reality.

Some people feel that overuse of online activities can lead to a breakdown in normal human interaction which can have a detrimental effect on the life of a community.

▶ Impact on the way organisations are run

More people are likely to become flexible tele-workers as communications continue to improve. There will also be a growth in collaborative working as speed of accessing the Internet increases. There could also be a growth in **outsourcing** and **off-shoring** (see Chapter 15).

The personnel needed by an organisation is changing. In a large organisation, there is likely to be a Chief Information Officer on the board of directors (see Chapter 4) as well as an IT Director who will manage the ICT development and support teams within the organisation. In any organisation, it is crucial that a person at the most senior level has a good understanding of what ICT can and cannot deliver and the associated implications. **Compliance** with the ever-increasing legislation relating to ICT will continue to play a major role in the work of an organisation.

▶ Impact on individuals as consumers and as workers

The growth in the use of mobile phones has made it harder for an individual to be out of touch. If a person is travelling in a car by themselves when the car breaks down, they can instantly summon help. If someone is running late for a meeting with a friend or colleague, perhaps in a restaurant or outside a shop, they can ring the other person to warn them, so that they do not have to wait around.

Individuals with easy access to the Internet have a huge range of information and services available to them. Those who find travel difficult or who live at a distance from shops can make many purchases online. It is much easier to research the best deal – for insurance, when purchasing products such as washing machines or cars – using comparison websites.

Interactive services

A range of **interactive services** is available via the Internet. There are fewer and fewer services in the UK that are not now available online – it is possible to: get a car licensed; submit a tax return; book tickets for flights, concerts or other events; carry out banking transactions and order goods. The HM Revenue and Customs website, as well as providing a great deal of information, provides a taxpayer with the opportunity of filling in their self-assessment **tax return** online.

Online gambling

There are many online **betting sites** where an individual can place bets on a wide range of events such as the outcome of football matches or television programmes such as *Big Brother*. There is a trend for continuing to make bets during a match with the odds shifting as the game progresses.

Between 2001 and 2006, the amount gambled in the UK rose from about £7bn per year to £40bn. This is thought to be due partly to the removal of betting tax and partly to the growth of online betting. During the same period, there has been a rapid growth in the use of an online-gambling advice service. The average amount owed by people seeking advice was £25,000.

Online gambling using the betting sites can create a particular problem for isolated and lonely people who may find it difficult to interact with people; they can find themselves spending more than they can afford.

case study 7
▶ US online gambling ban

(From Andrew Clark, *Guardian*, 27 April 2007, http://www.guardian.co.uk/technology/2007/apr/27/news)

In October 2006, the US Congress passed a bill outlawing online gambling. A Republican congressman described online gambling as, "You just click the mouse and lose your house", adding that people could even lose money on their BlackBerrys while waiting in line at the movies.

But, in the six months since the ban, an online petition was gathering steam with a goal of attracting 400,000 signatures. A congressman who was trying to repeal the ban stated, "The existing legislation is an inappropriate interference on the personal freedom of Americans and this interference should be undone".

The chief executive of an online betting company was unexpectedly arrested while he changed planes in the US last summer. He has been under house arrest at a hotel in Missouri ever since.

1. Find out about the current state of the law relating to online gambling in the US and the UK.

2. Summarise the arguments for and against online gambling.

Online voting

Online voting is now used in a variety of situations. Some countries have allowed online voting in national elections. This form of voting is commonplace in organisations such as universities, where it is used to elect members of the student union.

Many people believe that online voting would be good for democracy. The current turnout for local and general elections is poor, particularly amongst young people. Recent research has shown that 66% percent of the British citizens who did not vote in the 2005 election would have been more likely to have voted if online voting was available.

Online voting can be used in many other situations. In 2005, a competition was held to find the winner of a £50 million National Lottery grant. The grant was to be awarded to a special project that would inspire a community to revitalise the area in which it lived. There were 33 entries to the competition. Four projects were chosen to go through to the final. The finalists were put to the public vote, which was carried out online and by telephone. A total of 286,285 votes was received.

Activity 2

1. Find five further examples of online voting.
2. Many people have concerns about the use of online voting in a national election. Describe what these concerns are likely to be.

Issues surrounding the rapid development of ICT

▶ Social issues

People get left behind due to lack of skills and resources. In the AS course, you looked at the problem of the "Digital Divide". In the UK, people who do not have access to a computer and the Internet are at a disadvantage as more and more services become available online. For example, there is really no equivalent to online price comparison sites for people without Internet access. Price reductions are often given to people who view bank or utility statements online rather than having a printed version delivered by post.

A small local charity has 50 members, all but two of whom have access to the Internet. Much of the day-to-day communication of the charity is carried out by email. Copies of minutes and other documents are sent as attachments. Although members usually intend to send messages by post to the two without access to the Internet, inevitably they miss out on a considerable amount of information.

Many jobs in the UK can only be applied for by filling in an online form. Whilst anyone without a home computer with Internet access can make use of one in a local public library, many libraries limit use to half an hour at a time. It usually takes much more time than this to fill in a job application and most do not offer the opportunity to save partially-completed forms.

There are still considerable concerns over the potential effects of lengthy exposure to violent video games.

▶ Legal issues

In the main, the law lags behind technological development. There has been a considerable amount of recent legislation relating to ICT that makes the issue of compliance a crucial one for organisations (see Chapter 7). This rapidly changing legislative environment means that organisations have to spend considerable time and expense in ensuring that they keep within all the laws.

Digital Rights Management (DRM) is a set of technologies that allows copyright owners (of media such as music and film) to ensure that they get paid for use of their property. DRM uses encryption to protect the content and authentication systems to make sure that only authorised users are able to decrypt the files. Data transmitted over the Internet is scrambled and cannot be read by anyone who does not have the correct key. This means that music files, for example, can be sold over the Internet and the companies can stop piracy by limiting the users' ability to copy it.

However, there are also websites that allow the illegal downloading of music without payment.

case study 8
▶ **Ministers plan clampdown on "unsuitable" video games**

(From Patrick Wintour, *Guardian*, 9 February 2008, http://www.guardian.co.uk/technology/2008/feb/09/games.digitalmedia)

Figure 1.5 Children playing a computer game

A legally enforceable cinema-style classification system is to be introduced for video games in an effort to keep children from playing damaging games unsuitable for their age. Under the proposals, it would be illegal for shops to sell classified games to a child below the recommended age.

Ministers are also expected to advise parents and guardians to keep computers and games consoles away from children's bedrooms as much as possible and ask them to play games in living rooms or kitchens, facing outward so that carers can see what is being played.

Ministers are anxious to strike a balance between the entertainment, knowledge and pleasure children gain from highly profitable Internet and computer games, and the dangers inherent in the unregulated world of the net and its overuse by children.

1. Explain the classification system currently used for films.

2. Discuss potential dangers to children when using the Internet.

3. Describe useful skills and knowledge that certain specified games can provide for children.

4. Why would it be difficult to police such a system?

▶ Technical issues

As ICT develops, a greater range of technical skills at different levels is required. Skills can quickly become outdated; new software requires re-training and can also change the whole way in which a job is carried out. There are approximately one and a half million ICT professionals who actually create and run organisations' ICT systems. They need to keep up to date with technological changes. Business managers and leaders need to be able to understand how technological advances can help them to meet their business objectives.

For millions of workers who are not ICT professionals, knowledge and use of certain ICT systems is a large part of their work. If someone is out of the workplace for a few years, the ICT skills that they had might have become out of date. For example, they may have been using older versions of common packages that are now obsolete or may not have used specific software that is now common in their field of work. For example, a nurse returning to work after a career break might find that there are a number of ICT systems relating to patient care and drug treatment that were not in use before.

▶ Ethical issues

A number of ethical issues arise from developments in ICT and are currently being debated.

An individual's movements and actions can now be tracked in many ways. If a mobile phone is switched on, its location can be picked up by logging the nearest base station; thus a record of an individual's movements with the phone can be built up. Mobile phone companies record the time and number of every call that is made. This data is kept from between six months and six years, depending on the network. CCTV recordings also can be used to track a person's movements.

Whenever an email is sent, the user's **Internet service provider (ISP)** stores the recipient's address, the subject line and the exact time that the email was sent. An ISP also logs the times when a user goes online and offline as well as the sites that are visited. This data is kept by the ISP for several months.

Who is able to access this information and the uses to which it can be put are important issues. In the UK, there is a range of recent legislation that allows government agencies, such as security services and local councils, to access most of this information. Many people are concerned that this is a breach of civil liberties and infringes an individual's freedom.

There are also fears that such information could be accessed and used by commercial organisations. Sir Tim Berners-Lee, known as the father of the web, is alarmed by a new technology called **Phorm**, which can record a user's Internet browsing habits and use the information gained to target advertisements as the user browses. He argues that if he searches for information on a particular kind of cancer, he doesn't want his health insurance company to know this and perhaps increase his premiums as a result.

case study 9 ► Mobile phone privacy	A well-known, high-street mobile phone supplier recently sold a second-hand, refurbished phone to a buyer. The original owner of the phone had exchanged it for a more up-to-date model. The purchaser was pleased to have got a good phone at a cheap price. When he used the phone he found that all the previous owner's details were still on the phone – saved messages and all the contacts. ■ What is the problem here?

► Economic issues

There are economic implications arising from the rapid development of ICT. Businesses may need to keep up to date with technology in order to remain competitive, so they have to buy new hardware and implement more modern systems. There will also be a training cost to keep all employees up to date with new systems.

However, there are some financial benefits to organisations. As communication technology continues to advance, it is possible to establish call centres and other "offshore" business functions, where there is cheap labour (see Chapter 15). Selling goods online and reducing the number of physical shops can reduce business costs. Other cost savings can be made by producing customer statements and invoices online instead of sending a printed copy in the post.

► Environmental issues

The growth in the use of mobile phones results in an increase in the number of phone masts located around the country. Many people feel that the masts are a health hazard for those living nearby; there is no conclusive evidence that this is so.

Computer equipment gets out of date quickly and disposal of it is an issue that was studied in the AS course.

The rapid worldwide growth of web-based services is increasing power demand and CO_2 emissions. Estimates give the total electricity used in powering and cooling the 2 million servers of the five major search engines to be about 5 gigawatts. There have been claims that ICT-related CO_2 emissions are nearly as great as those of the aviation industry. All stages of the lifecycle for ICT equipment (manufacturing, distribution, use and disposal) must be very carefully controlled in order to protect the environment and human health.

Energy savings could be achieved by:

- reduction in travel due to the use of video conferencing, audio conferencing and tele-working
- reduction in the use of paper due to online billing
- intelligent heating systems in buildings.

SUMMARY

There have been considerable recent developments in devices for remote and mobile working:

▶ **A personal digital assistant (PDA) acts as an electronic organiser.**

▶ **A smartphone combines the functions provided by a mobile phone and a PDA.**

▶ **Portable Internet devices combine the portability of a smartphone with the functionality of a PC.**

Benefits of advances in technology to business:

▶ **Technology can ease the process of travelling.**

▶ **Video conferencing can remove the need to travel.**

▶ **Goods can be sold online.**

▶ **Data can be collected faster.**

▶ **Tele-working allows for a wider pool of employees.**

▶ **Faster systems provide more efficient service for customers.**

The growth of ICT in society can be seen in:

▶ **gaming**

▶ **digital photography**

▶ **music**

▶ **online services.**

There are a range of social, legal, ethical, economic and environmental issues resulting from the rapid development of ICT.

Questions

◀

1. It is estimated that 825 million people worldwide access the Internet using their mobile phone and the majority of Internet access in Japan is wireless. Explain **three** reasons why wireless and mobile phone access to the Internet is increasing. (6)

2. Being able to talk to someone and being able to send text messages are two features of a mobile phone. List **ten** other features that might be found on a mobile phone. (10)

3. "Over the last few years there has been a convergence of IT and communication technologies." Discuss this statement with reference to recent new devices. (8)

4. Discuss the effects of the rapid development of ICT on society. (20)

5. ICT has developed rapidly over the past 20 years. Discuss the impact of developments in ICT on the way organisations are run in the 21st century. (20)

AQA Specimen Paper 3

6. "The rapid increase in the speed of broadband communications has changed the way in which we live our lives and do business." Discuss the impact of the increase in the speed of communication on business and society. (20)

2

Information and systems
AQA Unit 3 Section 2 (part 1)

◀

What is an organisation? ◀

An **organisation** is a group of people with a specific purpose. The following table contains some examples of organisations and their purpose:

Organisation	Purpose
A government pensions department	To pay pensions to pensioners
A multinational oil company	To make a profit
A college	To educate students

The purpose of an organisation, whether it is big or small, will determine how it operates. The information needs of any organisation are determined by its size, purpose and nature.

▶ Roles within an organisation

Individuals within an organisation will have defined roles. Activities and tasks are allocated according to these roles, enabling the organisation to take advantage of their personal specialisations and skills.

The allocation of tasks is called **division of labour**. By specialising, individuals can develop knowledge and expertise in a particular group of tasks. The larger the organisation, the more likely specialisation is to occur. For example, in a two-person business, the individuals concerned may share all the tasks. In a very large company, separate staff would specialise in accounts, personnel, marketing, sales, etc.

▶ Information needs

Different organisations have different information needs. The nature of these needs will depend upon the:

- type or structure of the organisation
- scale of the organisation
- nature of the organisation
- management style of the organisation
- tasks in the organisation.

Structure of an organisation

All organisations must have some structure. The structure determines who is responsible to whom. This can be shown in an **organisation chart** such as the one shown in Figure 2.1. The four telesales assistants all report to Sheila Burnside.

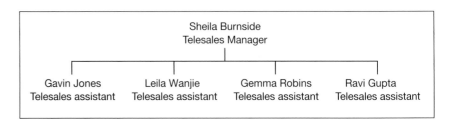

Figure 2.1 Organisation chart

This is only part of the organisational chart for the whole business. Sheila Burnside is responsible to the Marketing Manager. The Marketing Manager is responsible to the Marketing Director, and so on. At the top of the organisational chart is the managing director, the person who has ultimate responsibility for the organisation. This could be the Chief Executive Officer (CEO) or the owner.

The organisational structure:

- determines to whom an individual is answerable
- determines who can make what type of decision
- enables managers to co-ordinate, control and monitor the activities of their staff.

The **span of control** is the number of employees who are directly supervised by one person. Sheila Burnside's span of control is the four telesales assistants. Too wide a span of control leads to a lack of control and is inefficient. Too narrow a span wastes staff.

The nature of the roles of the staff being supervised will help to determine the appropriate span of control in any particular circumstance. A supervisor of supermarket checkout operators would be able to sustain a larger span of control than a personnel manager. The checkout operators are all carrying out the same, fairly straightforward, tasks while a personnel manager's subordinates would have a range of spheres of work, such as recruitment, industrial relations and remuneration. The span of control should be clear in the organisational structure.

The **chain of command** is the path through the levels of management, from the managing director downwards. Instructions go down the line of authority. Problems are referred up the lines to a higher level. Long lines of communication mean messages can be distorted and take time to reach their destination. The chain of command should be clear in the organisational structure.

▶ Pyramid or hierarchical structure

The pyramid or hierarchical structure (see Figure 2.2) is the traditional shape of an organisational structure in a large business. It is common in large public limited companies, the military and the civil service. Roles are clearly defined within a large number of layers, each responsible to the layer above.

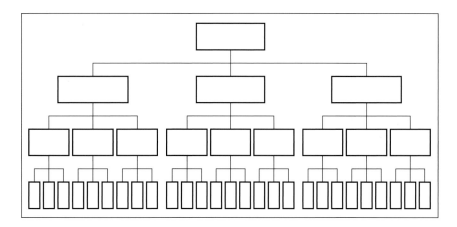

Figure 2.2 Hierarchical structure

At the top of the pyramid is the managing director or chief executive who is responsible for the success or failure of the organisation. Each manager has a relatively small span of control. The chain of command down from the managing director is long. The hierarchical structure is suitable for large organisations with centralised decision making by the strategic staff.

Advantages of the hierarchical structure

■ An individual's authority and responsibility are clearly defined.
■ The effective use of specialist managers is encouraged.
■ Employees can become very loyal to their department within the organisation.

Problems with the hierarchical structure

■ Decisions take a long time to be made and even longer to implement.
■ Communication across sections can be poor.
■ Senior staff can be very remote from the lower levels of the structure.

Organisations with a hierarchical structure are likely to be slow to change as important decisions have to be referred all the way up the line.

▶ Horizontal or flat structure

An alternative structure is the horizontal structure (see Figure 2.3). In a flat structure there are fewer layers, but the spans of control are much wider. As a result, problems being referred up the line can be resolved more quickly.

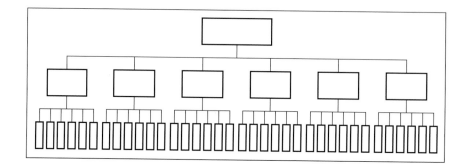

Figure 2.3 Flat structure

As more people are directly answerable to the managing director, the power to make decisions for themselves may need to be delegated. Parts of the organisation may tend to operate independently of the other parts but are still under the umbrella control of senior management.

Employees have more responsibility, which often leads to better motivation. It is more likely that employees can contribute more to decision making as there is better communication between staff working at different levels.

Advantages of the flat structure

- There is greater communication between management and workers.
- There is less bureaucracy and decision making is easier.
- There are lower costs associated with fewer levels of management – managers are generally paid more than workers.

Problems with the flat structure

- As departments are specialised, different departments may have little to do with each other, which can lead to poor communication across the organisation.
- Managers can be responsible for several departments so their role is not always clear. They can be responsible for areas beyond their own expertise.
- Control of top management could be weakened as they may have too wide a span of control. They may need to delegate more frequently.
- Fewer levels of management usually mean that there are fewer prospects of promotion.

The flat structure has become more popular. It gives considerable independence to different units, which means that these units can make decisions and change more rapidly.

Hierarchical organisations are static – changing the way the organisation operates is difficult. Flat organisations, on the other hand, tend to be more dynamic which means that they are more flexible and open to change.

▶ How has the development of ICT affected organisational structure?

The introduction of Information Communication Technology has tended to lead to flatter organisational structures. One reason is that the introduction of ICT and the pace of hardware and software development means that frequent change is inevitable and businesses must be dynamic to cope with the change.

ICT systems provide better information on staff performance, thus enabling managers to monitor more people and cope more easily with a wider span of control, a feature of flatter organisational structures.

Some jobs at lower levels may disappear altogether; for example, typists in a typing pool have disappeared as a result of the growth of word processing. New, direct methods of data entry reduce the number of clerical staff needed. All these changes have resulted in the reduction of the number of levels in an organisation.

Over the last 20 years, the jobs of middle managers have been eroded. Contributory causes include the developments in ICT and communications. These have enabled information to be produced, in a form suitable for strategic managers, directly from the operational level. This removes the need for manipulation and interpretation by middle managers.

Many decisions that used to be taken by middle managers are now taken by computer-based systems. For example, decisions regarding granting of loans to bank customers and stock ordering in supermarkets can all be made by computer-based systems. Increasingly, operational staff can work without needing as much direct middle-management involvement.

Scale of an organisation ◀

The specific nature of the information needs of an organisation varies depending on its size.

Very large organisations, such as Microsoft or Exxon, have far-reaching and diverse information needs. The CEO needs information that gives an overview of the whole organisation. Managers of divisions within the company just need information that is relevant to that division. Many such organisations operate globally; they face a particular set of problems and opportunities because they operate across international boundaries. In some ways the growth of multinational organisations has been made possible by electronic communications. Because such a large organisation will collect enormous amounts of data, ensuring that the right information is produced to the right person at the right time can be hard to achieve.

case study 1
▶ Morrisons supermarket chain

Morrisons is one of the UK's largest supermarket chains. It offers a range of goods including both branded and own label products. It aims to provide its customers with best value for money. All aspects of the business operation have been managed in-house, including fresh fruit and vegetables, meat processing and transport. They have their own fresh food factory that produces pizzas, pies, cooked meats and sausages. They serve nine million customers every week and have 117,000 employees.

Morrisons has recently decided to establish new systems using Oracle's suite of retail products. These include Oracle's retail-specific merchandising, planning and stores applications; related software for accounting, human resources (HR), payroll, manufacturing, database products and customer-relationship management (CRM) software (see Chapter 3). These systems will replace Morrisons' legacy systems, which are not able to support the company's plans for growth.

Morrisons has also signed a three-year contract with Cable and Wireless to set up a virtual private network system which will connect their 430 stores, petrol stations, distribution centres and data centres to their headquarters.

The systems will bring together all Morrisons' information in suitable forms for in-store operations, corporate strategy and supply-chain management. The information provided will be accurate and fully integrated between store, merchandising, and financial systems.

1. Find out more about the Oracle systems mentioned in the case study.

2. What information would be needed by a Morrisons' store manager?

3. What information would be needed by the manager of a petrol station?

A small organisation, such as a local charity or sports club, will have different information needs. A charity may be run by a very small number of employed staff together with some volunteers. They will all need information about income and expenditure. The other information needs will depend on the nature of the charity or club.

The Venturi Brothers, Mario and Marco, have run a home-decorating business for eight years. Until recently, they made no use of computers. However, their work has increased and they now employ three more decorators. As they were finding the paperwork more and more time consuming, Mario's wife agreed to set up some ICT systems using standard packages. First, she set up an accounts system using a spreadsheet package. In this, she recorded details of income received from the decorating jobs as well as money spent on materials, transport and wages.

Mario's wife also set up a database of customers, jobs quoted for and jobs done. For the first time, Mario and Marco were able to work out the real cost of jobs, which enabled them to make more realistic quotations for new jobs.

1. What information could be produced for the Venturi brothers from the data stored in the customers and jobs database?

2. What other systems could Mario's wife set up for the business?

3. What information could be produced from these systems?

Nature of an organisation ◀

Organisations have different purposes. Public sector organisations, such as health authorities, schools and local councils, are service-driven whereas retail businesses, banks and providers of services such as hairdressers aim to maximise profits. The nature of the organisation will also determine its information needs.

Activity 1

Describe the information needs of the following types of organisation:
- a school
- a small local hairdresser
- an international environmental charity
- a company that manages several holiday caravan sites
- a large dental practice.

Management style of an organisation ◀

There are many different styles of management that can bring success to an organisation; the management style will differ from company to company. To some extent, the organisation's management style will determine its information needs.

When Bill Gates managed Microsoft, he liked to be in total control and concerned himself with minute details of the business. To enable him to maintain this level of control, he would need information that provided very detailed breakdowns of every aspect of the business. His management style was an extreme version of a style known as **autocratic**, where senior managers of an organisation make all the decisions.

The other extreme of management style is **democratic**. Employees are expected to take part in decision-making; many decisions are agreed by the majority. Information will need to be widely available to many employees.

Many organisations have a management style that falls between the two described above. Senior managers will have areas of responsibility and delegate tasks to members of their teams. The ICT systems will need to provide each senior manager with the information that relates to his area (sales, personnel, accounts, etc.) whilst the CEO will be provided with an overview.

Activities within an organisation ◀

Different activities within an organisation have different information needs.

▶ Ordering systems

Order management systems allow businesses to manage the distribution of goods from supplier to customer in an automated way that saves time and minimises overheads. A typical order-management system will allow a manufacturer to manage and track orders from the desktop. They can also control any special sales promotions or offers. The sales-ordering system delivers these orders, electronically or by email, to the wholesaler. The system provides detailed reports on the types, volume and processing times of orders.

---

case study 3
▶ **Pullen's mail order clothing**

Pullen's is a company that sells clothing by mail order. It uses a specialist software system that supports multiple users from any Windows-based computer that is connected to the Internet. The software allows different employees to access the same information at the same time.

When a customer's order is received, the employee selects the codes of items chosen on the computer system. The size and quantity also have to be selected. Once the item has been selected, the stock level of the item is reduced immediately, so that if another employee tries to enter an order for the same item, there will be no chance of ordering an item that is out of stock.

case study (contd.)

The system then produces a **picking list** for the order and sends it to the warehouse. The picking list lists all the items included in an order, sorted so that the time taken to "pick" the items from the shelves is minimised. A **delivery note** is also generated; it contains details of delivery address, etc.

1. What information will the warehouse staff need from the order-processing system?

2. Discuss the types of report that would be useful to the sales manager of the company.

► Customer support

Customer support is an important part of many businesses – consumers and business customers have high expectations. Good customer support can result in future sales. To provide good customer support (see Chapter 14), a business needs to be able to provide information on a range of matters such as the progress of orders, past purchases and service history. Good customer support should be much more than a response to queries and complaints. Many businesses now provide online customer support through their website. They provide customers with self-service support tools, instant access to FAQs and other information and resources.

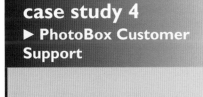

case study 4
► PhotoBox Customer Support

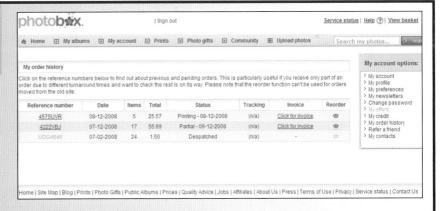

Figure 2.4 PhotoBox website

PhotoBox is a company that prints digital photographs that can be sent by customers over the Internet. They have a wide range of photo-gifts, from calendars to mugs and T-shirts to mouse mats. Customers can also share their photographs with friends.

PhotoBox provides a number of services to customers. When an order is placed online the customer is sent an email that contains confirmation of the sale together with a unique order number. As soon as all or part of the order is dispatched, another email is sent. A customer can check the progress of any order by accessing the "My account" section of the website. As Figure 2.4 shows, details of all recent orders are displayed. A customer can also be sent regular copies of a newsletter or access an extensive help section that has a number of FAQs, a blog that allows customers to give PhotoBox feedback, access to special offers and photographic competitions as well as regular photography news and tips.

1. What are the benefits to the customer of the services that PhotoBox provides?

2. What are the benefits to PhotoBox of these services?

Levels of task within an organisation ◀

There are generally three levels of personnel (strategic, tactical and operational) in a business organisation, although there may be many more layers. The personnel at each of the three levels have different information requirements. The dissemination and distribution of reports to the appropriate people at the appropriate time will be a crucial factor in meeting information needs. Reports must arrive at the right manager's desk at the time when a decision needs to be made, in a suitable format to be useable.

▶ Strategic level

The strategic level is the highest level. It consists of senior management, responsible for long-term planning and major decision making. The board of directors and the chief executive make decisions at the strategic level. This might include whether to:

- open a new factory
- move production to a new location, possibly overseas
- start to produce a completely new product.

Strategic information is used by senior managers, such as directors and the Managing Director or Chief Executive Officer (CEO) in a business, the head teacher and governors in a school, or the directors of a charity. Long-term planning is a key function at this level of management and most decisions made will reflect this. An overview of the operation of the whole organisation is required so that an assessment can be made of how well objectives are being met. Actual costs and profits need to be compared with forecasts for all sections of the business. A **management information system (MIS)** can produce projections and predictions based on current data, both internal and external, that relate to the business.

The nature of strategic management means that the information that is required at this level can be very varied, both in content and in timing. There will be a need for some regular reporting, but depending on the decision to be made, other, "one-off", information may be needed. External sources will often play a major role at this level.

For example, consider a company that produces and sells ice cream and other associated products. It has six factories located in different parts of the United Kingdom. The senior management may wish to close down one factory to reduce costs. This would be a strategic decision and the management would need a wide range of information. An example of internal information would be the increase in labour costs at each factory. External information would include the present site value of each factory.

A supermarket's chief executive is not interested in individual staff within a store but wants to know which stores are performing well and which are performing badly, which products are no longer popular and which products are increasing in sales. This information will be used when decisions about future strategies are made.

For a cinema chain, the management at head office will be interested in the overall performance of certain films as well as the revenue coming from individual cinemas.

▶ Tactical level

The tactical level consists of middle management who are, for example, in charge of one particular department or area of the business. Their titles could be Branch Manager or Department Manager; for example there would be a training manager in a factory and a head of department in a school.

The tactical decisions a head of department in a school might make include:

- what training courses to offer to staff
- timetable issues, such as who should teach which class
- what teaching materials, such as textbooks, to buy.

Middle managers, typically department heads, have roles that are tactical. They would be responsible for a certain section of a business and would be responsible to a senior manager. They would be likely to have a number of operational managers reporting to them. In some organisations, such a manager could be responsible for a sales region, a specific factory or group of shops. In another organisation, a middle manager could be in charge of training, customer accounting or ICT services.

Much of the information needed by such managers relates directly to the performance of the organisation and is used for monitoring and controlling purposes. An example would be sales figures for each of the company's sales representatives. Regular reports to assist making tactical decisions are common at this level in a variety of forms: **tabular**, **graphical** and **pictorial**. The information is usually prepared on a routine basis, perhaps weekly or monthly. A factory manager of an ice-cream company might consider running an extra shift during the summer months. Such a decision would be based on tactical information.

When making decisions, a supermarket manager will not be interested in individual sales but in sales trends and information on staff performance. Information may be aggregated using an MIS and the manager may have access to a range of graphical displays.

At a cinema, the local manager will be interested in the total sales for the various showings of different films. This information can be used to help make such decisions as whether to show a film for an extra week, move it into a larger or smaller auditorium, or alter the start times of the shows.

Exception reports, for example, a list of all sales figures which fall below their target level, provide managers with a powerful tool in establishing areas for further investigation. Successful decision making at this level often depends upon accurate forecasting, for example, cash-flow forecasts.

▶ Operational level

The operational level is the lowest level. This consists of the workforce who are making the product, taking sales orders, keeping the accounts, and so on.

Operational staff may be very well qualified. A surgeon in a hospital, a teacher in a school, and an airline pilot are examples of operational staff. ICT was first used at the operational level for data processing. It is still used extensively at this level. A supermarket checkout operator receives operational information, that is, the price of each product as it is bar-code scanned and the total price of a customer's purchases.

At a cinema, a person selling tickets will receive a request from a filmgoer for a number of seats to see a particular film at a chosen time. The seller will enter the data relating to the request into a computer and will receive operational information: which, if any, seats are available at the required showing, together with their price.

Operational managers are closely involved at the productive end of the operation. A supervisor overseeing the workforce on a particular production line may need to work out rotas and rest breaks, monitor the rate of production, ensure that hold-ups due to machine failure or delay in the arrival of spare parts are minimised and ensure that the quality of the finished product is maintained within acceptable levels. Information regarding the details of employee working hours and current stock levels would help in decision making.

Nowadays, many operational decisions, such as when to reorder stock, are made automatically by computer software. The reordering can itself be initiated automatically.

Simple lists and charts will play a major part in operational information. Such a list could be produced by sorting the transaction data that has been processed as part of the normal data-processing function.

At the operational level, information is characterised by a high level of detail. For example, in a shoe-shop chain, the local shop manager might require a daily, itemised list of all shoes sold, sorted into types, styles and quantities. The regional manager (at the tactical level) would require a weekly or monthly summary report showing the total sales for each shop in a region. At a strategic level, the marketing manager might wish to forecast sales trends over the next few years.

case study 5 ▶ West Yorkshire Police	West Yorkshire Police is the fourth largest metropolitan force in England and Wales with 8000 employees, police and support staff. With the introduction of the Government's Best Value regime, the force needed to use ICT for more efficient ways of working and to deliver better value for money.

Police overtime payments were the largest devolved part of the budget. Information given to the divisions about the amount of overtime worked was completely out of date by the time it was sent out. West Yorkshire Police were looking for a system that gave them better financial budgeting and could deliver management information.

The new system records how many hours each police officer has worked and exports the data directly into the payroll system. It includes an MIS (see Chapter 3) which is able to provide information to managers about the division, group and week in which the overtime is worked. As a result it is much easier to monitor spending.

1. Which information is used at an operational level?

2. Which information is used at a tactical level?

3. Think up some examples of decisions that could be made based on the tactical information provided.

▶ Worked exam question

The owner of an independent driving school, which employs six instructors, decides to get a local software house to write a bespoke package to manage client information, including the booking of lessons, the tracking of progress, and the recording of payments.

a) Identify **two** different potential users of this system. (2)

b) With the aid of examples, describe the different levels of information that each of these two users might require. (6)

January 2003 ICT4

▶ **EXAMINER'S GUIDANCE**   *Part (a) says 'identify' and there are only two marks. An example of a possible answer is:*

▶ **SAMPLE ANSWER**   Two potential users of this system are the owner of the driving school and the driving instructors.

▶ **EXAMINER'S GUIDANCE**   *There are three marks allocated for your answer for each user in part (b). You will get one mark for stating the relevant level of information, one for a description of why that is the appropriate level and one for an example. Have a go. Don't read the sample answer below until you have tried yourself!*

▶ **SAMPLE ANSWER**   The owner would require strategic information to support him in decision making, e.g. whether or not to employ more instructors.

▶ **EXAMINER'S GUIDANCE**   *Now write an answer for another user.*

Activity 2

1. For each of the following examples state whether the information is strategic, tactical or operational:

- contents of the managing director's diary for next week
- details of a car's former owners from the Police National Computer
- sales figures for a supermarket's 200 stores
- news that George will be off sick today
- 6000 widgets need to be delivered immediately.

2. Copy and complete the table below with your own examples of strategic, tactical or operational information. The examples should be different from those given in part 1 of the activity.

Scenario	Strategic information	Tactical information	Operational information

Information needs of different people

Different personnel within an organisation have different information needs. A member of the accounts department needs information relating to financial transactions (see Chapter 3). A production manager who is in charge of the manufacturing process requires information that relates to production levels, materials and parts costs, labour costs and stock levels. This information allows him to see how different teams are performing and whether costs are increasing or decreasing over time.

case study 6
► Cosifit carpets

Cosifit Carpets is a company that sells carpets direct to the public through warehouse stores on industrial estates throughout the UK. It stocks a number of carpets in the stores but also shows a number of patterns of carpets which can be ordered for customers.

Each store has a store manager who is in charge of a team of sales people. Cosifit Carpets has an integrated online sales and ordering system so that sales staff can order carpets for customers from the stores. All sales are recorded in the same online system which produces the invoice for the customer.

The Cosifit Carpets' headquarters houses:

- the Managing Director
- the Sales and Marketing Manager who decides on which carpets to stock and how to price them
- the ICT team that maintains the company's network and systems
- the operations team who deals with suppliers and the delivery of carpets to stores
- the accounts department
- the human resources department.

1. What information would the Managing Director need?

2. What information would the Sales and Marketing Manager need?

3. What information would the ICT Manager need?

4. What information would the Operations Manager need?

5. What information would the Chief Accountant need?

6. What information would the Head of Human Resources need?

7. What information would a Store Manager need?

A sales manager needs information that shows the number of sales per product over time so that he can spot trends in the popularity of products. Future pricing decisions also need to be made. He needs information showing the sales in each region. External information giving the pricing of rival products is also required for decision making.

The human resources department wants information about employees: for example, the turnover of staff, the gender and ethnic mix of both employees and job applicants.

Exchanging information with external bodies ◄

As well as producing information for use within the organisation, organisations have to exchange information with external bodies. Certain information will be needed by suppliers as well as by customers. Many organisations have set up an **extranet** to allow access to parts of their information system. For example, customers may be given access to details of stock to enable them to ascertain what items are available. A school may allow the parents of a pupil access to his attendance record. There will be issues of security and privacy that must be addressed. For example, customers should not be allowed to alter the price of a stock item before ordering it. A parent should only be able to access his or her own child's attendance record.

There is a range of taxes for which a company is liable, including PAYE income tax payments for employees, VAT and Corporation tax that is paid by limited companies on their profits. Information relating to tax needs to be provided to the Inland Revenue (see Chapter 3).

All organisations that hold personal data must provide information for the Information Commissioner under the Data Protection Act (see Chapter 7). Any charity must register with the Charity Commission and submit annual accounts.

Role of ICT systems ◄

The role of ICT systems is to improve the efficiency and effectiveness of business processes. It supports the activities of the organisation. ICT systems by themselves are of no use.

Different kinds of organisations have different information needs.

Organisations differ in:

▶ **type or structure**

▶ **scale**

▶ **nature**

▶ **management style.**

Different activities within an organisation have different information needs.

Different levels of task have different information needs:

▶ **strategic**

▶ **tactical**

▶ **operational.**

Different personnel have different information needs.

Organisations have to exchange information with external bodies.

ICT systems support the activities of organisations.

Questions

◀

1. Explain why it is necessary to have an organisational structure in a business. (2)

2. Information is communicated at three levels within an organisation. State these three levels. (3)

3. A message has to pass from the chief executive of a company to all the operational staff.
   a) Is the message likely to get through more quickly if the company has a hierarchical structure or a flat structure? (1)
   b) Explain your answer to part (a). (2)

4. Companies rely on their information systems to provide good quality information. Identify **three** different categories of users of information systems and state the level at which they operate. (6)

5. A company with a hierarchical structure is considering making a whole tier of middle management redundant and adopting a flatter structure. Give **two** advantages and **two** disadvantages of this action. (4)

6. "An organisation needs information like a human being needs blood. Information flows up and down the veins and arteries of an organisation."

   Discuss the above statements with reference to:
   ■ the organisational structure and style of an organisation
   ■ the importance of data collection, input and processing
   ■ the dissemination of information
   ■ the role of the people involved with creating and using information. (20)
   January 2008 AQA ICT 4

7. A large supermarket chain has a hierarchical organisation structure.
   a) State the three levels of staff within this organisation and, for each one, give an example job title. (6)
   b) Owing to the size of the supermarket chain, information is passed using formal methods of information flow. Define the term "formal information flow", giving an example in this context. (3)
   June 2007 AQA ICT 4

3

Types of ICT system
AQA Unit 3 Section 2 (part 2)

◀

Common ICT systems

◀

All businesses have to carry out some core activities, such as payroll, personnel and accounting. In all but the smallest businesses, such functions are usually carried out using an ICT system. When new systems are introduced it is very important that they are compatible with existing (known as **legacy**, see page 42) systems within the business. For example, a new payroll system must be able to interface with the existing personnel system that maintains records on employees, so that changes to pay scale can be made effective in both systems with a single change.

▶ Payroll systems

A **payroll system** consists of the records and calculations needed to work out the payments and deductions for every employee of a business. It is crucial that payroll systems are secure and reliable so that employees are paid the correct amounts at the right time.

Payments include:

- salary or wages
- overtime payments
- holiday payments
- bonuses
- statutory payments such as sick pay or maternity pay.

Deductions include:

- income tax
- National Insurance contributions
- student loans deductions.

Employees receive a payslip that itemises the payments and totals them to make the **gross income**. The deductions are also itemised and subtracted from the gross income to give the **net income**, the amount that is actually paid to them. Frequently, the net income is automatically transferred into the employee's bank account.

Very careful records need to be kept so that the correct amounts can be transferred both to employees and to **external bodies** such as the Inland Revenue. Managing payroll is a key task for any employer. Figures need to be produced at the end of the tax year – each employee must be given a slip that summarises their annual payments and deductions; overall summaries of total wage payments will be needed both by management and by external bodies such as Her Majesty's Revenue and Customs. Any payroll system must be able to deal with events such as when an employee leaves the business or when a tax rate changes.

Payroll can be:

- **out-sourced** (see Chapter 15), where all the necessary records, calculations and paperwork are carried out by a specialist company that is paid to do the job
- managed **in-house** using **electronic payroll** software that can be bought from a number of suppliers
- managed **in-house** using a **manual** system to keep written records of each employee's details and calculate tax and National Insurance contributions using tables supplied by the Inland Revenue.

▶ Personnel systems

The personnel or **Human Resources** department of a business deals with the recruitment, induction, training and disciplining of employees. It carries out the necessary procedures when an employee departs, manages holiday, maternity or other special forms of leave and monitors absence. The personnel department needs to keep record of a range of data relating to current employees that can include their personal histories, skills, capabilities and salary. Some systems can hold scanned images, such as application forms, driving licences or certificates linked to an employee record. Appraisals and review dates are also recorded. The recording of all absence, together with the reasons for absence, is necessary both to monitor individuals and highlight difficulties that they might have and to pick up problems within the organisation. Keeping detailed records allows the personnel department to use the ICT system to produce statistics on such things as staff turnover rates or absences (for individuals or departments).

An ICT system can be used to administer and track employee training and development within a business, in terms of the education, qualifications and skills of the employees and in terms of the training courses, books, CDs or web-based learning that are available to develop specific skills. It can also be used to support the administration of training courses organised by the business for its employees, storing details of speakers, venues, equipment requirements and room layouts. Appropriate courses can be offered at a specific session. An individual employee record would hold details of all the courses the person had undertaken.

A personnel department will need to register with the **Information Commissioner's Officer (ICO)**, listing all the categories of data that are to be stored for their various activities.

▶ Accounting systems

All companies need to keep formal accounts to keep track of financial transactions. They need to be kept for a number of reasons, including:

- to keep track of money paid out or in and any amounts owing or owed
- to ensure that the accounts reconcile (the amount coming in minus the amount going out equals the cash in hand) and that any errors are highlighted
- to allow management an overview of how well the company is doing
- to fulfil legal requirements.

For any but the smallest organisation, a computer system will be used for accounting. A company might purchase an off-the-shelf package, such as one offered by Sage (http://www.sage.co.uk/), or commission a bespoke system that is tailored to the company's specific needs.

Sage Instant Accounts is designed to make managing your money, including VAT, end of year accounts and invoicing as quick and easy as possible, giving you the information you need to manage your business at your fingertips:

- for new and small businesses
- quotations and invoicing
- VAT return, profit and loss reports
- health and safety advice.

Apart from recording day-to-day transactions, accounts software produces vital management information, such as details of profit and loss, that are needed by senior management. A variety of reports can highlight issues that may have arisen in different parts of the organisation.

case study 1
▶ Wildlife charity accounts

Figure 3.1 Woodland

A charity works to support wildlife in the local area and to raise public awareness of conservation issues. It has a team of volunteers who go into schools where they run workshops, carry out regular wildlife surveys and organise regular conferences. They also own an area of woodland and employ a full-time manager.

The charity raises money from three main sources: individual donations, grants from trusts and fundraising events such as concerts, jumble sales and sponsored runs.

One of the volunteers has the role of treasurer. She is an accountant and she uses a computer system to keep track of all income and expenditure. When she first started in her role, she used an Excel spreadsheet but decided to transfer to a specialised accounts package as it enabled her to produce a variety of reports quickly and easily.

The trustees of the charity have the responsibility of ensuring that the charity remains financially healthy. They meet every month and the treasurer provides them with a report that summarises their income and expenditure during the previous month. Every six months, she produces a report that breaks down income and expenditure into different categories (such as grant income, donations, income from events, etc.) as well as showing the comparable figures for the previous year.

1. Why is it necessary for the charity to keep accounts?

2. Explain why a spreadsheet is a suitable package for tracking the income and expenditure of a small organisation.

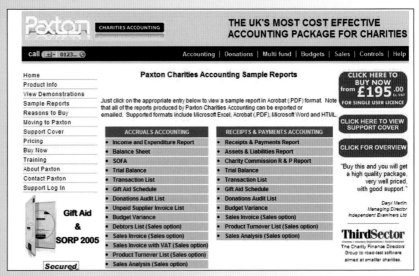

Figure 3.2 Accounting software for charities

Figure 3.2 shows the sample reports available from an accounts package designed for use by charities.

3. Explore the different reports that are available (www.paxtoncharities.co.uk/).

4. Identify three report formats that would be useful for the charity's board of trustees, explaining how each could be used.

▶ Transferring information between ICT systems

Very few business ICT systems are completely self-contained. Most systems will need to interface with other systems **internally**, within an organisation. For example, the payroll system within the personnel department will need to interface with the organisation's accounts system. It is very important that the relevant data from one system can be transferred electronically into the other.

It is also important for some interface with systems that are **external** to the organisation. All organisations with employees need to interact with banking systems to enable pay to be transferred into employees' bank accounts. All further education colleges need to transfer data relating to the number of students and courses undertaken to the Learning and Skills Council. Financial information from an organisation needs to be shared with the tax office.

An organisation can share information with external agencies through the use of an **extranet**. As you studied at AS level, an extranet is an intranet that is made partially accessible to authorised people outside an organisation. A business might share information with suppliers, customers, or other businesses.

The term **supply chain** describes the activities involved in taking a product from raw materials or the parts stage to a final product in the hands of a customer. The more efficient the supply chain, the more likely that a particular product will be profitable, as every stage in the chain adds to costs.

A manufacturer of cars may purchase parts from a number of suppliers around the world. These parts need to be transported from the supplier to the manufacturer's plant. It is important that supplies arrive at the right time. Late delivery could result in loss of income as the car plant may be unable to produce the cars needed to meet their orders. If parts arrive before they are needed, expensive warehouse space will be needed to store them until they are used. Transport options must be considered carefully to minimise costs.

Once the cars have been built, they need to be transported directly to the customer or to a showroom.

Supply chain management software is used by businesses to streamline all the activities in its supply chain. It ensures the most efficient use of transportation, labour and stock so that customer demands are met while keeping costs to a minimum.

case study 2
▶ Aeroplane engine manufacture

Figure 3.3 Jet engine

A company produces engines for aeroplanes. Parts come from suppliers located worldwide. They use **supply chain management software** to help to:

- make sure that the combination of the purchase price of parts and transportation costs are minimised
- keep parts at their factories at a minimum to reduce storage costs but make sure that parts are available when needed (**Just in Time (JIT) processing**)
- optimise the manufacturing process
- distribute the completed engines to the aeroplane manufacturers at minimum cost and on time.

1. Investigate what is involved in JIT processing. Why is JIT so important to the engine manufacturer?

2. Draw a diagram to illustrate the supply chain.

Interfacing with legacy systems

It is crucial that any new system that is developed will work together with any legacy systems. A **legacy system** is an existing system that is likely to have been used for several years. It may not be the latest technology but it can do the job it is supposed to do. Usually, legacy systems are not replaced and are still used because:

- to replace them would be expensive
- to replace them would be disruptive
- a new system may not improve the current system.

It is vital that any new system can link to any legacy sytems. For example, if a new recruitment package is developed for the HR department, it must interface with the existing personnel database.

Back-office systems ◀

A **back-office system** is the name given to a system that runs a company's business administration processes. The name refers to work that, before the use of computers, was carried out in the "back office", rather than in front of customers. Thus, they are not systems that deal directly with customers.

In a bank, back-office systems would deal with such tasks as producing customer statements, calculating interest and transferring payments between accounts and banks.

In a retail company, a back-office system would maintain a record of all sales transactions and purchases, updating stock records as appropriate and producing hard copies of invoices and receipts. The system could also produce management information from the data that is stored.

Day-to-day working systems ◄

Within any organisation there are many routine, day-to-day tasks that need to be carried out. The nature of the tasks will depend upon the character of the organisation. Many of these tasks are carried out with the aid of ICT systems.

A **transaction-processing system** deals with the routine, day-to-day transactions of an organisation. They carry out repetitive, routine business activities such as the sale of goods, recording the loan of books in a library or the recording of a cash withdrawal from a bank's ATM. Such systems are usually involved in large quantities of electronic data capture. As a transaction is carried out, the database records are updated appropriately before another transition is processed. With a multi-user system, such as a flight booking system, this form of processing is necessary to preserve the integrity of the data. As a transaction booking seats on a specific flight is processed, the number of available seats is reduced accordingly. This will affect the next transaction. So whenever a user interrogates the database about a particular flight the most up-to-date seat availability is returned.

Workflow is the process of how a document moves within an organisation. Using a type of system called **document approval workflow**, a document is passed between staff in an organisation to be reviewed and approved, for example, when an insurance claim or planning application is made. How workflow software can be used in practice is shown in Case Study 3.

Most organisations still use physical documents to store some of the company's data. For example, a large FE college will have thousands of handwritten application forms each year. A doctors' surgery may have paper-based medical information concerning each patient. A large firm of solicitors may have legal documents and letters relating to clients stored in several offices. Many documents, although no longer operationally needed, by law must be stored for a number of years. These documents need to be filed so that the information they hold can easily be retrieved when needed. Filing, storing and indexing the documents so that they can easily be accessed and protected from outsiders are major considerations for an organisation.

Large organisations need a **document management system** to control the flow, storage and retrieval of documents. Many organisations scan in and digitise all documents and store the digital record in a large database. The physical copies can be stored in a safe, off-site location as long as they are needed, or if they do not need to be kept they could be thrown away to save storage space.

Accessing physical records can become a problem if they are misfiled. Some important documents are given stickers that include transponders that allow a filing clerk to locate them.

As more data is created and shared on a daily basis there is a great demand on keeping it secure and available.

Document management systems vary in size and complexity. There are very large systems used by multi-national organisations and government departments as well as small applications that can be used by an individual. As all documents are stored electronically, links can easily be set up making it easy to **cross reference** between documents. An organisation can set up an online file archive which can provide everyone within the organisation with access to the files wherever they are working.

---

case study 3
▶ Duggan Steel Group

Figure 3.4 Kodak i1220 Scanner

Duggan Steel Group is an Irish company that produces steel roofing and cladding. The steel used comes from around the world and production is maintained so that stock can always be delivered to customers within 24 hours.

A new document scanning system using Kodak i1220 workgroup scanners (see Figure 3.4) has been installed. All business documents are scanned in. In the purchasing department, 4000 supplier invoices are processed annually.

Before the document management system was installed the supplier's invoice would go through a process taking up to three weeks:

- arrive at head office
- be sent to the appropriate part of the organisation for signoff
- be returned to head office for final payment
- be filed.

With the document management and workflow systems, when an invoice is received, it is scanned and sent at once to the appropriate manager with an on-screen "pop up" and email alerting the manager of its arrival. The manager can then digitally authorise payment. The scanned document is stored electronically on the system. Documents

case study (contd.)

can be stored in **Portable Document Format (PDF)**, developed by Adobe. PDF format maintains page layout, fonts, and graphics. PDF files are easily accessible with freely available software.

Sales staff are also big users of the scanners as each sale involves six documents, four of which are scanned into the system; the other two are produced by the system.

The new system allows Duggan Steel to shred most paperwork once it has been scanned, with only a few documents, those that hold a customer's signature, having to be kept for legal reasons. The number of people involved in paperwork management has been reduced from three to one. Paper produced as part of day-to-day trading has reduced considerably, and the speed of information retrieval is almost instantaneous whereas previously it was estimated that 14 hours per week were spent by administrative staff looking for paperwork. The company has been able to convert storage areas into new office space.

All imported steel and steel products need a steel test certificate; these are being produced at the rate of over 4000 a year. One certificate can relate to more than one product and the information may legally be required to be kept for up to seven years.

The system also includes a company-wide, bar-coding system. The steel arriving on site is assigned a unique identification number. Any related documents are linked using this code. In terms of stock control, all test certificates are now scanned for easy search and retrieval, along with bale IDs, in case of subsequent damage.

■ List the benefits of the document management and workflow systems to the company.

Collaborative working systems ◀

Very often, within any organisation several people need to access the same documents or other files. For example, the authors of this book share the documents for the chapters as they write them. A number of people can share a meeting online; common diaries are often used.

case study 4
▶ Shared diaries at Betta Toys

Betta Toys has a team of 25 salesmen, each of whom keeps an appointments diary. Requests for appointments can come from shops who phone in to the administrative assistant who has to phone the client back after tracking down a salesman and finding a suitable appointment time. The Sales Manager also allocates visits to salesmen. Every Friday, the salesman is handed a list of the following week's visits. Some salesmen have had a greater workload than others.

The Sales Manager decides to install a shared diary system. Such a system will allow the administrative assistant to make appointments, whilst talking with a customer, with a salesman whom she knows is free at that time. In fact, if the meeting involves more than one person it can be scheduled for everyone in one operation. When a meeting is scheduled for several people, a message can be sent to every participant informing them of it.

The new system still allows an individual salesman to make his own appointments. A salesman is likely to access his diary using his mobile phone. He can add appointments using the phone; the appointments are automatically synchronised with the diary stored on the office computer.

The new system holds further benefits. It allows for the set-up of repeat events. Reminders can be given in advance of a meeting. Reports can be produced for the Sales Manager that summarise the meetings of each of his salesmen. Absences through holidays or sickness can also be entered.

1. What problems could arise if meetings are arranged on behalf of others?

2. Why might a salesman be unhappy that other people can look at his diary?

3. Suggest useful reports that the diary system could produce for the Sales Manager.

Management information systems

A **Management Information System (MIS)** uses operational-level data to provide management-level information. The data can come from both internal and external sources and is combined and often presented in an easy-to-read format such as tables or graphs. The information is used by managers at different levels of the organisation to make effective decisions or plan appropriately.

An MIS aims to provide a manager with all the information needed to make decisions associated with the job as effectively as possible. The use of such systems has increased as a result of the rapid growth in the use of database systems. An MIS is usually based on data from one or more databases and allows managers at different levels to access information that is appropriate and in an easily understandable form.

The manager of a chocolate factory needs to decide the number and types of bars to be made in a particular week. The following information would help him make this decision:

- the number of each type currently in stock
- outstanding orders still to be delivered
- the sales of each type last week
- the sales of each type this time last year.

This information could be created from the data collected as part of the day-to-day operational data-processing system.

The sales manager for the same company requires information on products sold rather than products produced. He needs to be able to compare the performances of different members of the sales force. Information on each product's market share and the nature and performance of a rival manufacturer's products are needed by the manager so that he can make decisions on which product to promote and on the size and nature of any advertising campaign. Such information is **external**.

MISs provide information to be used by managers at a strategic or tactical level. The information is often grouped but the MIS allows the manager to 'drill down' and get the information in more detail, if required.

Most MISs provide summary statistical information suitable for senior management. Often, however, such summarising hides crucial detail. The need for such detail is impossible to predict as it depends on specific circumstances. This lack of appropriate detail could result in incorrect decisions.

A form of MIS called an **Executive Information System (EIS)** provides aggregated information for senior managers. Usually an EIS will have an extremely user-friendly, graphical interface. If the manager wishes to learn more about some information that is displayed, he can display the information in more detail by clicking on a point on the screen, called a **hot spot**. Such a system would bring together information from a range of internal and external sources.

For example, a senior manager is reviewing company expenditure over the past year, comparing it with the estimated budget. This information is displayed in a graphical form. One department is well over budget and the manager decides to investigate further. A click of the mouse on the appropriate figure results in the details of the budget and expenditure of the department in question being displayed. It appears that the overspend is greatest in the raw materials' expenditure, so the manager clicks on this figure to reveal that prices are as estimated, but the department has purchased more raw materials than planned. The manager can investigate sales and stock levels to find out whether these extra purchases were necessary.

Enterprise resource planning systems ◄

An **Enterprise Resource Planning (ERP)** system is an integrated suite of software applications that supports and automates the business processes in large businesses. It may consist of modules that deal with the manufacturing, distribution, inventory, shipping and invoicing as well finance, payroll and personnel. The particular modules required will depend upon the nature of the business.

An ERP is an example of back-office software and is designed to improve the efficiency of the business, reduce money tied up in stock and lower production, staffing and transport costs. The strength of ERP software lies in the fact that it ties together all business functions into one integrated system that has a common interface for the user; users from every department of the business can access the information they require in real time. All the data is held in a single database.

Customer relationship management systems ◄

Customer Relationship Management (CRM) software allows a business to collect, update, and maintain all of its customer data in one centralised location. Details of any contact with a customer could be recorded. The information is accessible to everyone in the company who needs customer information, such as members of the sales, marketing and customer services departments. By sharing up-to-date information in this way, improved customer service levels can be achieved. The aim of installing a CRM system is to increase customer satisfaction. Happy customers are likely to do business with the company again and recommend the company to others, thus increasing the company's profit. It can also reduce costs, wastage, and complaints and, as a result of better customer relations, staff stress can be reduced.

When a salesperson discusses a new purchase with a customer, the CRM software shows the status of any previous purchases, for example, whether there have been problems with delivery or payment. This information allows the salesperson to provide a better service to the customer.

The use of CRM software enables the customer to feel that they are dealing with one company, all of whose employees, in every department, are informed; people perceive the business as a single entity, despite often interacting with a variety of employees in different roles and departments.

case study 5
▶ **Banking customer relationship management system**

A high street bank has recently implemented a CRM system. The bank provides a customer, Naomi, with a number of services. She has current and savings accounts, a credit card and a mortgage. Her will is held at the bank and she arranges her household insurance through them. She also has a portfolio of stocks and shares that is managed by the bank.

Before the system was installed, every time Naomi went into the bank to make changes to an account she seemed to deal with a different person who had no access to all her other accounts. For example, when discussing her mortgage with a mortgage specialist, the details of her portfolio were not available.

After the bank installed a CRM system, Naomi noticed a change when she discussed her financial situation in the bank. Whoever she met had access to all the relevant information, which made her feel more valued.

Another advantage for Naomi was that she now received only targeted marketing material describing new products from the bank. These mailings were relevant to her situation; before the CRM system was installed she had received lots of mailings that were of no relevance to her.

She was surprised when a birthday card from the bank dropped through her letter box on the right day!

1. In your own words, explain what is meant by a Customer Relationship Management system.

2. Describe how a car sales and repair business could make use of a Customer Relationship Management system.

Activity 1

The B&I software website at http://www.bandisoftware.com/rsagescreenshots.htm displays a number of screenshots of a Customer Relationship Management system in use by a company selling and repairing clocks.

1. Study the screenshots.
2. For each, state who would use it and how it would help them in their job.
3. Investigate another set of screenshots (from the Screenshots page) in the same way.

Decision support systems ◀

The purpose of a **decision support system (DSS)** is to convert raw data from a variety of sources into information that will be used to make high-quality decisions and identify and solve problems.

To make a good business decision, a manager needs to have high-quality information based on good data. He then needs to analyse the data, finding links and trends, so that he can make appropriate decisions, find solutions to problems and build strategies. A DSS is an interactive application that can provide him with information in a form that makes the process of decision-making easier. A DSS processes data from a business system and outputs it in an easily understandable form. It presents information in the form of graphs and charts; it can include an **expert system**.

Most DSS systems are integrated into a company's day-to-day activities, using data that has been collected as part of an operational system. For example, a company selling cars might constantly download and analyse their sales data, budget sheets and forecasts into a DSS, then modify their strategy after analysing and evaluating the current results.

A form of DSS is an **executive dashboard**, business performance software that allows a manager to make certain decisions very quickly by identifying negative trends and allocating resources appropriately. An executive dashboard tells the manager the key information needed to run the company. It can display tailored information, such as how fast revenue is coming in, the level of expenses for the current month and the level of stock. An executive dashboard can give this information at a glance, in real time: the executive dashboard is automatically updated with the latest available data.

The design of an executive dashboard is determined by the needs of the executives for which it is designed. It is accessed through a web browser and is highly graphical in nature. The executive dashboard starts with an overview and, by clicking on the relevant graph or map, the user can drill down into more detail.

case study 6
► **Executive dashboard used by a US superstore chain**

The main screen of the dashboard displays a map of all the states in the US. The executive user can **drill down** by clicking on the state which concerns him.

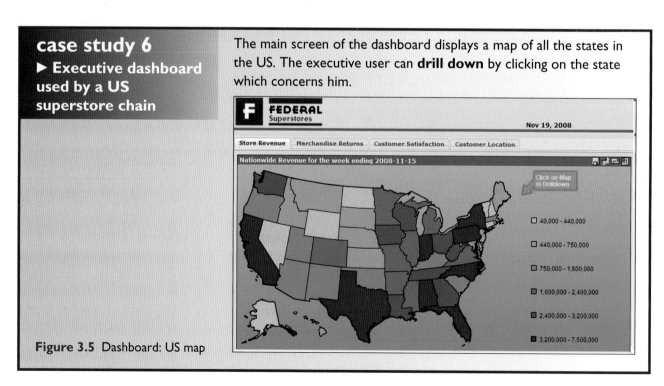

Figure 3.5 Dashboard: US map

He chooses West Virginia and clicks on that state. A map of the state is displayed, showing the location of towns that have stores. Below the map, the best and worst performing stores in the state are shown on a bar graph.

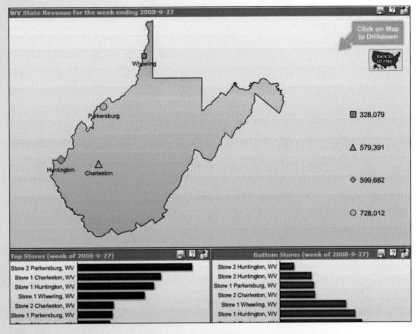

Figure 3.6 Dashboard: Revenue for West Virginia

He selects the town of Charleston and line graphs are displayed that show him how the revenue from each of the stores there has varied over the last 10 weeks. Pie charts show the breakdown of revenue from different categories of goods.

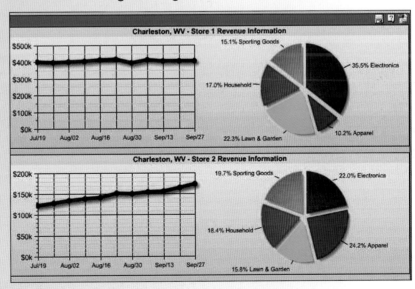

Figure 3.7 Dashboard: Revenue for Charleston stores

The executive selects the Customer Satisfaction tab which again displays the state map.

case study (contd.)

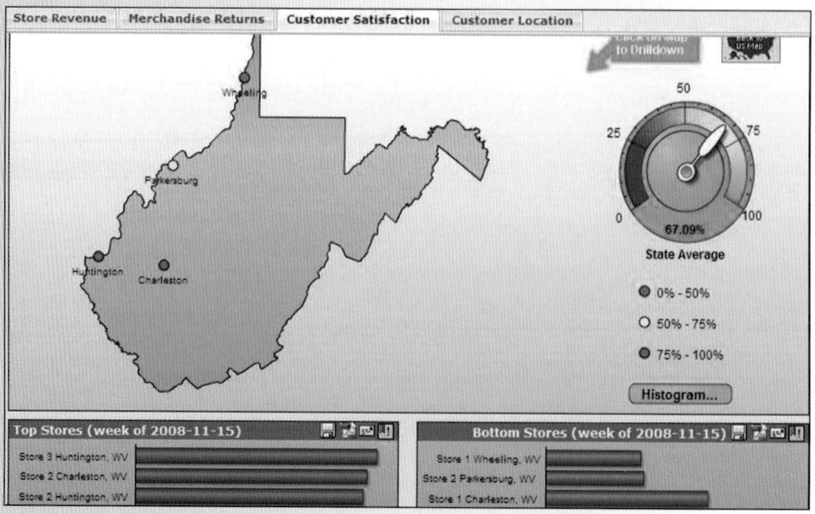

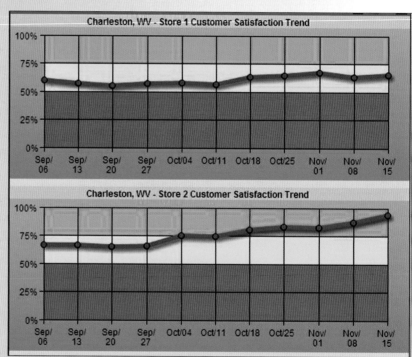

Figure 3.8 Dashboard: Customer satisfaction in West Virginia

He again selects Charleston. Line graphs are displayed showing the trend in customer satisfaction in each of the two stores.

Figure 3.9 Dashboard: Customer satisfaction for Charleston stores

1. Discuss what use the executive can make of the information displayed.

2. Discuss the strengths of using this form of Decision Support System (DSS).

3. Explain what systems would need to be in place to provide the data on which the information is based.

4. Describe two other situations when the use of a DSS would be appropriate.

DSSs are widely used in business, but are used in other fields too. **Medical Decision Support Systems (MDSSs)** are used to assist doctors in making clinical decisions and can improve the quality of medical care by providing more accurate, effective, and reliable diagnoses and treatments as well as by avoiding errors that can be caused by insufficient knowledge on behalf of the doctor. MDSSs can decrease the cost of healthcare by giving a faster diagnosis and minimising the need for consultations with specialist doctors.

A DSS can also be used by a bank employee working with a client who has requested a loan. The system can be used to decide whether or not the loan should be given, based on the client's financial details.

E-commerce systems

As you studied in the AS course, e-commerce has become an important part of many organisations' interaction with their customers and other external people.

The reservation of all kinds of tickets, for example those for flights, train journeys, concerts and cinema, are increasingly undertaken via the Internet. When all purchases are made through one system the possibility of double booking is removed and tickets can be reserved a very short time before they are used. The use of such systems means that the organisation requires fewer reservation staff.

More and more companies sell their products online. For some, this method of sales supplements their normal retail outlets while, for others, online is their only sales method. Selling online provides a company with a wide pool of possible customers as the website can be accessed from anywhere in the world. Unlike mail order, there is no need for costly posting of brochures to customers. Of course, online customers are not able to physically inspect products before buying. The cost of postage incurred for products bought online can be substantial.

UK tax returns can now be made online, making them much easier for the Inland Revenue to process as all data entry is carried out by the taxpayer.

Other services are provided online. TV licences can be bought or renewed (see Figure 3.10). This allows the licensing authority to save details directly on their database without employing staff to enter the data. The TV licence can be emailed automatically to the householder, thus saving postage costs.

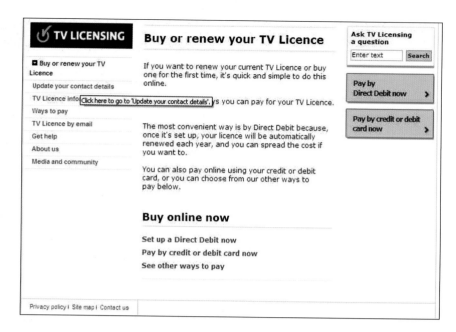

Figure 3.10 TV Licensing website

It is also easy to obtain vehicle registration for the DVLA online (see Figure 3.11).

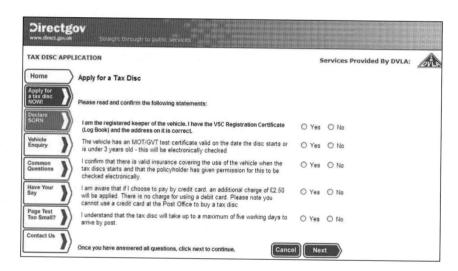

Figure 3.11 DVLA website

There are a number of types of system that are common to nearly every organisation. These include:

▶ **payroll** – the records and calculations needed to work out the payments and deductions for every employee of a business

▶ **personnel** – the recruitment, induction, training and disciplining of employees

▶ **accounting** – a formal record of all financial transactions.

There is a need for information to be transferred between information systems, both internally within an organisation and externally.

An organisation can share information with external agencies through the use of an **extranet**.

The "**supply chain**" is the activities involved in taking a product from raw materials or parts to a final product in the hands of a customer. **Supply chain management** software is used by businesses to streamline all the activities in its supply chain.

Any new system that is developed must interface with existing **legacy systems** within the organisation.

A **back-office system** is a system that runs a company's business administration processes behind the scenes, not involving direct interface with customers.

A **transaction-processing system** deals with the routine, day-to-day transactions of an organisation.

A **document management system** can be used to control the flow, storage and retrieval of documents.

A **Management Information System (MIS)** converts data from internal and external sources into information. This is communicated in an appropriate form to managers at different levels to enable them to make effective decisions.

An **Executive Information System (EIS)** provides aggregated information for senior managers. It is a form of **MIS**.

An **Enterprise Resource Planning (ERP)** system is an integrated suite of software applications that supports and automates the business processes in large businesses.

Customer Relationship Management (CRM) software allows a business to collect, update, and maintain all of its customer data in one centralised location.

The purpose of a **decision support system (DSS)** is to convert raw data from a variety of sources into information that will be used to make high quality decisions and identify and solve problems. An **executive dashboard** is a form of DSS.

There is a wide range of **e-commerce applications**, including online sales, licence applications and seat reservations.

Questions

◀

1. Describe what is meant by the following terms, and give an example of each:
   a) internal information (3)
   b) external information. (3)

2. a) Describe what is meant by a Management Information System (MIS). (2)
   b) Explain why an organisation would implement an MIS. (3)
   c) Give an example of where a Decision Support System (DSS) might be used and explain how the DSS would be used. (3)

   AQA Specimen Paper 3

3. A travel agency with outlets throughout the North of England decides to implement a Management Information System (MIS). Explain how the travel agency might benefit from having an MIS. (3)

4. Define the term "supply chain" and explain the importance of information transfer along the chain. (4)

5. Discuss ways in which e-commerce can be used. (6)

6. A wide range of software applications are available to support back-office systems.
   a) Explain the term "back-office system". (2)
   b) Discuss how such applications can benefit an organisation. In your answer you need to identify specific applications. (12)

   January 2008 AQA ICT 4

4

Managing ICT

AQA Unit 3 Section 3

◀

Managers have to make important decisions about ICT. It is important that the correct decisions are made. Nearly every organisation makes extensive use of ICT and is likely to become even more dependent on the use of computers in future. ICT equipment is expensive – if it is to be used effectively within an organisation there will be other costs as well as the hardware and software. Employees will need training and support in the ICT systems. ICT is a complex field – getting the best out of the equipment requires people with specialist technical skills. All but the smallest organisations will rely on ICT to manage its information; if this is not done well, the organisation is unlikely to meet its objectives.

Why is managing ICT important?

◀

If an organisation is to get the best of the ICT systems that it installs then they must be managed effectively. Roles and responsibilities need to be clearly defined; specific people need to be accountable for specific aspects of ICT. Areas that need to be managed include:

- strategic development and management of ICT
- technical matters
- development projects.

Each employee should be clear what his responsibilities are – these could involve seemingly small things, such as keeping stocked with printer paper and changing the printer cartridge when necessary, following security procedures and organising files in a structured way.

It is important that the ICT-related decisions an employee is empowered to make are clearly established. At what management level a specific decision can be made – such as replacing an old PC or installing a new payroll system – will vary from organisation to organisation; it will depend upon the size of the organisation and the experience of the managers. However, who can make a decision must be clearly understood.

Most ICT development arises from the business needs of the organisation, but some comes as a result of technological advances. For example, the growth in the use of email has come about because the technology is now easily available. In many organisations, it was a technical ICT manager who proposed the installation of an email system. Good decision-making requires trust and dialogue between managers and technical people.

Organisation size ◀

The size of the organisation affects the degree of formality with which ICT is managed. Usually small organisations have **informal** systems for managing ICT while large organisations tend to have **formal** ones.

Formal systems are carefully planned in advance and should be strictly adhered to. A large organisation will have a clearly defined management structure with the relationship between different employees clearly laid out. As was discussed in Chapter 2, an organisation can have a hierarchical or a flat structure. Responsibility for ICT will be assigned to specific people with appropriate skills and training. Such an organisation is likely to have many employees whose role is purely ICT-related. Figure 4.1 shows a typical structure for an IT department within an organisation.

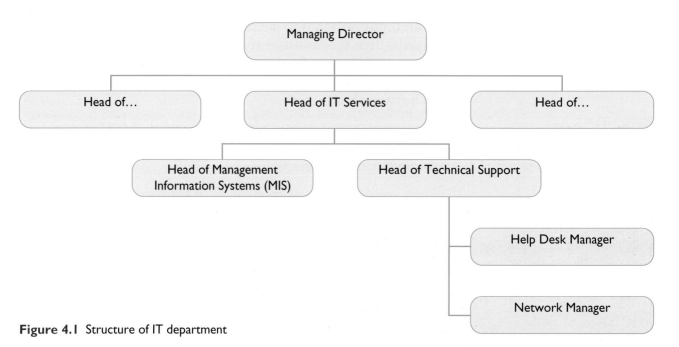

Figure 4.1 Structure of IT department

There will be technicians who manage the networks, install and maintain hardware and software, perform data backups, keep an inventory of equipment and licences and provide support to users. These technicians will need a manager who will organise and monitor their work.

If the organisation develops any new systems in-house it will establish project teams consisting of analysts, developers and testers. Each team will have a leader. There is likely to be an overall manager who oversees the work of all projects; the project leaders will report to him or her.

Formal job specifications will clearly lay down the responsibilities of each person.

A number of policies relating to ICT will be in place for areas such as security, training and procurement (see Chapter 6). Codes of practice for ICT workers will be established. Formal systems will need to be in place to ensure that the organisation complies with all legislation relating to ICT (see Chapter 7).

All organisations will need to maintain contacts with people external to the organisation who provide support, such as maintenance engineers, consultants and those providing software support. Some IT systems (e.g. payroll) may be **outsourced**. All of these will need to have formal contracts; someone within the organisation will need to manage the external personnel.

Within a small business, the manager or owner may be responsible for all aspects of the business: marketing, finance, employing assistants and any ICT matters. Even in a small business, it is important that the place of ICT is carefully thought through and that an ICT strategy, however limited, is established. ICT can bring great benefits to a small business. However, the costs of equipment and software and the time needed to set up a new system need to be weighed against the benefits.

---

case study 1
▶ **Charlie's Garden Tours**

Charlie owns a small business that runs coach tours to interesting gardens around the UK. He works from home and his job includes:

- researching new gardens to visit
- informing existing customers of new tours
- producing and distributing fliers to recruit new customers
- taking bookings for forthcoming tours
- maintaining his accounts
- hiring a coach with a driver for each visit.

Figure 4.2 Gardens

case study (contd.)

Charlie has little interest in computer technology and describes himself as "ICT illiterate". Fortunately, his wife Val used to teach ICT at an FE college. She has organised the purchase of hardware and software and set up a number of applications to help Charlie run the business.

1. Describe the applications that might help Charlie run his tour business.

2. What problems might arise from Charlie's lack of ICT knowledge and skills?

Information flow

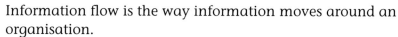

Information flow is the way information moves around an organisation.

Formal information flow is the flow of information created by the procedures of an organisation. Someone applying for a job would fill in a formal application form and send it to the company. Orders, dispatch notes and invoices are other examples of formal documents involving formal information flow.

There are a number of different formal methods by which information flows. Here are some examples:

- Formal meetings are a common way of disseminating information.
- Internal memos can be sent to individual employees or to a whole section or department.
- Noticeboards in common work areas, such as corridors, staff rooms or canteens, are often used for legal requirements such as health and safety regulations and fire notices.
- Presentations to groups of employees explain why something is going to happen.
- A company intranet can store all policies and other corporate information so that all employees can access them. Intranets are a fast-growing development.

Of course, there are less formal methods of information flow, which may be less reliable and less accurate but nevertheless cannot be ignored when looking at information flow within an organisation. **Informal information flow** is not structured but is naturally arising within the organisation. It can arise from:

- phone calls
- the office grapevine
- stories in the local press and rumours
- personal conversation or observation.

Email is an increasingly common way of communicating internally, particularly as emails can very easily be sent to a "global" mailing list of every employee. If email is tied in to proper procedures then it is part of the formal information flow. For example, an agenda for a meeting can be sent by email. However, it can easily be used for informal information flow, such as "Has anyone lost any keys?"

When an employee requires some stationery, he fills in a form that is sent to the Supplies Department, where the data is entered into a system that produces a weekly list of requests. Goods are then distributed and a report sent to the Accounts Department detailing the amounts to be charged to the appropriate departments. This is the formal information flow. When a member of staff needs an item of stationery urgently, she phones the Supplies Department with the request. This is an example of informal information flow.

A company information system must support the information flow of the company. For example, if the Marketing Department uses information on last month's sales to plan their next campaign, the department manager will require accurate information quickly on which to make decisions.

It is crucial that information arrives at its destination in time to be used. For this to happen, it is vital that the data and information flows within an organisation are carefully planned. These flows will differ between organisations and are dependent upon a number of factors.

The size, type and structure of an organisation will all play a large part. Within a small business the close proximity of employees means that formal systems for sharing information are not always necessary.

Quite different information flows will be required, depending on whether the organisational structure is hierarchical or flat. Within a large organisation with a hierarchical organisational structure, the flow of information needs to be carefully planned. As information normally flows up and down the chain of command, it often has to pass through many levels. This can lead to delays and distortions. If the organisational structure is poorly designed, one person may have to deal with more information than they can cope with. This creates a bottleneck and inevitably other people will be waiting for the information.

The amount of information will affect information flow. Obviously the more information, the longer it can take to process.

The nature of the data will have a major effect on information flow. How and where the data originates is a factor. It could be electronically generated, for example, through Point of Sale (POS) terminals and processed by powerful tools to produce information that is disseminated over a network to managers on their desktop computer. Alternatively, it could have originated from handwritten notes and telephone conversations.

ICT, particularly email, can make information flow more easily. Firstly, it is practically immediate. Secondly, it is easy to send to many recipients, such as every employee, and so can bypass the bottlenecks. Thirdly, it is easy to reply to, or forward, by clicking on one button. This may however lead to information overload. It is too easy to send the message to everybody even if it is not really relevant to them. Users in many organisations complain of email overload where the indiscriminate copying and forwarding of messages has caused an unmanageable volume.

Many large organisations now provide information internally using an intranet, enabling employees to share information.

Managing ICT strategy

Any ICT strategy should match the long-term aims of an organisation. For example, an aim of the organisation to increase its market share might necessitate the ICT strategy including the development of e-commerce. An FE college aiming to improve the attainment of students by increasing attendance in classes might require development and installation of an electronic attendance system. A manufacturing company that has just undergone a merger may need to develop a new order-processing system that is compatible with the legacy systems of each pre-merger company.

It is vital that such strategic decisions are taken at the highest level within the organisation. There is a common slogan used in ICT: "There are no ICT projects, only business projects". This emphasises the importance of the need for developing an ICT strategy that is in line with the organisation's business objectives.

Once an ICT strategy has been devised, ICT policies will need to be written that outline how the strategy will be put into operation.

ICT management and business strategy ◀

A large organisation is likely to have a **Chief Information Officer (CIO)** as member of the company's executive. In a way, the CIO acts as a bridge between the business goals of the organisation and the implementation of the ICT solutions that are needed to meet those goals. He or she will be instrumental in writing the ICT strategy and then overseeing its implementation within budget.

The CIO is unlikely to make all the technical decisions regarding ICT systems; these will be delegated to specialists. The CIO of a large pharmaceutical company defines his or her role as overseeing the overall framework of the company's ICT strategy and policies and empowering the company staff to deliver the necessary systems and services. A CIO should develop the priorities, objectives and targets so that ICT can deliver value to the organisation.

case study 2 ▶ **Role of chief information officer**	The following formed part of a recent advertisement for the post of CIO in a university: **The Chief Information Officer (CIO) is a member of the senior management team of the University and is responsible for the strategic development and co-ordination of all information services and technology in the University. This includes leading strategic IT projects and initiatives. In this work, integration, streamlining of work processes and resources, and co-ordinating users' views should be a priority.** **The CIO is expected to lead the University to become an exemplary higher education institution in the application of IT and to create an environment within which IT can become a natural support to both its academic and administrative activities.** 1. Describe in your own words the job of a CIO. 2. Explain why the CIO needs to be a member of the senior management team. 3. What is strategic development? 4. How can ICT support the staff and students of a university?

SUMMARY

ICT systems must be managed effectively if the organisation is to gain the most benefit from them.

ICT-related roles and responsibilities need to be clearly defined, with specific people accountable for specific aspects.

Areas that need to be managed include:

▶ strategic development and management of ICT

▶ technical matters

▶ development projects.

Small organisations usually have informal systems for managing ICT while large organisations tend to have formal ones.

An ICT strategy should match the long-term aims of an organisation.

Its policies outline how a strategy would be put into operation.

Formal information flow is the flow of information created by the procedures of an organisation.

Informal information flow is not structured; it arises naturally within the organisation.

A large organisation is likely to have a Chief Information Officer (CIO) as a member of the company's executive.

Questions

1. Explain the differences between informal and formal information flow within an organisation. Include in your answer examples of formal and informal information flow mechanisms. (10)

2. A company has an ICT strategy and a number of ICT policies.
   a) Explain the difference between an ICT strategy and an ICT policy. (6)
   b) Describe the role of a Chief Information Officer (CIO). (4)

3. Discuss how the following factors might influence choices made by management when writing a corporate information systems strategy:
   ■ organisational structure
   ■ legal and audit requirements
   ■ hardware and software
   ■ behavioural factors. (20)

   June 2008 AQA ICT 4

4. Figure 4.3 shows the hierarchy of a further education college. The number of staff in each role is shown in brackets.

   a) For each of the following levels of staff, give **two** examples from the hierarchy shown in Figure 4.3 of someone who would be using information from college ICT systems at that level:
      (i) strategic (2)
      (ii) tactical (2)
      (iii) operational. (2)
   b) Information flows around an organisation in a variety of ways, using both formal and informal methods. For the college shown in Figure 4.3, suggest a method, using ICT, of providing the following information to the intended recipients, stating whether this method is formal or informal:
      (i) monthly attendance figures for the whole college to the Student Vice-Principal (2)
      (ii) weekly attendance figures for individual students to Course Team Leaders (2)
      (iii) annual income and expenditure to the College Principal (2)
      (iv) date of the annual college Open Day to all college staff (2)
      (v) details of a student disciplinary action and its outcome to the Student Vice-Principal. (2)

      January 2008 AQA ICT 4

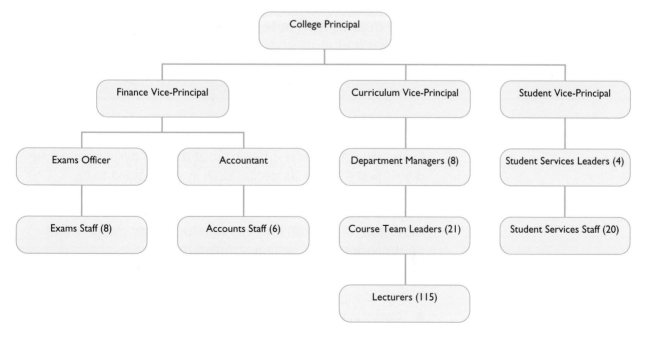

Figure 4.3 Hierarchy of a college

5

ICT Strategy
AQA Unit 3 Section 4

◀

All organisations have objectives which determine the way in which they function. For many organisations, an objective may be to make a profit, whilst for others providing a service may be the main objective. Breaking even, survival, growth or maximising sales are all possible objectives.

Businesses need a strategy to help them to achieve these objectives. The strategy may define what the business will do to become or remain successful. For example, the strategy might plan areas of expansion and anticipate areas of growth.

An ICT system is only a means to an end. It exists to support the organisation in pursuit of its objectives. A company manufacturing automotive parts will have different objectives from one selling insurance. This will affect the sort of ICT systems required. Chapter 4 explored the different objectives that an organisation could have. An organisation needs to establish an ICT systems strategy so that the information needs of everyone in the organisation can be met.

A well known saying goes: "There are only two reasons to use ICT: to do things better or to do better things". There is no point in having ICT for its own sake – indeed, there are situations where using ICT is not the best solution. Any ICT development should bring real, measurable benefits to users, to the organisation or to the organisation's clients. The best specified and most up-to-date system is of no use unless it meets the needs of the organisation.

Factors influencing an ICT strategy

◀

Every organisation is different and the ICT systems must be developed to meet its needs. Such systems need to be strategically planned. Most factors that determine the strategy arise from the nature of the organisation. Among these **internal** factors influencing the choice and design of an organisation's ICT system strategy are:

- business goals
- available finance
- legacy systems
- the geography of clients
- business fulfilment
- the structure of the organisation.

The ICT system strategy will also depend on some **external** factors, including:

- compliance
- legal issues.

▶ Business goals

The business goals of an organisation will have a major effect on its ICT system strategy. If an organisation has a business goal to reduce overall administrative costs, the ICT strategy might include the development of a system that replaces a current system that requires many hours of clerical data entry with a document scanning system. A supermarket may have a goal to increase customer throughput in its shops without increasing the number of POS tills. The ICT strategy might include the development of self-scanning systems. An insurance company may have a goal to reduce the volume of data input by their employees by allowing potential customers to enter the data directly. The ICT strategy could include the development of online forms for their website.

case study I	High Hill Secondary school has eight classrooms that are equipped

case study I
▶ Computers in every classroom

High Hill Secondary school has eight classrooms that are equipped with a computer for every pupil in the class. All the classrooms are timetabled for all lessons.

The humanities department, which teaches in five classrooms each equipped with two computers and a smart whiteboard, have put in a request to the senior management team to have each of their classrooms equipped with a suite of networked computers to enable pupils to make use of the school's intranet and other software. The management team agree that the humanities department have a good case, but the proposal is too expensive – the school does not have enough money to finance such a large purchase.

In consultation with the ICT manager, they decide to purchase a trolley that can hold 20 wireless-enabled laptops. This trolley will be stored in the humanities area and can be wheeled in when needed for use by a class.

1. Discuss the benefits and drawbacks of such a solution.

2. What alternative solutions could the management team have implemented?

▶ Finance

The amount of finance that is available is important in determining what can be achieved. A small charity working with old, second-hand, stand-alone computers could benefit from a networked system with new, fast computers. However, the very limited finance available for administrative tasks does not allow this development to be undertaken.

An insurance company wishes to implement a range of new developments, such as supplying all sales staff with wireless-enabled laptops and providing clients with online access to the current state of their policies. The company might have to phase the developments over several years to meet financial constraints.

▶ Legacy systems

Any new system must be compatible with an organisation's **legacy systems** (see Chapter 3). Any new ICT system must be able to read existing data files. New software must be compatible with old software. To change to another package could cause unnecessary anxiety and require further training. Hardware must be appropriate. In buying new hardware, it is essential that old software and data can be used easily. Continuity is important. It is important that any change is managed and carefully planned for. The use of standard file types will enable files that have been produced by one system to be read by another.

case study 2
▶ Mail order sales

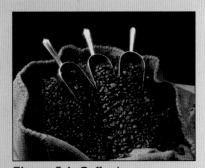

Figure 5.1 Coffee beans

PureAroma is a small company that currently sells specialist coffee and teas by mail order.

The company wished to increase its sales by developing a new e-commerce system that would allow customers to purchase goods online. They intended to maintain the mail-order operation as many customers would wish to continue ordering in this way.

The company hired an external developer to set up a website with an online ordering system. The system went live and proved popular, gaining extra custom for PureAroma.

However, after a few days, problems became apparent. Orders were taken for items that were out of stock and there were delays in delivery as PureAroma had to replenish their stocks by making expensive special orders to their suppliers.

1. What went wrong?

2. How could the problem have been avoided?

► Geography

The geography of clients – where they are located – will influence the ICT strategy. A small family business that builds customised dolls' houses sells them from a single shop in a large market town. Customers come to them from the local area. A decision to expand the business, by developing into e-commerce where customers can specify and order a dolls' house online, will expand their potential customer base worldwide.

► Business fulfilment

ICT helps a business fulfil its goals at all levels, from efficiency gains in day-to-day office work to very large new ICT systems. In a doctors' surgery, queues at reception can be reduced by introducing a touch-screen system that patients can use to log their arrival. On a large scale, an online patient records system can be produced that links into a financial system.

► Structure of the organisation

The way in which the organisation is structured and the various business functions managed will need to be taken into account when developing an ICT strategy. A description of the current departments and how information is used will need to be studied carefully.

Any information system needs to provide information to the right person at the right level in the right detail. For example, an organisation which is managed geographically will have regional managers who require reports summarising the performance of all functions within that region. In an organisation that is structured functionally, a production manager would require summaries of the performance at all factories in the organisation.

A formal hierarchical structure will require a method for ensuring information is passed up and down the structure appropriately and in a timely manner.

An information system should enable good communication within the organisation. The design of an information system must take account of information flow around the organisation. For example, the use of a company-wide intranet or email system can be used to get information to all employees quickly and efficiently.

► Compliance

Government rules and regulations lay down how data should be managed. Organisations must be in compliance with these regulations. The officers of a company are responsible for ensuring that their organisation complies with the law. Any ICT system strategy must ensure that all such legislation is followed. Some new legislation requires an organisation to develop a new ICT system to ensure that compliance is met: for example, there are laws relating to the archiving and encryption of data that may demand new technology.

As compliance becomes more complicated, with more regulations relating to ICT coming into force, many organisations use external consultants or specialist software to help them be compliant. Some very large organisations have even appointed a Chief Compliance Officer.

An important area of compliance is **software licensing**; it is vital that an organisation purchases an adequate number of licences for the number of users. If an organisation fails to do this they will be in breach of copyright law. This is true even if a manager is totally unaware that illegal use of software is occurring within the organisation.

To meet the **data protection regulations**, wide-ranging security measures are needed that go beyond standard firewalls and antivirus software. Extensive and robust backup and recovery procedures must be established; effective systems that can identify permitted users and manage appropriate access to information are needed.

Any public sector organisation must make sure that systems are in place to enable them to comply with the demands of the **Freedom of Information Act**.

An organisation needs to ensure that systems are in place so that all regulations relating to the use of emails are complied with. Amendments to the Companies Act in 2007 state that all company emails must contain company contact information including a full address, company registration number and VAT number where applicable. UK financial services companies are required to store all business emails for up to six years.

An employer is liable for any wrongful acts committed by employees in the course of employment. This can apply to such offences as deliberately sending viruses. An organisation must ensure that adequate training and security measures are in place to ensure that its employees do not breach the **Computer Misuse Act**.

There are other regulations that, directly or indirectly, relate to the use of ICT within an organisation. Every one of these regulations will need to be considered and procedures put in place to ensure that the organisation is in compliance. Further discussion of some of the legislation is to be found in Chapter 7.

Activity 1

1. Find out details of legislation that relates to the use of ICT within an organisation.
2. Copy and complete the table below: list the legislation and outline the steps that an organisation should take to be in compliance.

Legislation	What a company must do
Data Protection Act	Register all data stores with the Information Officer; train all staff in related matters; ensure systems in place to keep data up to date
Computer Misuse Act	
Freedom of Information Act	

case study 3
▶ British Horseracing Board

Figure 5.2 Horse race

A case has been won by the British Horseracing Board against the bookmaker William Hill; it is the first such case to be won regarding the database regulations of 1997. William Hill have been forbidden from publishing lists of runners in forthcoming horse races on its website.

The Horseracing Board, the governing authority for horseracing in Great Britain, was given a ruling that the publication of lists of runners by William Hill on its betting website without consent infringed the Board's database right.

The case is the first to reach a verdict in a UK court under the Copyright and Rights in Databases Regulations 1997. The regulations protect data or other materials arranged in a manner that involved "substantial investment in obtaining, verifying or presenting the contents". In other words, if a database is used by someone else without permission, the owner could have grounds for legal action against that person.

1. Find out more about the Copyright and Rights in Databases Regulations 1997.

2. What are the implications of the regulation for a company?

▶ Auditing and legal issues

Any ICT system development must take account of legal and audit requirements. These will vary from business to business. An audit is a check. A financial audit is often required by law. An auditor is an independent person whose job is to check the accounts of an organisation to ensure that they comply with all laws and regulations and that no fraud has taken place. Any ICT system strategy will have to ensure that all audit requirements are met. This might involve purchasing an auditing software package.

An **auditor** must check that an organisation has procedures in place that provide protection against the misuse of ICT systems and data. Auditing systems should detect any misuse that has taken place, for example by uncovering anomalies or discrepancies through regular checking. Any misuse must be investigated through the use of such aids as monitoring systems and audit trails.

The auditor needs to be able to access all relevant records within the ICT system, for example, records of customer transactions, orders, payroll details, as well as the overall end of year statement of accounts. To carry out an audit, an auditor will need to examine the data files. However, files on magnetic media such as disk cannot be read as easily as traditional paper ledgers. Old files are not normally kept for more than a few days before being overwritten. The system must be designed with the work of the auditor in mind; records of transactions must be stored. This is known as an **audit trail**.

An audit trail is an automatic record made of any transactions carried out by a computer system (for example, all updates of files). An audit trail is a means of tracing all activities relating to a piece of information from the time it enters a system to the time that it leaves. An audit trail should provide sufficient information to establish or verify the sequence of events. It enables the effects of any errors in the accounting information to be traced and the causes determined.

For example, if five items of a product are removed from stock, the number in stock stored in the record for that item will be reduced by five. For audit purposes, a record of the transaction that resulted in that reduction must also be stored. This will have fields: stock number to identify the product, the type of transaction (e.g. adding to or removing from stock), the quantity of items and the date and time of the transaction. This ensures that auditing is an integral part of the system.

A further example of an audit trail in use is the Police National Computer. This is used to trace the history of owners of a motor vehicle. Before computerisation, every car was issued with a paper log book which had to be kept by the car owner. The log book had details of all the previous owners of the car recorded in it. The current computer system has been designed to hold the same information so that the names of all past owners can be found on request.

case study 4
▶ Humberts garage

Figure 5.3 Garage

Humberts is a local garage company that has many regular customers who bring their cars for a service or repair.

A customer of theirs, Mrs Gillis, brought in her car for a service and agreed that any problems that were detected should be put right. The mechanics found that the brakes of her car were worn and so they replaced two brake pads.

When Mrs Gillis collected the car, she was very worried that there was something seriously wrong with her car as she could remember paying to have brake pads on several recent occasions. She talked to the manager of Humberts who was able to view the trail of past transactions relating to Mrs Gillis' car and the specific repairs that had been carried out. With this information, he was able to assess whether or not there had been an underlying problem with the braking system.

1. List the data items that would need to have been kept in order for the audit trail to have been carried out so successfully.

2. Humberts have a computer-based stock control system. A member of staff carries out regular audits on their stock, checking the physical number of items in stock against the number stored on the system for that item. Explain why such an audit is necessary.

An audit trail will tell an auditor what exact data was amended, by whom and when. An audit trail keeps track of:

- what has happened in a system
- who has been using it
- for how long they have been using it
- who did what with what data.

Online systems provide problems for the auditor for a number of reasons. Transaction details can be entered at many points on a WAN. Source documents may not exist; this could occur if an order was made by phone. Controls such as validation and verification may not be used as they may waste time in a time-critical system. Very often, immediate processing may make an audit trail impossible.

The auditor must check the software thoroughly. In particular he or she must pay attention to the validation checks made on input data. Careful checks should be made that passwords are used properly and that any suspicious transactions are reported.

The management of an organisation will need to be able to check that its employees are not misusing the organisation's computer network. If an employee is suspected of breaching the company's corporate ICT security policy then it must be possible to check an audit trail that keeps a record of all activities at network stations. The data items that will need to be recorded whenever a user accesses the network will include:

- user ID, to identify the user
- address of the workstation being used
- date and time of the access and the time spent logged on
- number of login attempts
- applications accessed
- data accessed.

The maintenance of audit trails does not come without a price. Additional computer storage will be needed to hold the extra data of the trail. The need to record data in an audit trail may well slow down transaction processing.

Managing information assets over time ◀

Most organisations change over time. It is important to be able to predict any likely growth so that planning can be effective. Growth might result in the employment of a number of new members of staff who will need to be provided with appropriate ICT equipment and network access. Substantial growth might result in the need to move to a new building, which will require substantial expenditure in new hardware and network installation. These are all changes to the ICT provision within the organisation.

Long-term use of ICT systems also demands the need for the management of information over time. Any organisation is likely to need to manage an increasing volume of data as they use ICT systems. Records will build up over time, whether they relate to sales, courses attended by employees, emails sent and received, details of symptoms and treatments for a patient or account transactions in a banking system. There are legal requirements as to how long certain records need to be kept, including certain categories of emails. Thus the volume of data stored will grow, taking up increasing amounts of storage space.

There are several options available in managing the older data:

- **Deleting records.** This at first glance seems the simplest option. Once a product that has been ordered has been delivered, it would surely be simple just to delete it. However, this is unlikely to be an appropriate solution for a number of reasons: there may be later enquiries from the customer regarding the purchase; details of all sales will be needed to produce future reports; records will be needed for auditing purposes. Many records need to be kept for several years for legal purposes.
- **Archiving records.** This involves storing records that are no longer needed for day-to-day use offline, not under direct control of the computer. On a home computer, this could be using a CD-ROM. Archive data can still be retrieved if it is needed. A school might archive all the computer records of pupils who have left the school, perhaps grouped together by their year. A bank will archive copies of account statements over a year or two old.
- **Expanding storage space** to accommodate increased data volume. If the increase in data is needed to be kept online, then the amount of storage space allocated will need to be increased accordingly.

As the volume of data grows, so the systems that produce the information must be carefully managed. Imagine a wedding photographer who stores photographs, emails and personal documents on her computer. After a couple of years she may have thousands of photos, hundreds of emails and many assorted documents. Without using a planned filing system, using a structure of directories (folders) and subdirectories to store all her information she will have great difficulty in finding a specific photo, email or document.

In a large organisation, similar problems could arise if not enough attention is given to information management. Databases that have grown too large can impair the performance of the applications that run on them and so impact on the service provided. Software products have been developed that will automatically archive historical transaction records and store them securely and in a more cost-effective way. The business application will have less data to deal with and so will operate faster and more efficiently.

Not only do organisations have databases that are growing in size, most will also have a huge increase in the amount of **unstructured data**, such as document files and emails. Such data can be very important to an organisation and needs to have the same level of protection and storage as other data. Currently, much of such data is stored on expensive disks; its large volume affects the performance of other systems as well as increasing backup and recovery times. Software tools exist that will automate the movement of data from expensive disks to lower-cost storage while retaining fast access to the data if it is required.

case study 5
▶ BT call centres

Figure 5.4 A call centre

case study (contd.)

British Telecom (BT) Group is a large provider of global telecommunications services. Its activities include:

■ networked ICT services

■ local, national and international telecommunications services

■ broadband products and services.

BT maintains 50 **call centres** and runs software that allows call centre personnel to access customer records. Customers can phone for a great variety of reasons, including: queries over bills; requests for new services; complaints or help. Around 12,000 call centre staff could be using the system concurrently. Records are kept on all customer accounts with details of transactions carried out as a result of the calls.

The system was designed to cope with up to 7 **terabytes (TB)** of data. The amount of new data is being created at a very fast rate. Archiving is a very important activity because the very large volumes of data being processed each day increases the amount of data being stored. Several million records are archived every 24 hours.

1. Explain the term "archiving".

2. Find out how much data is stored in a terabyte.

3. Explain why fast access to data is necessary in the call centres.

4. Why is archiving the chosen option for dealing with data growth?

The need for a corporate ICT strategy

Any large organisation needs to have a corporate strategy in place that ensures that it can take advantage of developments in technology as they arise. Technology does not stand still – there is continued movement to new, faster hardware; storage devices with a large capacity are being developed; new devices that were not in existence a short time ago are now readily available.

Through its ICT strategy, an organisation must plan ahead so that it can take advantage of new developments when appropriate, in a measured way, rather than reacting without proper consideration by purchasing every new development as soon as it becomes available.

Procurement is the acquisition of hardware at the best possible price for the use of an organisation. Hardware can either be purchased outright or leased. This is often achieved through a contract. ICT procurement plays an important role in achieving the objectives of an organisation. Appropriate services can only be delivered if suitable ICT hardware resources are in place. The amount of money that can be spent on ICT is limited so it is important that the correct purchasing decisions are made.

Future-proofing concerns finding ways of making sure that a system has a reasonable life and does not need to be totally replaced too soon. Systems must be designed so that they can cope with predicted changes and growth.

Computers have developed so rapidly that machines that are four or five years old seem slow and cannot cope with recent software. When installing a new ICT system, it is important to buy one that won't be out of date too soon.

Old data must be able to be transferred to a new system. For a small business, programs must have backward compatibility (the ability to read files from previous versions). DVD drives must also be able to read CD-ROMs. New computers no longer have a built-in floppy disk drive as the technology has become outdated. However, external floppy disk drives that work from the USB port can be used so that any files that have been stored on a floppy disk can still be read.

In a similar way, a large organisation must ensure that any new hardware that is installed can still cope with data held on earlier systems.

Considering future needs is very important when setting up a network. When establishing the cabling in and between buildings, care must be taken that future growth in network traffic is catered for. The development of wireless networking is growing very fast so it is important that any new network is set up to allow wireless access. The network infrastructure of cables, switches, servers and so on, is costly to purchase and install. Frequent changes to these basic, underlying services can be disruptive to work and need to be avoided through careful forward planning. There must be flexibility in the number and positioning of workstations so that changing requirements can be catered for.

▶ Upgrading hardware and software

After some years of use, a company may wish to upgrade their computers. Changes in available devices, such as the development of flat screens, may make upgrading desirable. An increased volume of data or a desire to decrease processing time could make it necessary to replace a computer with one that has a faster clock speed and more RAM. Required changes in software might make a hardware upgrade necessary as new versions of software often have greater resource requirements.

If computers are kept for a long time, they can become obsolete and spare parts become unavailable so that they cannot be repaired when they break down.

As technology advances, tasks can be carried out in a way that could not once have been achieved. This could result from such developments as increased processor speed, increased memory capacity or enhanced transfer speed over a network. For example, improved technology may have resulted in the production of printers that produce a better quality of print than was available previously.

Alongside the increase in hardware performance, software development has also made rapid progress. There has been a move towards software that has a greater range of functionality as well as graphical user interfaces which provide an interface that is easier and less frustrating to use.

The organisation may have a policy to upgrade hardware after a certain time in order to provide an up-to-date image for the company or to maintain good staff morale.

Having up-to-date ICT resources can inspire confidence in customers and other business contacts. It should also provide the best service to customers.

This is a particularly important reason for regular upgrading in a company whose business is in ICT, for example, in hardware manufacture, software development or support. Such an organisation needs to portray an image that is "ahead of the game" and at the forefront of ICT development.

Changes in the way that tasks within the organisation are carried out might force an upgrade of hardware or software. For example, a decision that salespersons should collect all information regarding clients directly would require them to be issued with laptop computers. The current software would have to be upgraded to allow for the transfer of necessary data to and from the laptops on a daily or weekly basis. A decision by senior management to provide the facility for Internet sales to customers would have networking and software upgrade implications.

Many commercial software packages are regularly updated and new versions brought on to the market. An organisation will have to decide if and when it is appropriate to move to the new version. Consideration will have to be given to whether the extra features offered by the new version will be of real benefit to the organisation's users. It is advisable to wait until the new version is tried and tested so that it will prove to be robust in use.

Occasionally, it is appropriate to change to new software which provides the same functionality as that currently used, but more cost effectively, as the licences for the new software are cheaper. If the new version has a different look and feel from the old version, as well as having extra features, it might be necessary to undertake a programme of staff retraining to ensure that everyone is able to make efficient use of the software.

A new version of a software application frequently has a greater systems resource requirement than an older version. It is likely to take up more hard disk space than the old version, require more RAM and may need a faster processor to run it. Problems can arise when not all the workstations in an organisation are able to run the new version and have to keep using an older version. This can lead to some file incompatibility as it is likely that files produced by the new version cannot be read by the old.

Users may require training in the use of the new version of the software if it includes new features. Although new features could be ignored until the user feels ready to find out about them, upgrades can also include changes to existing features which could cause confusion and irritation. Unless training is provided, users will initially take longer to perform familiar tasks. Extra support will be needed for users when software upgrades have been made.

In a large organisation, an upgrade can be trialled in one department before use throughout the whole organisation. In this way expertise can be built up and problems highlighted on a small scale. However, if this is done there are likely to be complications in file transfer between departments.

Very often, it is not necessary to purchase a full copy of a new version of software; an "upgrade" version will convert the current version to the new one. This is usually a cheaper option, but does have some disadvantages.

---

case study 6
▶ **Howse, Hulme and Byer (HHB) estate agent**

HHB is a small estate agent that has eight offices within a 50-mile radius. Information on customers and the details of houses for sale are stored locally at the nearest office. Customer details and data regarding the houses, such as the number of rooms and their dimensions, locality etc., are stored in a spreadsheet in a four-year-old computer. Photographs of properties are stored in filing cabinets.

HHB wishes to upgrade its methods to enable the photos to be stored on the computer together with short video clips. Details of all houses that they are currently trying to sell should be available online in all their offices.

1. What hardware is HHB likely to need if they upgrade their system?

2. Discuss the extra functionality that would be needed in the software.

3. What benefits would there be for HHB if they upgrade their current system?

When an organisation undertakes a major system upgrading a decision has to be made on the new hardware platform. Ideally, it should be compatible with the old platform. When different hardware manufacturers produce machines that all support the same software and data files the machines are said to be compatible. The processors of compatible systems will have a similar architecture with the same instruction set.

Some applications are dependent upon a particular hardware configuration (e.g. processor type or clock speed, memory configuration, VDU configuration). For example, Microsoft Office 2003 will only run on a PC with a minimum clock speed of 233 MHz. The term "compatible hardware" is often used to refer to hardware systems that conform to a particular minimum hardware specification, having similar architecture and supporting the same peripheral devices.

▶ Worked exam question

A school ICT coordinator wants to upgrade the school computer network, which consists of a large number of workstations and two servers, all of which are at least three years old. The operating system (OS) is over five years old.

State **five** reasons she could give to her senior management that would reinforce her case for upgrading. (5)

ICT 5 June 2001

▶ SAMPLE ANSWER   Possible reasons include:

- additional functionality
- shorter time for users to log on
- access for students from home
- similar software on students' home computers
- unreliability of old equipment
- improving the image of the school.

▶ Technology lifecycle

All ICT technology has a distinct lifecycle. New technology is developed that allows problems to be solved in new ways. It can be implemented within an organisation, meeting its needs in a way that the preceding technology no longer does. This new technology will be expensive to acquire as the manufacturer will need to recoup its research and development costs. However, an organisation that acquires new, cutting-edge technology may well gain advantage over its competitors.

When a new technology has been available for a while it will become cheaper to acquire. For many organisations, purchasing technology at the mature stage in its lifecycle makes the most sense as it is likely to be well supported and any early problems will have been sorted out.

Eventually, technology becomes obsolete. Obsolete technology is replaced with new products and is no longer produced or supported by manufacturers. Organisations using obsolete technology will be likely to replace it as soon as possible. The lifespan of much ICT technology is very short – maybe just a few years.

▶ Standards

In the AS course you learnt that a standard is a common way of doing something, for example, storing data in a particular format or transferring data in a predetermined way.

Strategic choices concerning the purchase of hardware and software can be affected by the existence of standards. A business might decide to have a standard hardware platform running the same operating system throughout the organisation. Software packages used will be standardised too. This decision will reduce costs as better financial deals can be made with suppliers, there will be no compatibility problems, and ICT maintenance and support demands will be easier to manage.

A company might decide to use standard formats for storing business documents so that they can easily exchange data with other organisations through **Electronic Data Interchange (EDI)**. The ability to transfer data to or from another package or hardware platform in electronic form, known as **portability**, is a feature that is a very important requirement. It is likely to influence decisions relating to an organisation's IT strategy. Without portability, data may need to be re-typed, which would waste time and could lead to errors.

Data sharing might need to occur at a single-user level, between two software packages on the same PC, between two PCs using the same software, between two different platforms running different software, or even transferring data from an external device.

Portability can only exist if different manufacturers agree to adopt standards. Without these standards it would not be possible to transfer data between different computers or between other devices such as palmtops, mobile phones, digital cameras, video cameras and MP3 players.

Portability is an important sales feature for hardware and software companies. If a company upgrades its PCs, it expects to be able to transfer data from its old ones. If a more recent software version is purchased, it is expected that it would be able to read data from the previous version.

An organisation needs to establish an **ICT** system strategy so that the information needs of everyone in the organisation can be met.

Software, hardware and configuration choices have strategic implications for an organisation.

Factors influencing an **ICT** systems strategy within an organisation include:

▶ business goals

▶ available finance

▶ legacy systems

▶ the geography of clients

▶ business fulfilment

▶ the organisational structure of the organisation

▶ compliance

▶ legal issues.

The long-term use of **ICT** systems involves the need to manage an increasing volume of data.

There are several options available for managing older data:

▶ deleting records

▶ archiving records

▶ expanding storage space.

Procurement is the acquisition of hardware at the best possible price for the use of an organisation.

Organisations decide to upgrade their hardware or software provision for a number of reasons, including:

▶ hardware/software development

▶ organisational ethos

▶ task-driven change

▶ software change.

When upgrading, compatibility with existing systems needs to be considered.

Questions

◀

1. Give **four** reasons why a school might upgrade the hardware and/or software of its information systems. (4)

2. "Every organisation's ICT strategy is different". Discuss the factors that should be considered when writing an ICT strategy. (20)

3. Compliance is a most important issue for an organisation. Discuss the measures that a company must take to ensure compliance. (12)

4. When writing a corporate information systems strategy for an organisation, various factors have to be taken into account, including the structure of the organisation. Discuss other factors that might be considered when writing a corporate information systems strategy. (10)

5. A long-standing national chain of shoe shops has built up its information systems one at a time and without an overall plan. It is now having difficulty in getting these systems to work together effectively and has therefore decided to create a corporate information systems strategy.

Discuss the influence of the following factors when planning a corporate information systems strategy:
- the structure of the organisation
- information flow around the organisation
- personnel in the organisation.

The quality of written communication will be assessed in your answer. (20)

6

ICT Policies

AQA Unit 3 Section 5

An organisation will have a number of policies covering different aspects of the use of ICT, including:

- training
- security
- procurement.

All policies should be reviewed regularly to ensure that they still meet the objectives of the organisation and follow the overall ICT system strategy.

ICT training policy

An organisation's ICT training policy will include a statement of who needs to be trained, what training they need and how this training will be delivered. Any organisation that wishes to make the best use of its employees should have an IT Training Policy that is committed to staff development. It will be important to cater for the **Continuing Professional Development (CPD)** of staff to allow them to acquire the skills to progress in their field of work.

CPD is a systematic updating and extending of skills and knowledge relating to the workplace. As the term CPD implies, development should continue throughout an individual's career regardless of their age or role. The goal of CPD is to improve personal performance and enhance career progression. CPD can take a variety of forms; it includes much more than just formal training courses.

The training policy should fit in with other policies within the organisation. ICT training in a company needs to be planned and developed, based on that company's objectives. Training is often vulnerable to budget cutting as management sometimes sees it as an expensive luxury that has to be dropped when times are hard. This can lead to a reduction in the amount of training altogether or management may look to deliver training in different ways: perhaps a move to e-learning rather than sending employees on expensive courses at distant locations that also bring travel and living costs. However, if a training strategy is to be successful, it is important that decisions involving the ways in which training should be acquired fully take into account the needs of both the organisation and the individual employee. It is likely that a range of different methods will be used.

Training must be planned to complement the installation of new hardware and software. In some organisations the training of personnel when new software is installed is left to the IT department. This does not always result in the needs of the user being met in an appropriate way.

When a national museum implemented an email system for the first time, the training of the new users was not carefully planned and did not take into account the real needs of these users. The IT department decided when the training sessions should occur and the form that they should take without talking to the users to find out what would be most appropriate. As a result, many people were unable to attend any of the sessions due to other commitments. The content of the training sessions was also inappropriate and did not address the protocols and procedures that need to be established if email is to be successfully implemented within an organisation. It took a number of months to overcome the ill-feeling and confusion caused by the mishandled training.

New legislation may bring new training needs and these must be planned for in advance. New ventures within an organisation may also generate ICT training needs. These need to be identified early and planned for.

The ICT training needs of specific jobs must be established. These are often highlighted through the annual appraisal process, where an employee discusses his progress with his line manager and sets targets for the forthcoming year. A periodic ICT skills audit or needs analysis could be carried out to compare the skills required by each post with the skills of the person holding the post; this process will highlight training needs.

As employees are becoming more computer literate, so their training needs are changing over time. Many people are likely to demand more ICT training because they are interested in developing their skills further.

The ICT training needs of all new employees and current employees taking on new roles must be carefully assessed. Their current skill level should be compared with the requirements of the role and training put in place to plug the gaps.

The skills required, both from current employees and future recruits, will be established. A major training programme may be required. For many employees this training may just show them how to do their current jobs in a different way.

Activity 1 – ICT training needs analysis

The table below shows a sample page from a company's training needs analysis questionnaire. This page relates to Internet access; other software is covered on other pages.

In the questionnaire, employees are asked to score each specific skill. The scorings of all employees in a department could be added up for each specific skill; training could then be provided, targeting the low-scoring areas. An individual's overall score for a page shows whether or not he needs further training in that area.

The Internet and online activities *Tick the appropriate column: 0 – no skills; 3 – high skills*	**0**	**1**	**2**	**3**	**Need for job Y/N**
I can connect to the Internet					
I think I am a competent user of the Internet					
I use the Internet proactively					
I can open my web browser software					
I know where to put a URL in the browser to find the page I'm looking for					
I know how to find the information that I require					
I can add pages to my favourites/bookmarks					
I know how to download a document					
I know how to download software					
I can unzip programmes that I download					
I know how to save pictures to my hard drive					
I know how to change the appearance of my browser window					
I know how to set my default Home page					
I can send the page I am viewing to another person by email					
I know how to use a search engine, like Google or Ask					
I know how to navigate a website					
I know how to view and download Adobe Acrobat (PDF) documents					
I can use an online discussion forum					
I can change the security settings of my browser					

1. Work out your own score for "Internet and online activities".

2. Share the results with members of your class. Which specific skills scored the lowest?

3. Devise a similar training needs analysis table for another software package that you use regularly.

An ICT training policy is likely to contain some or all of the following:

- Review the ICT skills gap for the organisation – carry out a regular review.
- Review an individual's training needs annually – carry out an ICT training needs analyis to find out the specific needs of an employee.
- Encourage an atmosphere of on-going ICT learning within the organisation.

- Build in time for an employee to consolidate newly acquired ICT skills.
- Ensure that the organisation benefits as much as possible when an employee attends a training course by arranging for them to pass on some of their new knowledge and skills to colleagues.
- Build in a consideration of training costs to all hardware and software purchasing decisions.
- Provide all new employees with an introduction to ICT systems as part of their job induction; all employees should know where to go to if they have ICT problems.
- Take immediate steps to replace any valuable ICT skills held by an employee leaving the organisation. This is particularly crucial if no one else within the organisation has these skills.

ICT security policy ◀

If an organisation does not take adequate security measures then its operations will be at risk. Potential security threats exist to hardware, software and data and such threats can occur from within or outside an organisation.

Knowledge and data are probably the most important assets of any organisation. Companies must make sure that the confidentiality, integrity and availability of their data is maintained at all times. Three key security questions are:

- Who sees the data?
- Has the data been corrupted?
- Can I access data when I need it?

Although there are certainly many external threats to security, such as viruses or illegal access to systems by hackers, many experts think that the greatest security threat to ICT systems comes from people working within an organisation itself. Breaches of security can be caused through incompetence, for example: a failure to encrypt data sent over public networks; networks that are poorly implemented and protected only by simple passwords that are easy to crack; a firewall that stops nothing or protection software that is never updated.

On the other hand, breaches in security could be made on purpose by an employee, perhaps because they are unhappy with their job or their boss. Such situations sometimes result in the destruction of vital information. There could be an intent to steal information, either for personal use or for selling to others, such as a competitor.

The role of an ICT security policy is to lay down the procedures, guidelines and practices necessary to keep hardware, software and data safe from theft, misuse and unauthorised access. An organisation has a responsibility to maintain security measures to ensure that the requirements of the laws relating to ICT are not broken. An ICT security policy is established so that misuse can be prevented, with methods of detection and investigation being put in place.

Disciplinary procedures that will be used if a member of staff is found to be breaking the rules laid down in the policy will be explained. By enforcing the corporate security policy, organisations can minimise their ICT security risks.

Companies storing personal data are obliged to abide by the **Data Protection Act** which states that personal information must be kept secret. The company is responsible for ensuring that this data is not divulged and that staff are aware of the legal requirements.

An ICT security policy aims to:

- prevent misuse
- detect misuse through regular checking
- investigate misuse through the use of monitoring software and audit trails
- prevent unauthorised access
- lay down staff responsibilities in the prevention of misuse
- lay down disciplinary procedures for breaches of security.

An ICT security policy will need to be modified as new systems are introduced and old ones altered. For example, when insurance sellers are issued with laptops for the first time, to take with them when they visit clients, the company's security policy will have to be extended to contain rules to protect the data, the hardware and the software.

▶ Content of a security policy

The introduction of one company's ICT security booklet states: "The company is in a highly competitive industry in which the loss or unauthorised disclosure of sensitive information could be extremely detrimental to the company. These guidelines have been prepared to ensure that all staff understand the importance of safeguarding company information and the protective measures that need to be taken."

A security policy is likely first to state the purpose of the policy so that employees reading the policy are aware of why it is needed and the threats to security that could arise.

Staff responsibilities should be drawn up and disciplinary procedures agreed so that any misuse is dealt with. A staff ICT security document is likely to specify who can use company computer systems and to set out the password policy. It will lay down the steps that should be taken to provide protection against viruses and the physical security of computer systems. Rules will be provided to ensure that all computer use is within the law.

▶ Improving awareness of a security policy

For a security policy to be effective, the staff must be fully aware of its contents and it must be enforced. All users, including the most senior employees, must be seen to be keeping to the policy.

Many organisations ensure that staff receive a lecture from the security manager on issues of security when they join the organisation as part of an **induction training** programme for all new employees. They should have the contents of the policy carefully explained to them in an atmosphere that encourages them to ask questions.

The employee is usually given a handbook or leaflet with a copy of the policy to keep and read. They may also be given a CD-ROM or DVD that contains further information so that they can refer to the matter at a later time. In addition, every new employee will be expected to sign a copy of the corporate ICT security policy.

However, an introduction to the policy on induction day is unlikely to be enough. Guidance on the policy should be available to staff when it is required. In some organisations a new recruit is not allowed near a computer terminal until they have been successfully tested on the security matters relating to the tasks in their job.

It is vital that employees remember and absorb what is contained within the ICT security policy so that they do not break the rules through ignorance. A number of methods can be used to ensure that all staff are aware of the contents of the ICT security policy and of any changes that have recently been made. An organisation is likely to use a combination of these methods:

- a staff meeting at which the staff of the whole organisation or department can be reminded of security issues or introduced to new aspects
- training given to individuals through the use of an internal course
- a leaflet containing details of the policy in an easy-to-digest form, distributed to all staff
- the organisation's intranet or bulletin boards
- posters displayed throughout the buildings of the organisation to bring the importance of ICT security to the attention of employees
- emails sent to all staff reminding them of the policy.

In the USA, a new interactive training tool has been developed that tests employees' understanding of the organisation's corporate ICT security policy through the use of multiple choice tests. The new employee can only sign the policy when he passes the test.

case study 1	The Prudential Assurance Company has introduced an education scheme throughout the company to improve its ICT security. Their Head of Information Risk is reported to have said that companies are often too reliant on the technology of firewalls, antivirus software and intrusion detection systems, focusing too much on the technology and not enough on the people issues. "It is not that the technology isn't working, but it can't legislate for stupidity," he said.
▶ **Marketing security**	

Different approaches need to be taken to ensure the board and the staff take security seriously. The executives have direct legal responsibilities. If they are forcibly made aware of these they are likely to support security measures to remove any risk of being sent to prison.

The Prudential's computer-based training programme is reinforced through posters and coasters. It is important to use a variety of ways to educate staff; once a year is not sufficient; a more frequent approach has greater effect.

1. Why do you think the use of posters and coasters was included in the education plan?

2. Describe some ways in which ICT security could be breached due to user stupidity or lack of thought.

3. Devise slogans for ICT security that would fit on a coaster.

▶ Disciplinary measures

If an employee is discovered to have broken a rule in the corporate ICT security policy, for example, by installing unauthorised software on the organisation's network, they are likely to be subject to one of a number of sanctions.

They are likely to have network usage monitored very carefully and their access rights restricted. They may be given a verbal or a formal written warning. If the offence were of a serious nature, it could lead to suspension or even termination of employment. The employee could face legal action under the **Computer Misuse Act**.

Activity 2

A template for a corporate ICT security policy is shown below. Any organisation could use this as a basis for their own policy, customising it to meet the specific needs of their own organisation.

1. This document outlines guidelines for use of the computing systems and facilities located at or operated by [COMPANY NAME].

2. Use of the computer facilities includes the use of data and programs stored on [COMPANY NAME] computing systems, data and programs stored on magnetic tape, floppy disk, CD-ROM, or any storage media that is owned and maintained by [COMPANY NAME].

3. The purpose of these guidelines is to ensure that all [COMPANY NAME] users (business users, support personnel, technical users, and management) use the [COMPANY NAME] computing facilities in an effective, efficient, ethical and lawful manner.

4. [COMPANY NAME] computer accounts are to be used only for the purpose for which they are authorised and are not to be used for non-[COMPANY NAME]-related activities.

5. Users are responsible for protecting any information used in or stored on their [COMPANY NAME] accounts. Consult the [COMPANY NAME] User Guide for guidelines on protecting your account and information using the standard system-protection mechanisms.

6. Users shall not attempt to access any data, projects or programs contained on [COMPANY NAME] systems for which they do not have authorisation or explicit consent of the owner of the data, project or program.

7. Users shall not share their [COMPANY NAME] accounts with anyone. This includes sharing the password to the account or other means of sharing.

8. Users shall not make unauthorised copies of copyrighted software, except as permitted by law or by the owner of the copyright.

9. Users shall not make copies of system configuration files for their own, unauthorised personal use or to provide to other people or users for unauthorised uses.

10. Users shall not purposely engage in activities with the intent to: harass other users, degrade the performance of systems, deprive an authorised [COMPANY NAME] user access to a [COMPANY NAME] resource, obtain extra resources beyond those allocated, circumvent [COMPANY NAME] computer security measures or gain access to a [COMPANY NAME] system for which proper authorisation has not been given.

11. Electronic communication facilities (such as email or newsgroups) are for authorised [COMPANY NAME] use only. Fraudulent, harassing or obscene messages or materials shall not be sent from, to or stored on [COMPANY NAME] systems.

12. Users shall not download, install or run security programs or utilities that could potentially reveal weaknesses in the security of a system. For example, [COMPANY NAME] users shall not run password-cracking, key-logging, or any other potentially malicious programs on [COMPANY NAME] computing systems.

13. Any non-compliance with these requirements will constitute a security violation and will be reported to the management of [COMPANY NAME] and will result in short-term or permanent loss of access to [COMPANY NAME] computing systems. Serious violations may result in civil or criminal prosecution.

Signature: Date:

1. Define the terms "template" and "user account".
2. What activities could be referred to in Paragraph 4?
3. Draw up a table listing all the actions that a user must not take; for each give a clear reason why it should be avoided.
4. What sanctions for breaking the rules have been included? Can you include any other possible sanctions?
5. State what you would put into the User Guide referred to in Paragraph 5 of the policy to guide users.
6. Use the template to create an ICT security policy for your school or college. You might need to leave out some conditions, modify others and add further ones of your own.

case study 2
▶ Employees need training in security

A security company claims that businesses could cut external hacking attacks by 80 per cent by more effective enforcement of security policies among staff. They demonstrated how weak security can be when they carried out a spot survey of 150 people at Victoria Station in London that prompted two-thirds to reveal their network passwords.

Another recent survey found that 75 per cent of staff in the UK have not received any training on the security issues of using email and accessing the Internet at work. Although most were aware of the risk from viruses, few were able to identify or deal with potential threats.

1. What are the dangers that come from spam (the junk mail of the Internet) and jokes and other such mail being forwarded by friends?

2. Identify other common practices by members of staff that can lead to an ICT security risk.

3. Produce a plan for making and keeping the staff at your school or college aware of the ICT security policy.

4. Draw up a training needs analysis document for using email and accessing the Internet safely.

Figure 6.2 Victoria station

case study 3
▶ **MI5 laptop snatched at Paddington**

A few years ago, a desperate search went underway for a computer belonging to MI5, which was stolen from an agent at Paddington station. The laptop was believed to contain sensitive information relating to Northern Ireland.

The machine was snatched on the main concourse when the agent left it for a moment to help a group of youths. The security worker chased the thief but lost him in the station crowds.

The Home Office said that the information was highly encrypted and the theft did not pose a risk to national security.

1. Explain what is meant by encryption.

2. What other security measures could have prevented the thief from accessing vital information?

3. What disciplinary measure was likely to have been taken against the agent?

4. There have been many similar, recent cases of lost data. Summarise three examples.

ICT procurement policy ◀

Procuring means acquiring – an ICT procurement policy is about the ways in which ICT hardware and software is obtained for the organisation.

Organisations spend a lot of money on ICT: for the hardware, the software and the people who support it. Any large organisation should have an ICT procurement policy to ensure that best use is made of their investment in ICT and that any systems introduced are of benefit to the organisation. The senior management of an organisation needs to take a long-term view of ICT management.

A well thought-out and implemented ICT procurement policy will help an organisation to meet its objectives at the corporate as well as departmental level. Without an appropriate policy, services will not be delivered as intended, as the ICT resources will not be in place. ICT resources are expensive and budgets are limited – making the right purchasing decision is critical.

Without a centralised policy, as an organisation grows, different sections can develop their own systems that meet their specific needs; they may choose different hardware platforms and different software. This can lead to difficulties, making it hard to transfer data and information throughout the organisation because of hardware or software incompatibility. Without careful planning, systems can grow in an unstructured way, leading to inefficiency, redundancy and incompatibility. Although each department might work effectively and produce the information needed for their particular function, integration of the systems would be hard or impossible to achieve. Thus the overall information that the organisation would need for its management information system could not be brought together.

Having a clearly defined ICT procurement policy that ensures that there is a consistency of hardware and software across the organisation should make it possible to provide appropriate maintenance and support at a realistic cost. ICT technicians within the organisation will need to be familiar with only a limited range of hardware and software. A well embedded ICT procurement policy should establish order within an organisation so that different systems within the organisation complement each other.

A timescale needs to be laid down for the replacement of hardware. For example, desktop PCs may be given a life of three years. Other equipment may be given a longer or shorter life, as appropriate. This allows the managers involved with purchasing equipment to plan ahead as the replacement costs of hardware can be anticipated. With centralised control, new technology can be implemented over a reasonable period without having to change every piece of equipment at the same time.

An organisation may first realise that it needs an ICT procurement policy when it grows in size and the management becomes aware that ICT systems have been established in a rather haphazard way with no central planning. Often, the need for a policy is not felt until many problems arise within the organisation. Sometimes a new overall procurement policy has to be established when two organisations merge.

It is crucial that consultation takes place before policy decisions are made, particularly relating to the purchasing strategies for hardware and software. In order to make sure that departmental requirements are met, discussions must take place with departmental managers as they know what is needed within their own departments. Different departments within an organisation will have differing requirements that may result in them preferring to have different hardware or software. Including user departments in the decision making should result in the departments supporting and implementing the decision because they feel that they have ownership of it.

There can often be a conflict between the user and the organisational needs. In some cases, a "one solution for all" policy is just not appropriate. There will be specialist software requirements that are required for one department only due to the nature of the work done. For example, the accounts department within an organisation will require specialist accounting software that no one else in the organisation will need. It is very important that discussions take place with the head of department so that an agreement can be reached on the software to be used. If possible, software should be chosen that is able to export data files in a format that can be imported into the other software used within the organisation.

The choices that are made concerning the purchase of hardware and software, and also the kind of network infrastructure and operating system that are installed are likely to have major implications within the company. Such purchases are very costly and represent a major investment. New systems are unlikely to be totally replaced very frequently, so major purchasing choices will dictate the ICT structure and direction of the organisation for some time.

An organisation may become reliant upon the support given by the supplier or manufacturer. If a supplier or manufacturer is changed, then new relationships will need to be made with personnel in the new organisation.

When making a configuration choice for the network infrastructure and operating system, it is important to choose a set-up that is both flexible to use and able to be expanded as requirements change and grow. Organisations do not stay the same. They can diversify into new areas that will make new, extra demands on the ICT systems.

Decisions have to be made as to whether appropriate software already exists which can be bought and modified if necessary or whether it must be developed from scratch.

When choosing generic software that is likely to be used by all sections of an organisation, standardisation is usually important. The use of a standard office software suite and other commonly used software allows easy maintenance and support from the ICT technical team within the organisation. Documents and other data can be shared easily between users. Training can be standardised across all departments for the relevant applications.

The use of a standard operating system across a whole organisation will provide a standard look and feel. Software can support certain file formats; if the same standard software is used, all departments can share documents and guarantee that they can be understood.

Ideally, an organisation's ICT technical department would have identical workstations for all users. This would simplify maintenance and would allow the best discount deal to be worked out with the manufacturer. However, in reality, such a situation is unlikely to occur, except in very small organisations. To replace all workstations in one go is likely to prove too costly. Most organisations carry out a rolling programme of replacement to spread costs more evenly.

Even when the hardware purchases are standardised within an organisation, maintenance problems can arise if computers are configured in different ways.

In a rapidly changing environment where hardware and software become out of date very quickly, it is vital to plan ahead. Future expansion needs must always be considered, although these are unlikely to be exactly known.

case study 4
▶ Software change

A new head of department, Sean, was recruited to run the sales department of a business, StrongRope, that manufactures and sells rope. The spreadsheet software that was used at StrongRope was different from the one that was used in Sean's previous job. As he felt more comfortable with the old software, he persuaded his team to change to the package that he was more familiar with and purchased the required licences from his own budget.

All seemed to go well for a while, but soon some of his team became frustrated as they could not use the new software as well as they wished and there was no help available within StrongRope, as everyone else used a different package. The in-house support team did not have expertise with the new spreadsheet software, the cost of providing specific support was beyond Sean's budget and the company was not prepared to pay either.

The issue blew up when the Managing Director found out that his PA had been unable to produce a report, that should have included linked data from the sales department spreadsheets, as there was no common data format for transfer. He told Raj, the head of ICT, who was unaware that Sean had installed a different software package.

Raj realised that there were likely to be problems with the spreadsheet software as the company had a special agreement with the original spreadsheet provider that gave them the required licences at a lower rate so long as the company did not use any other spreadsheet.

The Managing Director immediately told Sean to get rid of the new software and to revert to using the original.

1. List the reasons why Sean should not have used the new software.

2. How could the problem described above have been prevented?

case study 5
▶ **Pump up the program**

(Based on an article by Brian Clegg, *PC Week*)
Software upgrades are a mixed blessing. Upgrading is plagued with hidden costs and difficulties such as incompatibilities with previous versions or other installed software and insufficient system resources. Even the users who beg for the latest version will need extra training and support.

An important consideration of upgrading is the cost of new software licences. The amount paid can be subject to negotiation: vendors have a variety of approaches. Oracle's support agreement for server products includes free upgrading. This removes any concern about the cost of new licences, but limits the ICT manager's choice. IBM effectively insures against upgrades, offering a protection scheme to provide low-cost upgrades provided you pay 15 per cent extra on the original licence.

The biggest upgrade expense can be training users. If benefits are to be gained, there is a training need, and companies that aren't prepared to provide that training will have hidden costs in the time taken to perform once familiar tasks.

However, training is the most disputed area. At one large company, a manager comments, "We do not put much resource into user training. It does not work for most people and they can't afford the time out from fee-earning work. We find most people who want to use software pick it up and use it to a level they are happy with themselves. If they get really desperate they can call my department for help."

Sometimes an upgrade will generate hidden training requirements. A senior network analyst with the same company recalls problems with a new version of Microsoft Project: "There were differences in the way Project handled changes, for example, tasks that had slipped. We treated the upgrade as if it was a matter of pure extra benefits, but ignored the differences in the way the product worked, resulting in problems."

The message from the ICT managers is that you should take charge of upgrading – don't leave it to the vendors to tell you when to do it.

1. List the costs of upgrading software identified in this article.

2. Describe the training needs that can arise from upgrading software.

3. Explain the reasons why software vendors make such frequent changes to their software.

An organisation needs to have an **ICT** training strategy to ensure that each employee has the skills necessary to carry out his job.

An organisation needs to have a corporate **ICT** security policy. Its aim would be:

▶ to prevent misuse from occurring

▶ to enable any misuse that did occur to be detected and investigated

▶ to lay down procedures that should prevent misuse

▶ to establish disciplinary procedures to be used when an employee has been found committing an act of misuse.

Software, hardware and configuration choices have strategic implications for an organisation.

Within a company, hardware and software procurement should be standardised to ensure:

▶ compatibility with existing data

▶ compatibility with existing hardware

▶ that colleagues can share data where necessary

▶ that colleagues can communicate where necessary (e.g. by email)

▶ that technical support is available

▶ that legal software licensing requirements are met

▶ that training is available

▶ that the hardware can cope with possible future demands.

Questions

◀

1. A publishing company wishes to standardise its ICT systems. Managers from all departments of this company are consulted before any standardisation takes place.

   a) Describe, using an example, **one** reason why this consultation is necessary. (2)

   b) As part of this standardisation strategy, it is decided that:
   - no computer hardware will be used for more than a fixed number of years
   - all departments will have a standard set of applications software
   - the software must support a certain set of file formats.

      Explain **two** reasons why the company has decided to adopt this strategy. (4)

   January 2004 AQA ICT 5

2. An estate agency company has a chain of 15 offices all situated in the South of England. It has recently merged with a smaller agency in the area that has five offices. Both agencies have computer systems that have been in use for several years. The management have decided to upgrade the hardware and software for all the offices.

   Discuss the implications of upgrading, paying attention to the following:

   a) the hardware requirements and the factors that will affect the choice

   b) the software requirements and the factors that will affect the choice

   c) any particular problems that will arise as a result of merging two different computer systems used by the merging organisations.

   The quality of written communication will be assessed in your answer. (20)

3. A dental practice has installed a new information system that links patient records to the financial systems of the practice. The financial records must be secure against fraud.

   Describe the factors that should be included in an ICT security policy for the practice. (8)

4. "Within an organisation, successful ICT training doesn't just happen, it has to be planned for."

   Discuss the need for and content of an ICT training policy. (20)

5. A soft drinks' manufacturer uses one particular hardware, operating system and applications package combination throughout its organisation. One department finds that this particular set-up does not suit its needs. The manager of this department decides to purchase a different hardware and operating system combination and the specialist applications that he requires.

   The manufacturer has an ICT procurement policy. Explain why the manager should consult this policy and give reasons why he might decide to change his decision after reading the policy. (10)

7

Legislation
AQA Unit 3 Section 6

Impact of legislation on ICT policies   ◀

Laws are a major influence constraining the operations of businesses. The procedures within a company must reflect the requirements of the legislation to ensure that all laws are being adhered to. When new legislation is passed, an organisation needs to look at current practice to check that new requirements are being met and, if necessary, modify procedures accordingly.

If a company's employee breaks the law while at work, the company is legally responsible as well as the individual, unless it can be proved that the company has done everything reasonable to prevent the employee breaking the law. For example, if an employee discloses personal information and unwittingly breaks the Data Protection Act, the company can be prosecuted.

Several companies have ended up in court because of the actions of their employees. As well as the possibility of a large fine, the company is likely to suffer through bad publicity.

Companies must ensure that employees are aware of:

■ the law
■ what employees must and must not do
■ sanctions against employees if they are found to have broken the law.

The requirement of an organisation to ensure that all its employees are aware of their legal responsibilities includes those laws that relate to ICT:

■ Data Protection Acts of 1984 and 1998
■ Computer Misuse Act 1990
■ Copyright Designs and Patent Act 1988
■ Health and Safety at Work Act 1974 and the EU Health and Safety Directive 87/391
■ Regulation of Investigatory Powers Act 2000 (Interception of private communications)
■ Electronic Commerce (EC Directive) Regulations 2002
■ Freedom of Information Act 2000
■ Copyright and Rights in Databases Regulations 1997.

You will have studied the details of some of these acts as part of your ICT AS Level course.

The **Regulation of Investigatory Powers Act (RIPA) 2000** concerns the use of a range of investigative powers by government security services and law enforcement authorities. Its purpose is to help the prevention of crime, including terrorism. RIPA updates previous legislation concerning the interception of communications as it takes into account technological change, for example, the expanding use of email and the growth of the Internet.

As a result of the act, the Secretary of State was able to make regulations allowing businesses, in specific circumstances, to intercept electronic communications in the course of normal business activities, without the consent of either the sender or the recipient. The business might need to do this to investigate or detect any unauthorised use of its systems, to check that employees are abiding by its own policies or to prevent or detect crime, such as breaches of the Computer Misuse or Data Protection Acts. These regulations are called the Telecommunications (Lawful Business Practice) (Interception of Communications) Regulations 2000. A business does not need to gain consent before intercepting for the purposes given in the Regulations, but first must inform users that interceptions may take place. There are safeguards under the Regulations so interception is only permitted under certain conditions.

The **Electronic Commerce (EC Directive) Regulations 2002** requires that all commercial websites must provide certain minimum information about the supplier, its products and services.

If the site accepts online transactions, it must also provide information about the ordering process and the contract and details of the technical steps a customer will need to go through to conclude the contract. The data entry screen must allow the customer to identify and correct input errors before placing the order; the supplier must acknowledge receipt of the order without undue delay.

The designer of any commercial website must ensure that it complies with the requirements of the Electronic Commerce (EC Directive) Regulations 2002.

The **Freedom of Information Act** came into force on 1 January 2005. It gives an individual the right to request from any public body all the information they have on any subject chosen by the individual. The organisation is obliged to supply the information within a month, unless there is a good reason not to do so. Public bodies must also maintain publication schemes to ensure the regular release of information.

Activity I

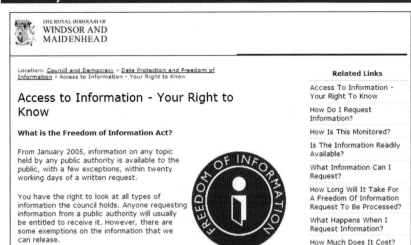

Figure 7.1 Freedom of Information Act

1. Explore the Royal Borough of Windsor and Maidenhead's website http://www.rbwm.gov.uk/web/foi_access.htm.

2. In your own words summarise the following:
   - How can a member of the public obtain information?
   - What exempts information from being accessed?
   - When might a request for information take longer than 20 days to be met?
   - How much will it cost?

3. Explain how the Freedom of Information Enquiry process flowchart would be used.

The **Copyright and Rights in Databases Regulations 1997**, which implement the EC Database Directive on the legal protection of databases, is designed to protect the investment of money, time and effort that goes into compiling databases. The Regulations create an important right to prevent the unauthorised extraction of the whole or a substantial part of the contents of a database.

Impact of legislation on procedures ◄

An organisation might need to alter many of its procedures to ensure that the laws are kept. For example, to comply with the Copyright Designs and Patent Act, it might be necessary to prevent individual users from purchasing and installing their own software. Instead, all such software purchases should be centralised with the ICT support department so that careful records can be kept to ensure that the correct licences are held for all the software installed on the organisation's computers.

New employees usually undergo an induction course which provides them with a background to the organisation as well as giving specific training about the job. This course should include a discussion of the legal requirements of the post. All employees should be given a handbook which lays out their legal responsibilities. It is useful to provide a list of "dos and don'ts".

It is vital that managers take an active role to ensure that legislation is enforced within an organisation. Employees should be reminded of the law through individual memos, public notices posted on walls, and the organisation's intranet. Employees should be expected to sign an agreement that lists the rules and procedures that apply to ensure that the requirements of all relevant legislation are met.

The Data Protection Act (DPA) was created to provide individuals with rights that protect them against the misuse of personal data held about them. The main aspects of the DPA are that all personal data held should be secure, accurate and should only be used for the purpose for which it was gathered. Individuals have the right to see data kept about them and can demand that errors in the data be corrected.

Methods of enforcing legislation ◄

▶ Data Protection Act (1984 and 1998)

Every organisation must ensure that they **register** with the Information Commissioner all **data stores** that fall under the DPA. It should be clearly stated how the data is to be used and to whom it is to be passed on. Enquiries should be made to the Commissioner in any cases of doubt about the need to register personal data. The organisation should draw up a written data protection policy which should make clear what data can be kept and for how long.

Each department should appoint a Data Protection Officer who is responsible for monitoring practices and making sure they are following the requirements of the act. Procedures need to be set up to allow for the investigation of possible breaches within the department.

The person whose personal data is being stored is referred to as the **data subject** in the DPA. An organisation should make public its privacy policy and the rights of data subjects. They should be made aware of the use to which their personal data is to be put and no unnecessary data should be collected. **No data can be sold to other organisations** without the data subject's consent. This is often obtained by adding a tick box to the form on which the data is being collected – if the subject does not tick the box then the personal data cannot be given or sold to other organisations.

Data collection methods should be designed to ensure that the data stored is **accurate** and methods need to be put in place to ensure that accuracy is maintained. Systems often fall down in this respect: the initial data collection is accurate but subsequent changes to the data are not recorded systematically. It is most important that a systems analyst takes data protection requirements fully into account at the design stage of any new system. The **intended "life"** of data should be established and procedures put in place to ensure that the data is destroyed when this time has expired.

Procedures need to be in place within the organisation to allow the data subject to **access the information** stored about them. The facilities to make corrections if errors are found must be in place.

It is important that all employees are aware of rulings of the act and of their responsibilities. An organisation must use a variety of methods to remind all staff of their responsibilities in keeping data private. Matters of data protection should be included in the organisation's security policy where the responsibilities and liabilities of employees should be highlighted. Every employee should be expected to sign a copy of the policy on joining the organisation.

Each employee should only be given access to the data that they require to carry out the tasks as laid out in their job description. This should be reflected in the access level assigned to them.

An individual should be responsible within a work area for ensuring that data security and privacy is maintained; this could be the Data Protection Officer himself, or it could be delegated to another manager. Spot checks could be made to ensure that the act is being complied with and staff should be reminded on a regular basis of the need for care and compliance.

The employees' code of practice should state that they should not create their own individual databases, perhaps on their own workstation, that contain personal data without telling the organisation's Data Protection Officer who will register the database with the Commissioner.

Data should be **protected** through the use of password protection, physical security methods, firewalls and encryption. However, such protection by itself will not be enough. Careful **operational procedures** need to be set up to ensure that personal data is not disclosed to unauthorised people. Employees need to be trained not to disclose personal information, either in person or over the telephone, without carrying out careful checks that the person they are speaking to is permitted to be given the information. Paper copies of data that have been printed out must always be stored in a secure place out of sight of prying eyes.

Disciplinary procedures, that will be used when an employee breaches the code of practice, need to be in place within the organisation.

---

case study 1

▶ **M&S admits to being in breach of Data Protection Act for 15 years**

Some years ago, Marks & Spencer was forced to tighten its procedures for dealing with charge-card holders after learning it had been acting in breach of the Data Protection Act for almost 15 years.

The company will now only disclose information relating to charge-card accounts to the primary account holder, who is legally liable for paying the bill. In the past, supplementary card holders who are authorised to charge goods to another person's account but are not responsible for paying the bill, were given access to this data and were allowed to alter personal details, such as mailing addresses.

This could constitute a breach of the eighth data protection principle, which calls for organisations to take steps to prevent unauthorised access to personal data.

A Marks & Spencer spokesman stated that the retailer had been acting in breach of the original DPA since it was passed in 1984, but added that it was unlikely to be alone in this regard.

Marks & Spencer had always sought to both comply with legislation and meet customers' requirements, a second spokesman added. An account holder whose details were altered by a supplementary card holder could allege that the store was in breach of this principle if problems arose afterwards, the spokesman said. He added that stores needed to juggle their desire to be customer-friendly with the requirement to protect customers' personal data.

■ What steps would Marks & Spencer have to take to keep within the DPA?

Activity 2

1. Prepare a slideshow to present to employees in an organisation showing how the DPA affects them. You should include all the measures that they should be taking to ensure that they comply with the DPA in their work.
2. Find three examples of where personal data is collected. For each example, describe how the data subject is informed of their rights under the DPA.
3. Explore the website www.ico.gov.uk.

▶ **Computer Misuse Act (1990)**

This act aims to protect computer users against malicious vandalism and information theft. Hacking and knowingly spreading computer viruses were made crimes under the act, which aims to secure computer material against unauthorised access and modification.

An organisation needs to make its employees aware of the act and to establish procedures that will make it difficult for employees to break the law.

Employees should be banned from using external disks, USB memory sticks and other removable storage media on the organisation's computers. They should not be allowed to install any software of their own on to their workstation. It is important that software downloaded from the Internet is included in this ban. Such a rule can be enforced by spot checks of the hard disks of employees to detect any unauthorised software and backed up with appropriate disciplinary action if an employee is found to have broken the rules.

Dividing up a job so that no one individual has access to all parts of the system is necessary so that no employee is put in a position where they can carry out a fraud. Some banks insist that key staff take a minimum of two weeks of their annual leave at one time to make it harder for them to sustain a fraud.

▶ Copyright Designs and Patent Act (1988)

Copyright laws protect the intellectual rights of authors, composers and artists. They also apply to computer software. When you buy software you do not buy the program, only the right to use it under the terms of the licence. It is illegal to copy or use software without having obtained the appropriate licence.

Every organisation needs to take positive steps to establish procedures that will ensure that the Copyright Designs and Patent Act is not being broken. No software should be used without the appropriate licences being in place. Particular care needs to be taken when LANs are used as sufficient licences for the number of users must have been obtained. The use of software should be monitored; it is possible to buy network software that will keep track of the number of users of a particular piece of software and limit the number of concurrent users to the number of licences held. Once the licensed number of users are accessing a piece of software, other users will be denied access to the software.

Software should only be installed with permission. **Spot checks** can be made to check that employees have not installed programs illegally. If unauthorised software is found on a user's workstation it should be removed immediately and appropriate disciplinary measures taken. Laptop computers should be collected in by the ICT department on a regular basis and checks made to ensure that the software installed has been correctly authorised. Employees should not be allowed to copy software for unlicensed home use. Disciplinary action should be taken if they are found to be doing so.

Software purchasing and control should be centralised. All requests for software should be made to one person or team who has the responsibility for ordering and overseeing the installation of the software. They will be able to ensure that all installed software is correctly licensed. An **inventory** should be kept that holds details of all software that is installed on computers within the organisation and the licences that are held. Such centralisation also allows reliable, known suppliers to be used and makes the checking that no unauthorised software has been installed a relatively straightforward matter.

What is unauthorised software in an organisation? It could be:

- software that has been installed without the permission of the network manager
- software that does not have the necessary licence
- software that is authorised, but has had its source code changed without permission
- software personally owned by the employee
- software that is not standard within the organisation
- software downloaded from the Internet
- pirated software
- software that might affect the network security.

Regular and systematic audits should be taken to ensure that the central inventory holds a correct record of software installation.

Software theft

Software theft can be divided into two categories: piracy and counterfeiting.

- **Piracy** occurs when more copies of software are made than the number of licences purchased. Many users do not realise that it is illegal and can sometimes do this unwittingly.
- **Counterfeiting** is when software is illegally copied for sale to other users. Often, counterfeit software comes without manuals, user guides or tutorials. The software cannot be registered, so there is no technical support or upgrade service available. An added problem for users is that such software carries a high risk of carrying a virus.

Figure 7.2 Federation Against Software Theft

▶ Health and safety legislation

Figure 7.3 Health and safety

Organisations must maintain a healthy and safe environment for work. The role of a **health and safety officer**, who checks that the appropriate laws are complied with, must be established. The safety officer should review health and safety issues. A safety committee, with representatives from all parts of the organisation, should discuss safety matters on a regular basis. Management should encourage and give recognition to a trade union health and safety representative who could act on and report the concerns of colleagues. Such representatives should be given a very thorough training.

It is the management's responsibility to ensure that **risk assessments** are carried out on a regular basis.

All staff need to be reminded regularly of the importance of health and safety issues. Posters can be displayed which show potential hazards and precautions to be taken. A health and safety policy should be produced and a copy given to all staff. Regular training should be undertaken to inform and remind employees of potential health and safety hazards when working with computers, especially VDUs, and their responsibilities in preventing them.

Regular **inspections** of workstations should be carried out against health and safety criteria, such as VDU emissions and electrical safety. Procedures must be in place to replace faulty equipment in a timely manner. Inspection of workstations should also take place against ergonomic criteria such as seat positioning, sight levels and the use of wrist supports; any deficiencies should be followed up.

In workplaces where mistakes can be life threatening, such as oil refineries, **safety incentive schemes** are often introduced. In one such scheme, the team or location with the best safety record each year is rewarded with a bonus payment.

When installing a new computer or designing the layout for a new office, it is important that space guidelines are complied with. Care should be taken to make sure that equipment and furniture are **ergonomically** designed for the required use.

For employees who are using a computer for most of their working day, there needs to be a clear understanding that appropriate breaks are built in and facilities for refreshment and relaxation away from the computer should be provided.

An organisation should establish a policy that specifies the human–computer interface (HCI) requirements for software design that should be adhered to whenever new systems are developed.

case study 2
▶ **Computer-based training for health and safety**

A large multinational retail company had problems keeping its in-store employees up to date with health and safety issues. The company did not employ dedicated trainers for its stores; the responsibility for keeping staff up to date fell on the store managers.

Most employees were given a thorough and appropriate induction training programme when they first joined the store, but ongoing and refresher training was more haphazard.

To get around this problem, an online computer-based training package was devised that staff could use at times convenient to them. A log of employee use was maintained centrally that recorded both access to the system by individuals and details of their performance while working through the material. In this way, employees could be reminded when they needed a refresher.

■ In what ways would the computer-based training ensure that the company met its obligations for staff training in health and safety?

▶ Freedom of Information Act (2000)

On receiving a request for information, public authorities must acknowledge and log it. The request must be answered within 20 working days unless the requested information is exempt from disclosure. The organisation will need to put a system in place that will ensure that any requests are dealt with appropriately and promptly.

Any organisation that is covered by the Act must establish an active publication scheme; these are generally made accessible on the organisation's website. The active publication scheme must be approved by the Information Commissioner. They should be regularly reviewed and updated.

case study 3
▶ Natural History Museum

To comply with the Freedom of Information Act, the Natural History Museum maintains a section on its website that provides details of how access to a range of information about the museum can be obtained.

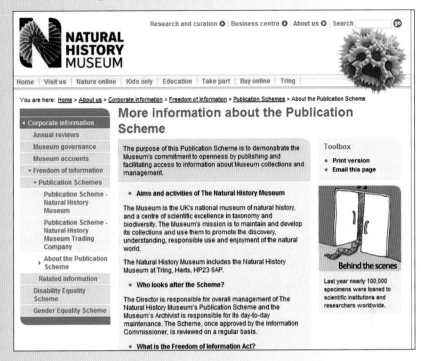

Figure 7.4 National History Museum website

1. Explore the contents of the website at http://www.nhm.ac.uk/about-us/corporate-information/freedom-of-information/publication-schemes/publication-scheme/visitor-services/general.html.

2. Discuss the implications for the museum of maintaining this active publication scheme.

SUMMARY

An organisation has a responsibility to ensure that all its employees are aware of laws relating to ICT and their responsibilities under these laws:

▶ **Data Protection Acts 1984 and 1998**

▶ **Computer Misuse Act 1990**

▶ **Copyright Designs and Patent Act 1988**

▶ **Health and Safety at Work Act 1974**

▶ **EU Health and Safety Directive 87/391**

▶ **The Regulation of Investigatory Powers Act 2000 (Interception of private communications)**

▶ **Electronic Commerce (EC Directive) Regulations 2002**

▶ **Freedom of Information Act 2000.**

Methods of enforcing and controlling data protection within an organisation include:

▶ appointing a **Data Protection Officer** to monitor systems

▶ establishing procedures to follow up possible breaches

▶ establishing security methods such as firewalls, the use of passwords and data encryption

▶ including a clause in the code of practice stating that employees should not build up their own databases of personal data

▶ using a variety of methods to educate all staff of their responsibilities in keeping data private

▶ establishing and circulating disciplinary measures that will be undertaken if an employee does not comply with the **DPA.**

Methods of enforcing and controlling software misuse within an organisation include:

▶ banning employees from installing unauthorised, unlicensed software

▶ banning employees from copying software for unlicensed home use

▶ separating duties between employees so that no one person does the complete job

▶ centrally controlling the purchase and maintenance of all software licences

▶ carrying out spot checks, as well as regular audits, to ensure that no unauthorised software is stored on individual computers

▶ disciplining employees who break the rules.

Methods of enforcing and controlling health and safety legislation within an organisation include:

▶ appointing a safety officer

▶ regularly inspecting workstations against health and safety criteria

▶ regularly inspecting workstations against ergonomic criteria

▶ carrying out regular staff training regarding health and safety legislation with respect to computer use

▶ ensuring that all software used is appropriately designed

▶ establishing procedures that ensure that faulty equipment is replaced in a timely manner

▶ producing memos, leaflets or posters to advise on good health and safety practice

▶ establishing disciplinary procedures to use when health and safety rules are breached.

Questions

1. Describe methods that an organisation can use to ensure that health and safety legislation is enforced within the organisation. (8)

2. Current data protection legislation lays down the requirements that an organisation must follow in relation to the personal data relating to customers and employees that it holds. Staff training is one method of raising awareness of the legislation.

   a) Describe **three** ways in which the training could be provided. (6)

   b) Describe **three** further methods, other than training, that an organisation should use to ensure that the requirements of data protection legislation are met. (6)

3. Organisations that make use of information technology and use ICT systems have to ensure that they comply with the relevant legislation currently in place.

Discuss the implications of complying with such legislation on the operation of an organisation, showing how these may impact on the procedures used by the organisation.

The quality of written communication will be assessed in your answer. (20)

8

Developing ICT solutions

AQA Unit 3 Section 7

In spite of many technical advances and the investment of huge amounts of money, time and effort, many ICT systems have not fulfilled their promise and have failed to provide the organisation with the solution that they needed. Most such systems involve complex and extensive software and are very often designed specifically for the end users.

What exactly do we mean by a successful ICT project? Probably the best way of defining one is a project that does what the organisation intended, on time and within budget. An ICT solution is not an end in its own right – ICT should be used to enable a business to perform better and the benefits that a new system is to bring need to be expressed very clearly. Unfortunately, what an organisation requires from a new system is not always plain.

Factors that contribute to successful development ◄

For an ICT solution to be successful then, it is important that very clear and realistic goals are set out at the start of the project and agreed by all involved. All those involved need to be clear exactly what is wanted and why – ICT solutions have to meet a need within the organisation and it is crucial that the reason for its development is clear to all. For example, a solution designed to lessen the stress and strain on end users by reducing data entry would be different from one designed to increase management information. The benefits that the ICT solution needs to produce should be explicitly stated before the start of the project. Specific objectives should include the timescale for completion, exactly what the development team has agreed to deliver and the size of budget available.

▶ Management involvement

Senior management must be involved throughout the project. At the inception of the project, when the objectives are being established and the scope of the ICT solution is being defined, senior management has a crucial role. Managers need to understand clearly what specific problem the solution is aiming to solve. The costs and benefits to the organisation need to be weighed carefully before any decision is made to proceed with the project. Once agreed, the project goals need to be explained clearly and unambiguously to all involved.

It is vital too that the management is involved at all subsequent stages of the system development. They need to have input at the design phase of the development process so that they can be sure that the proposed ICT solution will meet the agreed requirements. The management will need to be kept informed of developments as the project progresses; regular updates on budgeting and timescale issues should be referred to them on a regular basis.

To be able to make informed decisions, members of management will need to have an up-to-date knowledge of current ICT systems and their capabilities. They will need to be able to make decisions that are not blinded by the ICT experts' knowledge and use of jargon. With such knowledge they will be less likely to make inappropriate or excessive demands of the developing system.

Projects are successful when ICT is seen as an integral part of the organisation rather than as a stand-alone discipline. Ideally, at least one member of the board should have a strong background in ICT.

► End user involvement

Just as it is important to involve management in every stage of an ICT project's development, so it is important to involve the end users, who will use the system once it has been developed. If they are involved and their opinions sought as the system develops, they will feel ownership of the system and be keen for it to succeed.

End-users have a very important part to play in the analysis stage, when the requirements for any new ICT solution are being drawn up. The end user is the person who is carrying out the tasks for which a new ICT solution is being found. He or she will have detailed knowledge of what is involved in those tasks. When a new system is being designed, end users should be very involved. They will be able to tell the developers whether or not suggested design features are practical and will be able to suggest modifications and improvements.

Everyone likes to feel involved and have their opinions valued. An ICT team, especially if it is made up of experts from outside the organisation, will find it hard to implement a new system successfully if it has not built up the right working relationship with the system's end users. Just coming in and telling them how the new system will work and change their jobs is unlikely to gain their cooperation. If the end users are listened to from the start and their ideas and opinions are used to shape the project, they are likely to back the project with enthusiasm and feel committed to make it work. The ICT team should set up user groups which should meet regularly to discuss the project's progress.

▶ Effective ICT team work

ICT projects are usually so large that they cannot be implemented by just one person. Some large projects, such as a new ticketing and passenger tracking system for the London Underground, require hundreds of thousands of man-hours to complete. ICT projects are normally undertaken by a team of people working together. No one person could do all the work on their own, even if they had the time, as a wide range of skills and knowledge will be required. The project team members should be selected with care to complement each other so that together they possess the drive, skills and knowledge necessary for implementation. It is crucial that, from the very beginning of the project, the whole team works to agreed standards.

A large project is likely to be broken down into a number of more manageable **subtasks** (or subprojects). Each subtask will be allocated to a smaller, more manageable team. Such a team should consist of a number that the team leader can control easily, perhaps four to six members. Breaking up a project into tasks makes it easier to control. Subtasks that are not dependent upon each other can be carried out concurrently (at the same time). This can bring down the overall completion time of the project and enables stricter control of the time spent on each sub area. Subtasks are more manageable as they have clearly defined and realisable objectives. Very often **milestones** are identified. A milestone is an important point in a project. Examples of milestones could be when all coding has been completed, or when the network infrastructure has been installed. Reaching a milestone represents significant progress towards the completion of the project.

It is not surprising that the nature of the ICT team running a project has a marked effect on its successful outcome.

As part of the AS course, you studied the use and organisation of ICT teams (see *ICT for AS Level*, Chapter 16). A successful team was described as having the following characteristics:

- good leadership
- an appropriate balance of skills and areas of expertise amongst the members of the team, with suitable allocation of tasks
- adequate planning and scheduling of tasks
- adherence to agreed standards
- good communication skills both with users and within the team.

The overall project leader needs to have good technical knowledge and a clear understanding of the business as well as project management and logistical skills. A project needs to be well managed and have adequate resources and time allocated to it if it is to be successful. The leader needs to be able to make tough decisions and take responsibility for those decisions.

Inadequate teamwork can lead to the chain breaking at its weakest link. Unless colleagues cooperate, some work can be left undone and other work may be repeated. A successful implementation depends upon an effective and balanced team, with everyone working together on appropriate tasks, well controlled by good leadership.

case study 1
▶ eCourier

Figure 8.1 Motorcycle courier

eCourier are a courier service based in London that operates 24/7. It is an innovative company that delivers goods anywhere within the country within a day. It uses mobile devices and Global Positioning Systems (GPS) to track its couriers. Clients can arrange the transportation of a parcel online using eCourier's booking system. The ICT system that was developed to manage the organisation was ground-breaking.

eCourier set up from scratch in 2003 to provide an online booking system that allowed customers to track the progress of their parcels in real time on a map, showing the exact street where the parcel was at any time. Advanced ICT systems were needed to manage the couriers working for the company; the couriers used a wide range of vehicles. The system needed to allocate the most suitable courier for a delivery which would depend on couriers' current location relative to the pickup point, current road congestion, weather conditions and the size of the vehicles. Couriers were all to be provided with palmtop computers with global positioning systems (GPS) technology.

The business was set up by two people, one of whom led the project team to develop the ICT system. He had extensive experience of the courier business as well as excellent technical expertise. A small team of 15 people was established although not all the members were working for the whole time of its development. The team members were chosen on the basis of their extensive and complementary skills and experience; they all shared an enthusiasm and excitement about the new system they were developing. All the team members worked in the same London open-plan office.

Throughout the project development, the team undertook extensive discussions with potential customers to find out exactly what they would require from the system.

The new system was installed on time and the company has been very successful. eCourier is now the fastest-growing courier company in London and has won a number of awards as an innovative new business.

■ Explain why eCourier's ICT system was developed so successfully.

Factors that contribute to unsuccessful development ◄

As stated earlier, a successful project is one that implements a system that does what the organisation intended, on time and within budget. Unfortunately, not all projects can be categorised as successful. Many are implemented late or over budget. A number of projects, when finally implemented, fail to produce the solution for which they were developed.

► Inadequate analysis

The early stages of the development of a new system are crucial to its success. If inadequate analysis is undertaken there will be insufficient understanding of the nature of the problem; important factors will be missed that could make the final, implemented solution unworkable. Techniques of analysis involve observation of the current work being done, studying all documents in use and following them around as well as interviewing all those involved with the work. If insufficient time or attention is given to any of these aspects, an incomplete picture of the requirements of the new solution could be made.

It is important to follow an accepted methodology in a standard way to allow effective analysis, thus making sure that no important steps are missed.

► Unrealistic project plan

Every project has a plan that lays down which team member carries out which tasks. Clear **timescales** must be established so that a project can be monitored using **deadlines** for the completion of the various stages. These deadlines should be realistic and both parties must agree to them.

The management and the project team establish agreed deliverables. A **deliverable** is the name given to something that actually has to be produced (or delivered) by the project team and is likely to include fully tested and installed programs, full documentation and training material for users. Deliverables should fully meet the user's requirements and should be produced to agreed standards.

As discussed earlier, at the start of the project, **milestones** are agreed. A **milestone** is a stage in the project when the management must give **approval for the project to proceed** further. This ensures that the management is satisfied with the work to date. They would then give the go-ahead for the project to continue to the next stage.

Planning is crucial to the success of any project. It is very important that enough time and thought is given to realistic planning. If not, then essential tasks can be overlooked which can result in a project running over time or over budget. A careful analysis of risk should be carried out at the start of the project.

Scheduling involves allocating resources and facilities so that they are available when required. Resources can be human or physical. Delay in a resource being available may lead to slippage in deadlines which could incur extra expense. For example, the network cabling needs to be in place before the computers can be installed. Under-floor power cables need to be installed early on before the floor is laid. There are a number of project-planning techniques and associated software that are used with large projects.

▶ Insufficient monitoring

An important task for a project leader is to monitor the progress of the project as it proceeds and to report back to management. Inevitably, unexpected problems will arise and certain tasks will overrun. Sometimes extra tasks arise that were not identified at the start of the project. The project manager will have to adjust the schedule of tasks, perhaps changing around team members, authorising overtime or even contracting extra staff to ensure that deadlines are still met.

The leader must make certain that each member is working at the appropriate pace to complete their tasks on time. She must ensure that all team members are doing what they are supposed to do at the right level of effectiveness.

The project manager must control the project to make sure that it is delivering only what is required and has been agreed with management. She must ensure that any changes to the original specification that are agreed are incorporated into the current work or left for later stages as appropriate. It is the project manager's responsibility to ensure that the project is delivered to the original schedule.

The project manager will need to monitor the project costs to ensure that money has not been misused and to keep within the budget. She must be able to report back to management with the current position.

A good team will keep a careful watch on costs and should complete the project within budget. All aspects of work should be carefully costed. Progress should be monitored and alternative action taken whenever necessary, for example if progress is not being made according to plan. Regular review meetings, together with the use of charts and suitable software, can be crucial to monitoring progress and maintaining control.

Most projects will include **regular review sessions** where the team get together to compare current progress against the schedule's planned progress. Each team member will report on the progress of the tasks that he or she is currently working on. Any tasks completed since the last review will be noted. The review will enable problems to be highlighted and solutions found. If inadequate monitoring systems are established at the start of the project, it is likely that major problems will arise, leading to the loss of control of the project.

▶ Lack of standards

A lack of professional standards can lead to missed deadlines and a system that does not function as was intended. Without standards, different team members may be unclear of exactly which tasks their colleagues have completed and whether all aspects have been covered. Testing might not be carried out sufficiently thoroughly.

When professional standards are employed in a project, all team members know what processes and procedures to use during development. All stages of the project development are carried out using agreed methods that everyone works to; everyone will produce documentation in the same format; testing will be carried out in a standard way.

▶ Loss of control

Many projects fall behind schedule when the team leader loses control of the project plan. This can happen if agreed deliverables are not produced to deadline, or if, when a milestone is reached, the management is not satisfied with work done to date and does not approve moving on to the next stage.

A number of factors can lead to loss of project control:

- poor initial planning, with unrealistic timescales
- the wrong mix of skills within the team
- inadequate resource allocation
- poor leadership
- poor project coordination
- workplace inflexibility
- lack of trust between team members
- poor communication between team members, management and end users
- inadequate monitoring and control.

A poor system will be produced if there is too much emphasis on the computer system and not enough attention given to the whole system and the data flow throughout the organisation. The system should be designed around the information needs of the business rather than being based upon what the computer can easily produce.

case study 2
▶ **Dogged by failure**

In theory, ICT helps improve productivity, responsiveness and communication. In practice, ICT projects are often dogged by management problems that result in delays, cost overruns and failure to meet the original objectives.

ICT projects continue to have an extremely high failure rate according to a survey by OASIG, a group supported by the Department of Trade and Industry.

It concluded that between 80 and 90 per cent of ICT investments do not meet their performance goals, 80 per cent of systems are delivered late and over budget and about 40 per cent of developments fail or are abandoned.

1. Why do you think so many projects fail to meet their performance goals?

2. Describe the steps that should be taken to ensure that a project does meet its performance goals.

case study 3
▶ **Passport to nowhere**

Figure 8.2 UK passport

"Teething problems" with a new computer system at Britain's Passport Agency led to a backlog of over half a million would-be holidaymakers waiting for their passports.

The problem was made worse by changes in the regulations requiring all children to have their own passport and by a 20 per cent increase in applications for passports. Offices were taking nearly 40 working days to process an application, compared to a target of ten days.

Queues formed outside passport offices. In Glasgow, the first people started queuing one night at midnight. By 9.30 a.m. over 1000 people were waiting in the rain.

The new system was installed by the German company Siemens at a cost of £230 million. Siemens said: "It is misleading to suggest that the delays experienced by the public are primarily caused by failures in ICT systems. It is clear that the application demand has exceeded Home Office forecasts."

The new computer systems were installed first at offices in Liverpool and Newport. This was where the biggest backlogs occurred. Reports suggested that the need to install the whole system before the end of the year meant that the new system had not been fully tested.

So what went wrong? Many reasons were given for the Passport Agency's difficulties in issuing passports. The new ruling that children had to have their own passports undoubtedly made the problem worse. This obviously meant there would be an increase in the number of passports required and the number of passport applications. Was this taken into account in staffing levels and in the original hardware specification? The new computer system went

case study (contd.)

online at the start of the summer – the Passport Agency's busiest time. The rush to introduce the complete new system meant that full testing had not been carried out. The new system was piloted at two offices. There was inadequate integration with existing systems and procedures.

- Discuss the possible underlying causes that resulted in the failure of this new system.

Activity I

There is considerable debate concerning the development of the NHS's nationwide health information technology system, NPFIT.

Research the current progress of the project on the Web. Identify reasons why its development has not progressed as was originally planned.

SUMMARY

A successful ICT project is one that does what the organisation intended, on time and within budget.

A number of factors contribute to the successful development of an ICT system, including:

- ▶ **the involvement and understanding of management**
- ▶ **the involvement of users at appropriate points of development**
- ▶ **effective teamwork.**

Factors that can contribute to failure include:

- ▶ **loss of project control**
- ▶ **inadequate analysis of the problem**
- ▶ **lack of management involvement in design**
- ▶ **emphasis on the computer system**
- ▶ **concentration on low-level data processing**
- ▶ **lack of management knowledge of ICT systems and their capabilities**
- ▶ **inappropriate or excessive management demands**
- ▶ **lack of team work**
- ▶ **lack of professional standards.**

Questions

1. Many systems fail to deliver what is expected of them. One factor that can lead to failure is a lack of the use of professional standards in the development of the system.

    a) i. Explain what is meant by the term "professional standards". (2)

        ii. Describe why the lack of professional standards might lead to failure. (2)

    b) Describe **three** factors other than the lack of professional standards that might cause a system to fail. (6)

2. For the successful introduction of a new or updated information system, an organisation needs to have clear management objectives and effective staff teams.

Describe the aspects of an organisation that may need careful management during the introduction of a new or updated information system. (8)

9

Development methods
AQA Unit 3 Section 8

When a new computer-based system is introduced by a business, it is usually to replace an old system which may be a manual system or an out-dated, computer-based system.

The introduction of a new computer system is likely to be expensive and take some time. It is vital for the organisation that the new system:

■ is introduced smoothly
■ does not exceed the agreed budget
■ meets time deadlines
■ meets all the clients' needs
■ is fully working.

As the introduction of a new system is vital to the success of an organisation, formal methods for developing an information system have arisen to try to ensure the new system is a success.

This development is broken down into a number of stages, carried out in order. These stages do not have to be followed, but experience has shown that a project is more likely to be successful if they are followed. They ensure that nothing is missed out in the development process.

Systems development lifecycle

The stages of developing a new system are sometimes referred to as the "systems development lifecycle".

As the term "lifecycle" implies, producing a new information system is not a one-off exercise involving a few months of activity. A system, once developed, will need maintenance and eventually will be seen as inadequate to meet the users' needs so a new system will then need to be developed, and so on.

The stages of introducing a new system that have traditionally been used are shown in Figure 9.1. Although the lifecycle goes through a number of stages, a particular stage may need to be repeated a number of times. For example, when the design stage is apparently complete, the prospective users or developers may highlight problems that require the stage to be repeated.

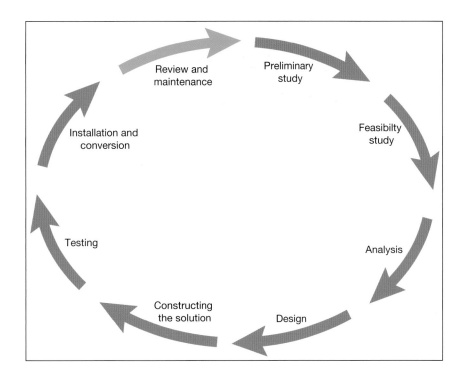

Figure 9.1 The traditional system lifecycle

▶ 1 Preliminary study

This is a brief study to look at whether or not a new system is needed. Managers initiate the study if they feel that the present system is not functioning well or that a new system might lead to improvements in productivity or quality.

▶ 2 Feasibility study

This study looks at the existing system and possible alternatives, including a new system or upgrading the old one. The study considers the following five factors:

- technical feasibility: will the new system work?
- economic feasibility: will a new system save us money?
- legal feasibility: does a new system comply with the law?
- operational feasibility: will a new system really solve the problem?
- schedule: can a new system be built in time to produce benefits?

Looking at these five factors is sometimes referred to as "TELOS" after the five initial letters. Coincidentally, *telos* is the Greek word for "goal" or "target".

A feasibility study produces a formal report for the management of the company, which then decides whether to give approval to continue. If approval is given, the management decides on a budget for the new system.

▶ 3 Analysis of the problem and proposed solution

Once approval has been given to go ahead with the project, the next stage is that an analysis of the system is carried out by a team of systems analysts. Analysis involves finding out about the current system and investigating the requirements of the users.

The four main ways of finding out about the current system are:

- interviewing staff and finding out what they do – this can be very time-consuming
- sending questionnaires to staff – this is very useful if there are large numbers of staff
- observation – watching what happens and how it happens
- examining existing documents, looking at issues such as:
  - who uses them
  - how often they are used
  - how the data is collected
  - who the documents are sent to
  - what they do with them.

Systems analysts use formal graphical and tabular methods such as data flow diagrams (DFDs) to represent the current system (see Chapter 10).

The systems analysts use the results of their findings to produce a set of **deliverables** for the new system which are agreed with the users.

Deliverables are a set of items promised under a contract, such as:

- system functionality list
- user interface designs
- details of provision of existing data
- conversion of existing data
- test plans
- user documentation
- technical documentation
- deliverables timetable.

It is important to agree and write down the deliverables because:

- they agree the content of the new system
- they ensure that work is produced to agreed standards
- they agree exactly what the users' requirements are
- they agree the documents that will be provided.

Agreeing the deliverables before the work starts will prevent arguments later.

▶ 4 Design

The design stage for the new system determines how the requirements specification is implemented. It involves breaking the problem down into smaller sub-problems, such as:

- the fields and tables of the database
- input formats
- output formats – both for screens and printed output
- validation checks
- macro designs
- the test plan.

A system specification is drawn up in sufficient detail for the programmers to create the system.

Clear timescales are needed to prevent the project from over-running. A project timetable and milestones – deadlines for each part of the work – will be included in the design.

▶ 5 Constructing the solution

This is the stage when the system is produced by the development of programs or customisation of software packages. Programs are coded, tested and documented. In all but the smallest projects, a team of programmers will be involved.

It is vital that the work is monitored very carefully, and that timescales are adhered to. Files need to be converted into a form suitable for the new system. Hardware must also be installed and thoroughly tested. Installation may require extensive cabling and alteration of buildings.

▶ 6 Testing

Testing is a crucial part of program development. Test data should test that all branches of the program perform to specification. Data should be used to test extreme cases. For example, if a temperature value can be any number in the range 0 to 25, the values 0 and 25 would be the extreme values. Testing should also include invalid data to ensure that it is rejected. (Temperature values of 26, -4 and 56 would be invalid.)

When testing, it is crucial that the results produced by the program are compared with expected results. Any discrepancies should be investigated and corrected if necessary.

Types of testing include:

- **module testing**, in which each module (or part) of a system is tested
- **functional testing** – sometimes called "black-box" testing – in which it is checked that the outputs are correct for given inputs
- **system testing** – sometimes called "alpha" testing – in which the developers test the system as a whole to make sure that it meets its specified requirements
- **user testing** (sometimes called "beta" testing) – in which potential users test the new software on their own computers using real data
- **operational testing** – in which software is tested in its normal operating environment.

User testing for software that is not being tailor-made for a particular organisation can involve thousands of users and many different platforms. As a result, it may spot errors missed by other forms of testing.

Why is beta testing used?

Beta testing is often used to test a new piece of commercial software before it goes on sale. The software company provides it free of charge to selected users from outside the company, who will test the new software. There are a number of advantages of getting real users involved in the testing of newly-developed software:

- The testers are independent of the producers and therefore impartial. They are interested in finding out whether the software actually does the job they want it to do.
- The product is tested in the "real world" under realistic conditions. There are many modes of use of software that reveal errors only to real end users. Users can sometimes try to do things that have not been thought of by the designers and programmers. Sometimes a particular, unusual, sequence of key presses or option choices can lead to an unexpected error. The volume of data and frequency of access may far exceed that used in alpha testing. More platforms can be used for testing than the software company is likely to possess.
- The users can provide valuable feedback to the developers so that problems can be put right before the software is distributed more widely.

Beta testers are able to try out new software before most people have access to it. For many people, it is rewarding to be involved in an important part of the production of new software. Some beta testers may even pay for the privilege so they can get early copies of the software.

Beta testing is a vital part of software development. A company needs a sufficient number of beta testers to test the product fully but not too many so that the product becomes too public before it is fully released.

Beta testers may enter into an agreement with the software house to test the software in certain situations. They must not distribute the software to any other users. The agreement might state that they will be entitled to a discount when the software is eventually marketed.

▶ 7 Installation and conversion

Once testing is complete, the new system can be implemented. Hardware must be purchased, staff trained, user documentation written and data files converted for the new system.

Direct changeover, that is scrapping the old system and replacing it immediately by the new one, is usually not a good idea. Although no time is wasted, there is a risk of something going wrong. For some systems, direct changeover is the only possible method. It is normally carried out at a suitable, quiet time such as when a shop is closed on a Sunday evening.

If possible, one of the following three methods should be used:

- **Parallel running:** Both the old and the new systems are run together for a certain time. When the new system is established and running smoothly, the old system is stopped. This is a safe method of conversion as a backup is available in case problems arise with the new system. If any bugs arise in the new system, they can be corrected. Users can learn the new system at their own pace, without the fear that making mistakes would be disastrous. However, parallel running can be very costly as extra time is required to run both systems concurrently. It can also lead to confusion.
- **Phased conversion:** The changeover occurs in stages. This is only appropriate for systems that can be broken down into separate sections that can be developed one after the other. In most systems this is not possible, as different sections of a system all interrelate.

■ **Pilot conversion:** The system is implemented in one department or location in advance of the whole organisation (see Case Study 1). Bugs and running problems can be cleared up and users' reactions to the system taken into account before the whole system is implemented. Training can also be modified in the light of experience. Such a method is only possible in organisations that have discrete sections or branches. It may prove necessary for the pilot sites to run the old system in parallel.

---

case study 1
▶ Chip and PIN cards

In October 2003, banks and credit card companies in the UK announced that they would change to a new chip and PIN method for payment from January 2005. Purchasers would have to type in a secret four-digit PIN. This was an attempt to reduce credit card fraud, which was running at over £500 million a year. A similar system in France had seen an 80 per cent reduction in plastic card fraud.

A successful pilot project was held in Northampton in 2003. Over a thousand businesses in the town were involved, including national retailers such as Marks and Spencer, Woolworths and Tesco.

The national changeover involved issuing more than 76 million new chip and PIN cards to over 36 million people. Over 600,000 tills had to be upgraded in shops and staff had to be trained.

Within a month of the introduction of the chip and PIN system, almost two-thirds of the public had used it. Of the people questioned, 83 per cent said the experience had been "positive" but nearly a quarter of them said they found it hard to remember their PIN.

1. Why was a pilot project held before the national changeover?

2. One module that had to be tested was that if the customer entered the correct PIN, the transaction went ahead. Can you think of three other modules that would need to be tested?

▶ 8 Review and maintenance

Once a system is in full operation it is monitored to check that it has met the objectives set out in the original specification. Inevitably, changes will need to be made to the systems. These changes are known as **systems maintenance**. More programming hours are spent on maintaining existing systems than in producing new systems.

It is also necessary to evaluate the success of the project and review its effectiveness. Such evaluation will involve returning to the original objectives and performance criteria to assess how well they have been met.

Evaluation will involve discussions with management and users of the system some time after it has been installed to gather their opinions as to the new system's effectiveness.

Other, objective, tests of performance should be made, such as testing that the speed of carrying out tasks is within the requirement set. Surveys can be used to find out if information flows are correct and whether or not the information that is delivered is of a high quality.

Activity 1

Use a search engine such as Google to search for sites that recruit beta testers. Find three different software developers who are recruiting beta testers. Copy the table below and answer the questions for each site.

	Site 1	Site 2	Site 3
Name of software developer			
Who can be a beta tester?			
What are the benefits to the tester?			
What does beta testing involve?			

case study 2
▶ An electronic registration system

A sixth form college in the south of England decided to install an electronic registration system for class attendance. Each teacher has an A4 wallet which holds a specialised computer device. Each device is battery-run and linked to the central computer by radio, a receiver/transmitter being mounted for each cluster of classrooms.

The new method of registration was chosen to replace the current, paper-based system. Transmitters were installed and wallets configured during the Easter holidays. For the first half of the summer term, the system was piloted by the Biology and English departments. Some bugs and operational problems were sorted out during this pilot run. The rest of the teachers were introduced to the system and trained in its use.

After the half term break, the system went live throughout the college. However, to ensure that backup would be available in the case of failure, the paper-based system was continued in parallel. Gradually the staff became more confident users and fewer mistakes were made and less support needed. The following September the old paper-based system was abandoned.

1. Explore the effects that computer failure of the electronic system could have on the college attendance system.

2. Describe three other electronic means of collecting attendance data. Explain the advantages and disadvantages of each method.

3. Examine the aspects that would have been considered by the college when undertaking a feasibility study.

Need for systematic formal methods ◀

There are a number of formal methods used in the development of a new system. One of the most important areas is **project management**. There is normally a project manager who is responsible for leading the project team, making sure that the project stays within budget and is completed on time.

Without formal project management methods, the project is likely to miss deadlines and go over budget. These methods involve:

- agreeing deliverables that state exactly what the new system must do, when it will be done by and what it will cost
- gaining approval to proceed, that is, approval from the client to start work
- creating a project plan stating what must be done and by when
- setting milestones – dates by which parts of the project must be achieved
- achieving sign-off – the client signing to say that the project is complete.

Development methodologies ◀

▶ Linear methodologies

Linear methodologies allow the development of a new system in a linear order or sequence. Stages of development have to be completed in a fixed order and the next stage cannot be started until the previous stage has been completed.

The *waterfall model*, first described by Winston W. Royce in 1970, was the first example of a linear methodology. Royce's model consisted of the following phases, in order:

1. Requirements specification
2. Design
3. Construction
4. Integration
5. Testing and debugging
6. Installation
7. Maintenance.

It was called the *waterfall model* because tasks flowed from the top to the bottom like water in a waterfall.

The waterfall model is still widely used today by large software houses but it has been criticised as being too rigid in a world that is rarely as simple as Royce's model.

▶ Iterative methodologies

Iteration means repeating something over and over until you get the solution.

Iterative methodologies have been developed to improve the waterfall model. The phases may be the same as in the waterfall model, but they may not be linear. Developers can go back and improve a previous stage using the results from a later stage.

Iteration can lead to the constant redesign and implementation of the system, reflecting what has been learned from the development of the system, its use and user feedback. This can be time-consuming and it is important to set timescales so this is not allowed to happen. The following table compares the waterfall model with iterative development.

Waterfall	Iterative
Rigid	Flexible
Easier to limit the time	Can be time-consuming
Inflexible solution	Better solution

▶ Worked exam question

Name and describe **two** stages in the ICT systems development process.   (6)

AQA Specimen paper 3

▶ EXAMINER'S GUIDANCE

This is a "bookwork" question. There is no substitute for learning the stages and what they do. You would get one mark for naming each stage and a further two for the description. A possible answer is:

▶ SAMPLE ANSWER

The feasibility study stage is an initial investigation which looks at the Technical, Economical, Legal, Operational and Schedule issues involved in introducing a new computer system.

The analysis stage involves analysing the current system (by interview, questionnaire, observation and document analysis) to find out the client's needs and documenting the proposed solution.

SUMMARY

The system lifecycle is the series of stages involved in replacing an old system with a new one. The stages are:

▶ **Preliminary study**

▶ **Feasibility study** – a preliminary investigation to look at the technical, economical, legal, operational and schedule (**TELOS**) feasibility of the required new system; at the end of this stage, senior management will decide whether or not to give the go-ahead

▶ **Analysis of the problem and proposed solution** – an investigation (by interview, questionnaire, observation and detailed study of documents) into the current system to find out how it works and what is required from a new system; deliverables need to be agreed at this stage

▶ **Design** – all the elements of the new system are planned and clear timescales and deadlines are set

▶ **Constructing the solution** – the application is built using an appropriate programming language or software development tools

▶ **Testing** – the new system is thoroughly tested, using a realistic volume of real data as well as extreme and invalid data

▶ **Installation and conversion** – the current system is replaced with the new system using an appropriate changeover method; new files are created, hardware is set up and users are trained

▶ **Review and maintenance.**

Types of testing include:

▶ module testing

▶ functional testing

▶ system testing or alpha testing

▶ user testing or beta testing

▶ operational testing.

Formal methods are important in ensuring that work is done to time.

There are two main types of development methodology: linear and iterative.

Questions

1. a) Explain why ICT projects are often sub-divided into tasks and allocated to teams. (3)

b) Within ICT projects, describe the need for:

(i) clear timescales (2)

(ii) agreed deliverables (2)

(iii) approval to proceed. (2)

ICT4 June 2007

2. The development of an effective new information system and its successful introduction into an organisation can be due to a combination of factors such as formal development methods and teamwork. Discuss these factors, paying particular attention to:

- the possible methods of acquiring, developing and implementing a new information system
- the people involved in the development
- the role of the organisation's management in the development and introduction of a new system.

The quality of written communication will be assessed in your answer. (20)

ICT4 January 2007

3. Southside College is going to implement a facilities booking system (see http://www.aqa.org.uk/qual/gce/pdf/AQA-INFO3-W-SQP-07.PDF, page 4).

a) Describe **three** methods that could be used when changing over to the new computerised facilities booking system. (6)

b) Choose one of the methods described in part a and discuss why you consider this method to be the most appropriate in this case. (4)

Specimen paper 3

4. During the development lifecycle of an information system, there is a need for agreed deliverables, e.g. a test plan with data that is produced at the design stage. Give **two** other examples of such deliverables, stating at which stage of the lifecycle each one would be produced. (4)

ICT4 June 2005

5. "Information systems are the life-blood of any organisation." Discuss this statement with the aid of examples. Include in your discussion:

- the role and relevance of an information system to aid decision making
- the development and lifecycle of an information system
- factors which lead to the success or failure of an information system.

The quality of written communication will be assessed in your answer. (20)

ICT4 June 2007

6. Give **two** reasons why it is necessary to use formal methods in the development of information systems. (4)

7. One of the stages in the development of a new computer system is the feasibility study.

a) Explain the purpose of a feasibility study. (2)

b) Describe the areas that should be considered in a feasibility study. (5)

8. Draw a diagram to illustrate the main phases of the traditional system lifecycle. (5)

9. Microsoft use beta testers to test their latest software. What are the advantages of this to:

a) the beta tester? (2)

b) Microsoft? (2)

10. A systems analyst has been employed to produce a computer-based system to replace the current manual one in a lending library. Describe **three** methods of investigating the current system; for each method explain what information the analyst would expect to gather. (9)

11. Discuss why a computer system that is developed using iterative methods is likely to be better than one developed using a linear model. (6)

10

Techniques and tools for system development

AQA Unit 3 Section 9

Over the years, various methods have been developed to help the creation of new information systems. Often, these methods have been developed and then improved as a result of mistakes and systems that fail to do what they should do.

Investigating and recording techniques

We saw in Chapter 9 that there are four main ways of investigating how a system works at present:

- interviews
- questionnaires
- observation
- document analysis.

▶ Interviews

It is important to interview key members of staff such as managers and users. The systems analyst should be a good listener. The information is flowing from the member of staff to the analyst – not the other way round.

There should be **no** leading questions, such as "Why do you think your computer system is so bad?" or "Your computer system is rubbish, isn't it?" Questions should be neutral, such as, "Can you tell me what you use the computer for?" The analyst should **not** ask, "Do you think the work could be done more easily by a new computer?" It is the analyst's job to find out!

The analyst should take notes and show them to the interviewee to make sure that they have got the details right.

▶ Questionnaires

Questionnaires are likely to be used where there are a very large number of users. There may not be time to interview everybody but it is still a good idea to interview the most important ones.

Questionnaires can include:

- open questions: questions with no specific answers in mind
- closed questions: questions where the user chooses an answer from a list.

It is much easier to analyse the answers to closed questions but users may not always find a suitable answer on the list.

▶ Observation

This simply involves watching users do their jobs, writing down what they do and looking for problems such as bottlenecks in the system. As the analysts are independent, they are not looking for something specific. Sometimes, someone seeing a situation for the first time can immediately spot something that the users have never considered to be a problem.

▶ Document analysis

This means looking at existing documents such as business forms, reports, records, orders, invoices, diaries, etc. Document analysis helps the analyst to understand:

- what information is used
- who uses it
- where the information is stored
- how the information is stored
- how long the information is used for.

As with observation, inefficiencies in the current system may be spotted straightaway by looking at documents. If a new system is to be developed, the new documents should be as similar as possible to the old ones so that users are comfortable with the new documents.

Business process modelling tools ◀

Diagrams can be used in the modelling of business processes. Like graphs, they enable anyone looking at them to get a picture of what is happening. Diagrams are often much quicker and easier to understand than the same information in text format.

You are probably familiar with **Gantt charts** and **flowcharts**. Gantt charts (named after their inventor Henry Laurence Gantt) are used to show project timetables and schedules. Flowcharts use lines and symbols to indicate the flow of data or the sequence of operations.

Another example of a business modelling tool is **Business Process Modelling Notation (BPMN)**, which is a graphical representation of workflow in a business. BPMN helps process management by representing complex processes in intuitive diagrams. You can use the Internet to download free software for the easy creation of BPMN diagrams (see Figure 10.1). Find out more about BPMN at: http://www.bpmn.org/.

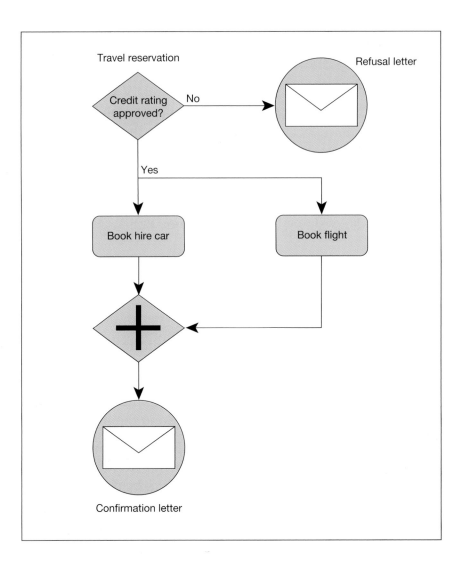

Figure 10.1 A BPMN diagram

Project managers have for a long time used Gantt charts (see Figure 10.2) to represent a project plan specifying tasks, resources and dates. Today they are likely to use project management software such as *Microsoft Project* or *OpenProj* to produce the diagrams for them. Find out more about *Openproj* at http://www.openproj.org/.

SSADM and PRINCE2 are two commonly used methodologies for managing projects:

- **Structured Systems Analysis and Design Methodology (SSADM)** was developed to provide a standard methodology for developing UK Government IT projects. It uses a set of structured techniques and tools to study data flows, data models and lifecycles.
- PRINCE2 is a structured methodology aimed at the successful management of a project, using procedures to manage budget, time, risk and quality.

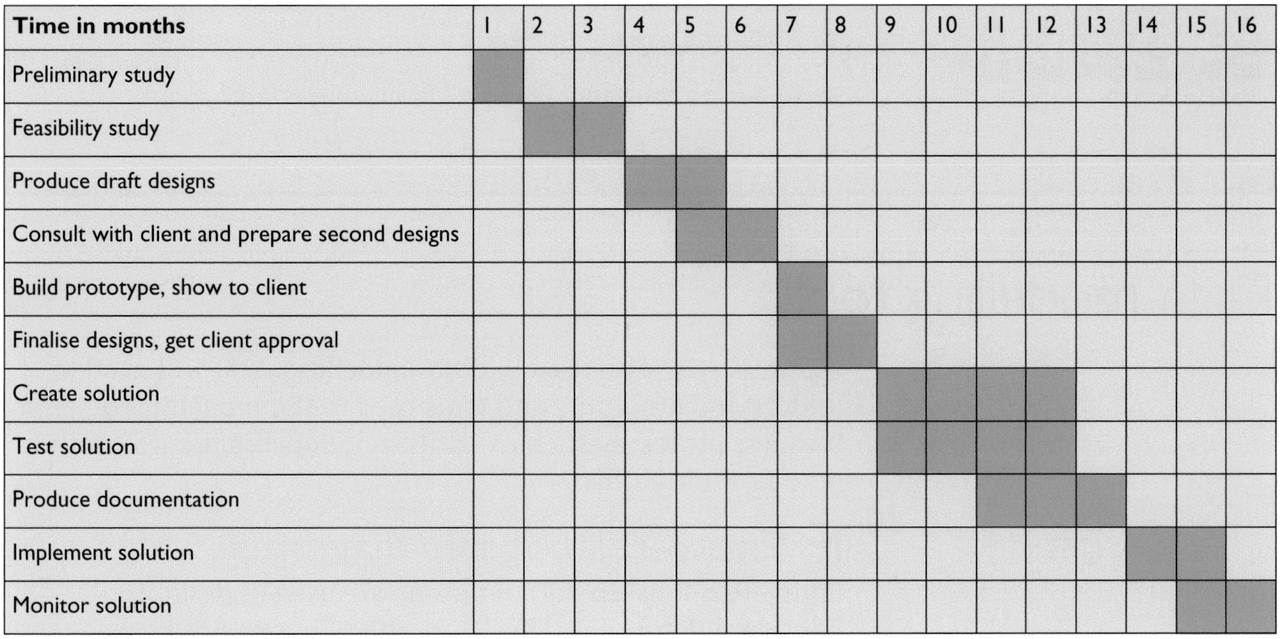

Time in months	1	2	3	4	5	6	7	8	9	10	11	12	13	14	15	16
Preliminary study	■															
Feasibility study		■														
Produce draft designs				■												
Consult with client and prepare second designs					■											
Build prototype, show to client							■									
Finalise designs, get client approval								■								
Create solution									■	■	■					
Test solution										■	■	■				
Produce documentation											■	■	■			
Implement solution														■	■	
Monitor solution															■	■

Figure 10.2 A Gantt chart

case study 1
▶ Reading Borough Council

(Source: http://www.projectperformance.co.uk/case_studies/reading.pdf)

Reading Borough Council provides services for 144,000 residents and employs 5500 staff.

From 2000, all councils had to make their services available electronically. For example, residents should be able to book a badminton court online. Providing such services electronically is known as **e-government**.

Councils provide a large number of services, such as schools, roads, parks, housing benefit and recycling. So, introducing e-government was a huge task. As a result, the informal project management methods used previously would not have been suitable. Reading Borough Council decided to use formal project management methods and, in particular, the PRINCE2 methodology.

The benefits of using PRINCE2 include:

■ The methodology is flexible and allows iterative methods.

■ There is a common approach which is easily understood and communicated to staff.

■ The common approach means that staff can be swapped over easily and knowledge is not lost when people leave.

■ Lessons learned can be passed on.

■ Workloads can be better managed.

■ Project documentation is easy to access.

■ Risks can be identified and managed.

case study (contd.)

- Auditing is easier.

- Find out more about PRINCE2 from www.prince2.com.

- List the main features offered by PRINCE2.

Data modelling tools ◀

Diagrams are also used in data modelling. You will need to understand diagrams and tools used in the modelling of business processes, such as entity–relationship diagrams and data flow diagrams.

▶ Entity–relationship diagrams

Entity–relationship (ER) diagrams are used in designing relational databases. They show the relationships between the data in different tables (the entities).

A booking system in a driving school may look like Figure 10.3. The "crow's feet" indicate that a student can have many appointments but an appointment would normally only have one student. This is a one-to-many relationship. Similarly, an instructor can have many appointments, but an appointment would normally only have one instructor. This is also a one-to-many relationship.

Figure 10.3 Entity–relationship diagram for a driving school

The relationships between tables and how they are linked is shown diagrammatically in Figure 10.4.

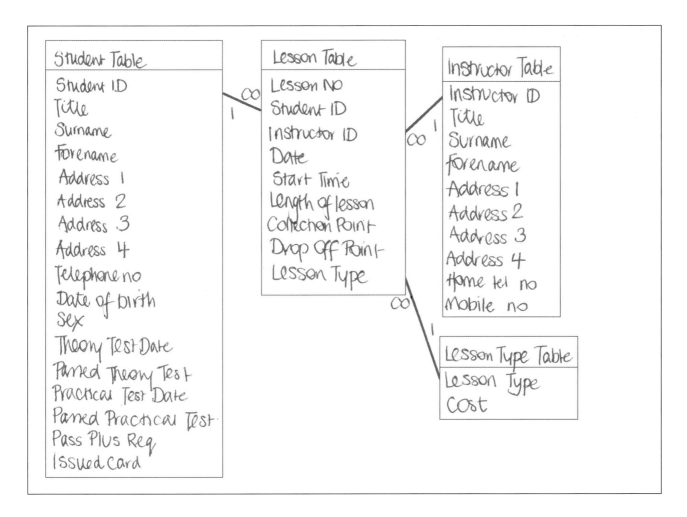

Figure 10.4 Tables for a driving school

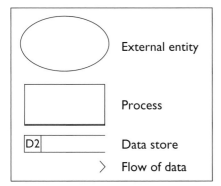

Figure 10.5 Data flow diagram symbols

▶ Data flow diagrams

Data flow diagrams (DFDs) show the movement of data through the whole organisation. DFDs are used in systems analysis to show how data moves through a system. The symbols shown in Figure 10.5 are used in data flow diagrams.

External sources of information and external recipients of information are called *external entities*. They are usually people such as customers, suppliers and users of the system.

In the driving-school system, there are two external entities: the student and the instructor.

Level 0 context diagram

The first diagram is the context diagram. This is very much a high-level overview of the system. Drawing a level 0 diagram starts with a rectangle in the middle of an A4 piece of paper. This rectangle represents the system. Next to it, oval shapes represent the external entiles (see Figure 10.6).

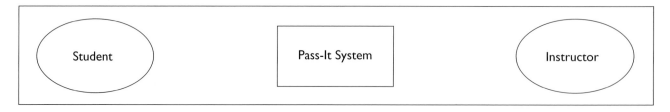

Figure 10.6 Starting a level 0 context diagram

Arrows show each of the data flows. It can help to make a list of all the data flows in the system. For example, when a new student joins the driving school, the external entity who is the source is the student. The arrow flows from the student to the system.

For each of the data flows, an arrow in the data flow diagram shows where the data is flowing. The finished level 0 diagram looks like Figure 10.7. The arrows should correspond to the data flows identified.

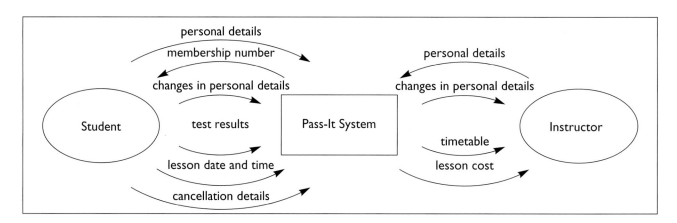

Figure 10.7 Complete level 0 context diagram

Level 1 diagram

At level 1, the DFD is broken down by dividing the processes into individual, more detailed, numbered processes. The DFD shows incoming data flow, outgoing data flow and the associated processes.

Each process refers to a separate part of the finished system. In the case of the Pass-It system, the four processes are student administration, lesson booking, instructor administration and general administration (see Figure 10.8).

Note that an external entity may appear more than once in a DFD. The diagonal line inside the oval shape shows that the entity appears elsewhere. The data stores are labelled D1, D2, etc. in Figure 10.8. Each data store represents a table in the final system.

- As data will be both written to and read from each data store, there must be at least one arrow going into each data store and at least one arrow leading from it.
- Data cannot flow directly from a data store to an external entity, only via a process.

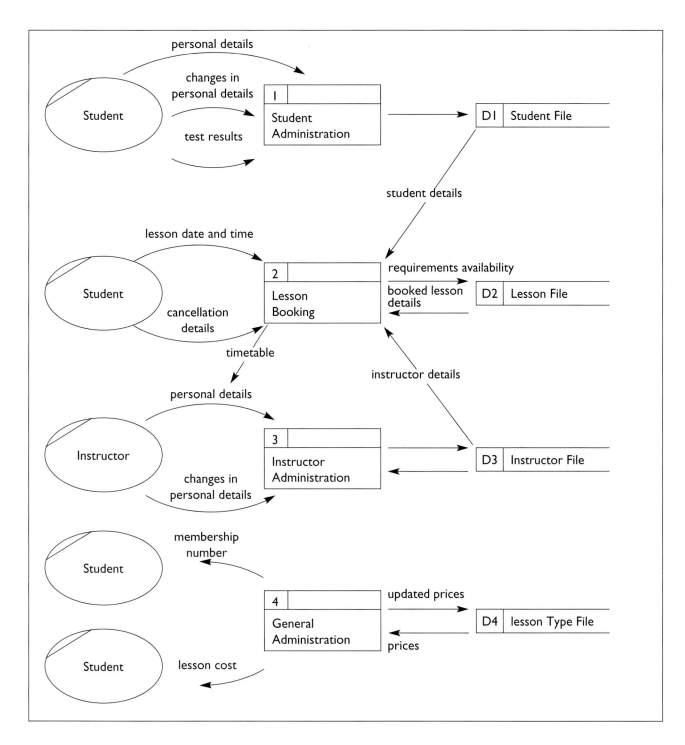

Figure 10.8 Level 1 data flow diagram

It is possible to go further and create level 2 diagrams, breaking the system down further into the various processes involved. Each process has its own DFD. However, we do not need to go this far for this course.

Data flow diagrams can be drawn in different ways. However you draw them, it is essential that the way you present your diagrams is consistent and that they have a key.

▼

Rules for DFDs

- There should be a data store for every entity.
- Information flows show data and not physical items.
- Entities don't link directly to data stores.
- What goes in must come out.

Techniques for testing ◀

There is a range of different testing techniques available to software developers. Here we look at a few examples:

- A **test harness** is a collection of software and test data configured to perform specific tests on a module of a program by running it under different conditions, comparing actual outputs with expected outputs.
- **Volume testing** tests that the new system works with large volumes of data. After a long period of use, data files may become very large. Volume testing tests that this does not affect the performance of the software.
- **Scalability testing** tests that a system will still perform as required even if the system has to deal with an increased workload such as increased numbers of users, large numbers of transactions, increased numbers of files and large volumes of data.
- **Prototyping** means producing a scaled-down, simple version of the software which is used to show how the new system will work. The prototype can be constructed and tested in a short time.
- **Multiplatform testing** ensures that software can be used with a variety of hardware specifications and operating systems. For example, new browser software for a PC should work in both Windows XP and Windows Vista. Clearly, new software will need to be tested with a variety of hardware and software before it can be released commercially.
- **Simulated environments** with various inputs and outputs can be used to test software in as realistic an environment as possible.

SUMMARY

The four main ways of investigating a system are:

▶ interviews

▶ questionnaires

▶ observation

▶ document analysis.

Modelling tools can be used to illustrate:

▶ business processes

▶ entities and relationships

▶ data flow.

Questions ▶

1. Southside College is going to implement a facilities booking system (see http://www.aqa.org.uk/qual/gce/pdf/AQA-INFO3-W-SQP-07.PDF, page 4).

One of the first tasks for the systems analyst is to produce a diagram of the context in which the facilities booking system will sit within Southside College. Draw a fully labelled context diagram for the facilities booking system, showing external entities and information flows.

(8)

Specimen paper 3

2. The systems analyst for Southside College has looked at the data required by the booking system and has found that the following rules apply:

- Any person or group can make a number of bookings.
- A booking is for one hall only (either the sports hall or the multi-functional hall).
- A booking may require many items of equipment.
- Each item of equipment belongs to one hall.

Complete the entity–relationship diagram in Figure 10.9 to show these relationships. Label all relationships. (8)

3. A company is introducing a new e-commerce system selling designer sunglasses over the Internet. Name and describe **two** testing techniques that would be appropriate.

(4)

4. A friend of yours has ordered new software from a programming company. She has been told that the programmers will create a prototype. She has sent you an e-mail asking you what is meant by "prototype". Compose an answer for her.

(3)

5. What is meant by "document analysis" and what is its purpose?

(3)

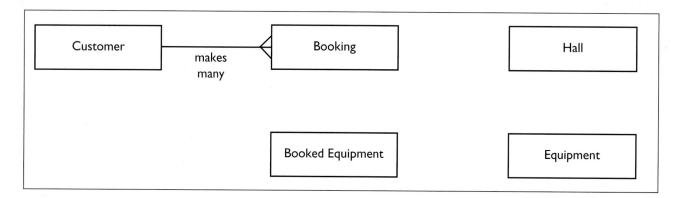

Figure 10.9 Incomplete entity–relationship diagram

Introducing large ICT systems into organisations

AQA Unit 3 Section 10 (Part 1)

Large organisations are likely to have large ICT systems in place. Global organisations such as Unilever or Exxon will have very extensive networked systems with computers in offices around the world. They will have their own, in-house ICT systems developed for them covering all aspects of their businesses.

Distributed systems

Large ICT systems can be used not only within a single organisation but also across multiple small organisations, all of which carry out similar functions.

The system used by newsagents to order newspapers from wholesalers can be one supplied by the wholesaler. Many newsagents will use the same system, accessing the wholesaler's database of products.

case study 1
▶ Smiths News plc

Smiths News plc is the leading wholesaler of magazines and newspapers in the UK. The company distributes newspapers on behalf of national publishers, as well as a large number of regional daily and weekly newspapers. It also distributes magazines for large and small publishers. Smiths News plc serves about 22,000 retailers across England and Wales. The company supplies general retailers and smaller independent newsagents.

Every week, Smiths News plc delivers about 60 million copies of newspapers and magazines. They receive them in bulk from publishers and distributors and then re-pack and send them out to retailers. The company has advanced IT systems that automatically pack the papers and hand-held scanning and tracking devices that allow the newspaper parcels to be tracked from a warehouse to a shop.

A part of the company, NewsWorks, provides the technology for wholesalers, publishers and distributors in the magazine and newspaper supply chain that allow them to use the tracking and also an order processing system. These IT systems enable the wholesalers, publishers and distributors to work more efficiently. NewsWorks also offers a maintenance and support service.

■ Why is it an advantage for a newspaper publisher to use NewsWorks' order processing and tracking system rather than to develop one of their own?

Each **National Health Service (NHS) trust** provides health services in a defined area in England or Wales. Each Trust consists of several hospitals and numerous general practitioner (GP) surgeries. A trust will have ICT systems that can be used by the practices for booking hospital appointments, accessing statistics and transferring data.

case study 2
▶ NHS ICT system

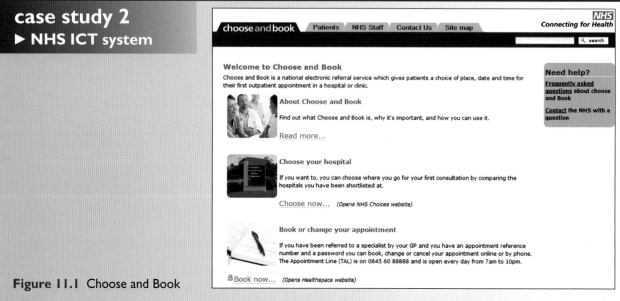

Figure 11.1 Choose and Book

The newly developed ICT system for the NHS system is made up of three parts:

■ a centralised records service that allows authorised people concerned with a patient's care to access appropriate general statistical information as well as clinical information about the specific patient

■ the Choose and Book system that allows a patient to select the place and time of their next hospital appointment

■ an electronic prescription system that allows drug requests from prescriptions to be sent from the prescribing doctor directly to the pharmacy where the patient has chosen to collect any prescribed drugs.

The Choose and Book system provides a patient with a choice of time, date and place of their first hospital outpatient appointment. The patient can select the appointment with an administrator using a computerised booking system at the GP surgery or at home using the Internet.

The patient is referred by their GP and allocated a referral number and password. The system displays all the hospitals in the area that can provide the service and the patient can choose where they would prefer to go. They can then select a date and time for their appointment that is suitable for them.

case study (contd.)

Choose and Book is used for around 50 per cent of all GP referrals to first outpatient appointment; 98 per cent of GP practices access the Choose and Book system. To do this they have to have a computer that can access the Internet.

1. Some people feel that the new systems could cause a threat to patient privacy. Can you justify their concerns?

2. Before the Choose and Book system was implemented, a GP would agree a hospital with his patient and then send a referral letter requesting an appointment. The patient would then be sent a letter by the hospital which gave the date and time of the appointment. Discuss the advantages of the Choose and Book system to the patient.

3. What are the benefits of the electronic prescription system to:

   ■ the GP surgery

   ■ the pharmacy

   ■ the patient?

case study 3
▶ UCAS

The Universities Central Admissions System (UCAS) processes all applications for UK universities. Applicants apply online and enter the name of their current school or college.

Each school uses the UCAS system to set up records for students. These records are grouped together in a way that suits the school. For example, a particular college that has several hundred university applicants allocates students to a tutor group which is a member of one of five faculties.

Students can only access part of their own record. A tutor has the rights to access the records for all members of the tutor group. The Head of Faculty can access the records for all the students in the faculty and can edit the part of the record that stores the student's reference. After checking the content of a student's application, the Head of Faculty authorises that it can be sent.

When the UCAS central computer receives a completed application, the student's record is forwarded to each of the selected universities.

Every year, the UCAS support team invites representatives from schools and colleges to a meeting at which any changes to the system are introduced. They also provide a help desk which schools can use if they encounter problems with the system.

1. Why does UCAS enable each school or college to customise their records system?

2. What problems could an organisation such as UCAS encounter when setting up this type of distributed system?

case study (contd.)

3. Discuss the training implications of the UCAS system.

4. Before the electronic application was implemented, university applications were sent on a paper form to UCAS. Describe the advantages of the electronic system.

These large systems, whether within a single organisation or used by many smaller organisations need very careful planning and management.

Reliability and testing

A large ICT system will have many users; it is particularly important that these large ICT systems always operate as expected. When a new system of this type is developed, extensive testing must be planned to ensure reliable operation. The testing will be very structured and may involve teams of people. Testing to high reliability is crucial; it is often the most expensive phase in the development of software.

case study 4
▶ **Air traffic control problems at Heathrow**

Several years ago a new computerised air traffic control system was installed at Heathrow airport. The software was tried and tested, having been in use for a number of years at several airports in the USA.

The original system took 1600 programmers years to write and a further 500 programmers years for developers to modify it for the more crowded skies of southern England.

When the system was put into action at Heathrow, there were a number of serious errors still remaining. One problem concerned the way in which the program dealt with the Greenwich meridian.

The program contained a model of the airspace it was controlling, that is, a map of the air lanes and beacons in the area. As the program was designed for use in the USA, the designers had not taken into account the possibility of a zero longitude, consequently the need to consider negative values was ignored. The software caused the computer to, in effect, fold the map of Britain in two at the Greenwich meridian, placing Norwich on top of Birmingham.

1. Describe, in your own words, the nature of the error and how it arose.

2. How could the problem have been avoided?

3. Describe the types of testing that should have been used.

► Developer testing

Testing takes place at many stages in the development of a system (see Chapter 10). The developers (programmers) use a range of tests to ensure that their code performs as required by the specification. This can involve a number of testing methods such as **code walkthrough**, which is a formal testing technique where the program code is worked through by a group with a small set of test cases; as this is done the state of program variables is manually monitored. This form of testing checks that the internal program logic is correct. Code walkthrough is an example of **white-box testing**. White-box testing concentrates on how the programs carry out what is expected.

Once the developers have completed their white-box testing, another round of testing takes place. This testing is known as **black-box testing**; the tests are based on what the software should do rather than how it is done. Black-box testing is carried out by the developers, often by a dedicated team of testers. **Functional testing** is a form of black-box testing that checks that the features and operations of the software adhere to the specifications and that it handles data and erroneous actions correctly. Large systems that support many users need to be tested under multi-user conditions. This testing is often carried out using an automated test tool to simulate a large number of users. The use of automated testing can save days of manual effort in testing. **Automated testing** employs software tools which execute tests without manual intervention.

It is crucial with large systems that they can survive unusual events without loss of data or functionality. Such events could include shortage of disk space or unexpected loss of communication or power. Special tests must be undertaken to check that the system performs correctly in such circumstances.

Many systems in a large organisation will be running in different platforms in different environments. Compatibility testing is done to ensure that software is compatible with the other parts of the system such as hardware and operating system.

When functional testing is complete, the software is said to be released. A release is the handover of the final version of an application from the developers to the client. A **software release** is generally the initial generation of a new or upgraded application. A large system is usually released in stages.

► User acceptance testing

User acceptance testing (UAT) is done after release, when other forms of testing have taken place. It is usually carried out by the client to determine whether or not to accept a software product. The acceptance criteria upon which the tests are based will be determined at the start of the project. The client is likely to use real data under a wide range of conditions for testing. Test cases are created to ensure proper coverage of all possible scenarios during testing. Acceptance testing concentrates on the functionality and the usability of the software. Ideally, acceptance testing should be carried out in an environment that is as similar to the real-world environment as possible.

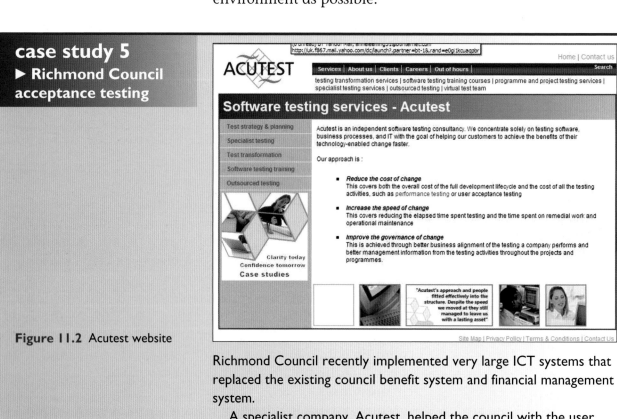

case study 5
► Richmond Council acceptance testing

Figure 11.2 Acutest website

Richmond Council recently implemented very large ICT systems that replaced the existing council benefit system and financial management system.

A specialist company, Acutest, helped the council with the user acceptance testing of the new systems as most of the council staff who had to carry out the testing had not previously been involved with such testing. They had to carry out the testing while doing their normal jobs.

Acutest set up a number of high-level test scenarios based on the business processes that the new systems should support. Acutest ran workshops to train the users in how to write and run suitable test scripts.

Acutest helped manage and coordinate the users during the acceptance testing stage, thus ensuring that the most effective use was made of the time spent testing and that the effect on the day-to-day business was kept to a minimum.

The user acceptance testing phase for both the systems was completed on schedule.

1. Why is user acceptance testing so crucial?

2. Why is it important to use real-life data and situations in acceptance testing?

3. How does acceptance testing differ from other forms of testing?

▶ Testing network systems

There are two additional aspects to testing network-based systems: the effect of the new system on the running of the network and the effect of the network structure on the running of the application.

For example, an organisation decides to add a new system, such as an online booking system, to run on its existing WAN. This extra system could generate considerably more traffic over the network, slowing up the response time of existing applications. Specialist skills and facilities are required for testing network-based systems.

case study 6
▶ **Advertisement for job in testing**

The advertisement in Figure 11.3 appeared recently.

Leader of Test Team wanted

Needs to be familiar with **Quality Centre** and **User Acceptance Testing (UAT)**.

This is a fantastic opportunity for an experienced Test Team Leader to join a highly successful finance house. The successful candidate will be leading a small team of highly technical manual testers, managing prioritisation and assignment of work for Test Analysts within the team.

The role will focus on the creation of Test Strategies, Test Plans, Test Scripts and Test Execution reports for testing Business Applications prior to release for UAT.

The successful candidate will have a proven background in coordinating complex UAT phases. An excellent working knowledge of Quality Center is also essential. Desirable skills include knowledge of automated test tools, including LoadRunner.

Salary: £45 – 48k

Figure 11.3 Job advertisement

case study (contd.)

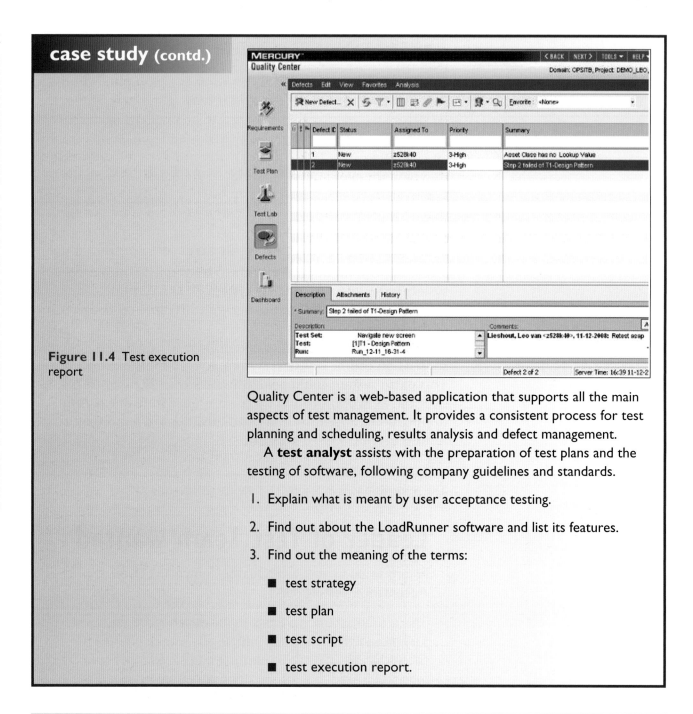

Figure 11.4 Test execution report

Quality Center is a web-based application that supports all the main aspects of test management. It provides a consistent process for test planning and scheduling, results analysis and defect management.

A **test analyst** assists with the preparation of test plans and the testing of software, following company guidelines and standards.

1. Explain what is meant by user acceptance testing.

2. Find out about the LoadRunner software and list its features.

3. Find out the meaning of the terms:

   ■ test strategy

   ■ test plan

   ■ test script

   ■ test execution report.

Installation

Replacing an ICT system with a new one is a difficult task. It demands very careful planning and attention to detail. All interested parties – the management, the users and the development team – need to be involved in producing the installation plan.

The use of planning software (see Chapter 10) is essential with the installation of a large scale system.

The different methods of introducing new systems were discussed fully in Chapter 9. Once all stages of conversion have taken place, the new system will have replaced the old system.

The period of change must be managed with extreme care; the people who will be using it will need to adapt to working with it. With a large-scale system, the number of computers and personnel using the system could be vast. For a new system to be successful, all these people need to be involved and trained.

The style of conversion used will pose different problems. Some systems can only be installed using **direct conversion**, in which the new system instantly replaces the old one. If the new system is very different from the old one then they cannot both run at the same time. For example, an airline that is installing a new online booking system cannot operate with two different systems in action. The logistics of installing a new system to go live at the same time on many thousands of computers over many sites are extremely complex.

Installing a very large system using **parallel conversion**, in which both old and new systems are in operation simultaneously for a time, is usually easier to manage. Very often a **pilot conversion**, in which a few locations are selected for installation, allows initial problems to be identified and put right and is followed by **phased conversion** where sets of locations are converted one after another. A large, multinational bank will install a new back-office system in its locations around the world using phased conversion. A separate roll out is planned for each location, a few weeks apart. A separate schedule is drawn up for each roll out and key personnel will travel to a location in advance to make sure that appropriate training is given before the system is installed.

Installation can involve a number of stages. New hardware may have to be installed and tested. With a very large system, this may involve many thousands of devices that must be ordered, delivered, connected and configured. Plans must be set up well in advance to ensure that the people needed to install the hardware are available when needed, that the space and room layout for equipment has been worked out and any necessary structural changes made in advance. It may be necessary to build or modify the network infrastructure, lay cables and install servers. Once the hardware is in place it will need to be thoroughly tested.

Once the hardware has been successfully tested and all apparent problems have been resolved, the software can be installed and tested.

Documentation ◀

Producing good documentation is essential for any system. For a large-scale system it is absolutely crucial. It takes time to develop good documentation and this time needs to be taken into account when planning the system development. The

▼

form of documentation needs to be agreed and designed; the text needs to be written, edited and refined; any diagrams must be drawn up and included.

Two main forms of documentation are needed:

- **System documentation** is produced for the programmers who will maintain the system. This will consist of structure and other diagrams, annotated program code and records relating to testing.
- **User documentation** is designed to enable the users to operate the system. It can consist of procedure manuals that describe how to perform business tasks; tutorials that teach a user how to use components of the system and reference manuals that allow a user to research a specific function. Much documentation is produced online. There is more about documentation in Chapter 14.

When a new system is installed the new users will need to be trained in its use. This topic is covered in Chapter 13.

Maintenance ◀

The job of developing new software is not complete when the software is handed to the users. Maintenance, which involves making changes to the software, will continue and is a major part of a system's life cycle. Changes to improve the functions offered by the software, or to correct detected errors, are a necessary part of the continued maintenance and development of systems. Indeed, development of software systems can make up only 20 to 40 per cent of the overall project cost; the rest is used in the maintenance phase.

The cost of maintenance is affected by a number of factors, including:

- how well structured the programs are
- the number of users of the system
- the number of undiscovered errors
- the quality of the documentation
- the skills of the maintenance team members.

When the development of the original project is successfully completed and handed over to the users, there is also a handover from the development team to a maintenance team. This maintenance team plays an essential part in the life of a system. The job of maintenance can be outsourced to an external organisation (see Chapter 15 for further information about outsourcing).

It is important that programmers who carry out the maintenance have a good understanding of the system. The maintenance programmers are unlikely to be the same people who developed the system. They cannot carry out any changes that are needed without this understanding of the structure and interaction between different pieces of software. The ability of a maintenance programmer to maintain an application will be dependent on the extent of the development programmers' planning and structuring of the application as well as the technical documentation.

Any requests for changes to a system need to be dealt with in a formal and systematic manner. A standard form will be used for reporting problems; these will be investigated and the necessary changes specified and agreed between the client and the maintenance team.

case study 7
▶ Project request for a change

Change Request Form						
Project Title			Project ID			
Change ID		Requested by		Date of Request		
Tick Priority		**Mandatory** – needed to operate the business function				
		Important – risk of lack of user acceptance or incorrect data				
		Desirable – system is usable but the change will improve the usability or functionality				
		Nice to have – cosmetic change that will enhance the look and feel of the system				
Description of the change						
Anticipated benefit to be gained from change						
Date of assessment			Evaluation completed by			
Change authorised by (customer)				Date		
Approval decision by manager				Date		
Approve			Reject		Hold	

Figure 11.5 Change request form

An ICT development company uses a form similar to the one in Figure 11.5 to record requests for changes to a system that it develops for a client. The form is filled in by a member of the team who wishes a change to be made, usually at the request of the client. All change requests need to be investigated before being agreed or rejected.

The progress of all change requests and changes are tracked. The company maintains a spreadsheet which holds details of the progress of all changes.

1. Design the layout for a tracking spreadsheet – think carefully about the data that would need to be stored for a change.

2. The form offers four categories of priority for changes – mandatory, important, desirable and nice to have. For each category, give an example of a possible system change.

3. Why might a change request be rejected?

Whenever any changes are made to a system further rigorous testing needs to take place. Very often the same test scripts and test data from before can be reused. A schedule of changes will be drawn up and agreed with the clients. Each change will be given a code number and a log will be kept of the progress. Once testing has been completed on a number of changes they will be released to users.

Systems maintenance can be grouped into three categories: adaptive, corrective and perfective.

▶ Adaptive maintenance

Adaptive maintenance is needed when circumstances change in the environment in which the system runs, such as modifications in the hardware or interacting software. For example, a change could occur in legislation or taxation that demands modifications to be made to software. Changes in other software that is used may have an impact. For example, an Internet application provides information about different mobile phone tariffs, allowing a user to find out and compare mobile phone packages offered by different providers. This Internet application has a high maintenance requirement as the structure of the system can change as the mobile phone market changes.

▶ Corrective maintenance

The term corrective maintenance refers to changes to software that have to be made because unexpected errors occur in the system that have to be put right. Even when a very extensive testing regime has been followed, errors can still occur. With a large-scale system there are millions of different possible paths that can be taken through a program and it is not always possible to test every one. In a multi-user system, the combination of a user's option choices in the software, the hardware configuration and the use that other users are making of the system at the same time may cause an unexpected failure in the system.

Errors that give rise to corrective maintenance are usually reported by end-users. Microsoft Office has a feature that asks the user to allow the computer to send information directly to the company if a fault occurs.

It may take time and considerable investigation to discover the source of the error so that it can be put right.

▶ Perfective maintenance

Perfective maintenance involves the addition of new and enhanced functions and features to the software. This is the most common type of maintenance. It will include insertions, changes, deletions, and extensions to a system to meet the changing needs of the user. A high number of requests for perfective maintenance can be seen as success for a piece of software. If users finds the software useful, they are likely to think of further enhancements beyond the scope of the initial development.

If major, extensive changes have to be made, then it is likely that a new, upgraded version of the software will be produced. This will involve extensive rewriting of the software, which will go through all the normal development stages, including thorough testing.

▶ Maintenance releases

The versions of a software package released after the initial release are called "maintenance releases" and they include changes to the original version of the software.

The software producer must ensure that all existing licensed users are given details of any maintenance changes. Very often a **software patch** is produced. A software patch is a mini program, a brief piece of code that will make the changes to overcome a specific problem in the software.

Patches are usually offered as downloads from the Internet. Many software packages now automatically search for updates online which can be accepted or rejected by the user. Within an organisation, such downloads would need to be managed centrally on a company-wide basis to make sure that different parts of the company are not running differing versions of the software.

User support

▲

The users of any system will need support. This is likely to be at a high level when a new system has been handed over. With a very large system, there will be a large number of users located at different sites. The users will be at different levels in the organisation and will be using different parts of the system. There may be a very wide range of skills within the user base. All users, wherever they are located, will need the same standard of training which must be completed within a reasonable time scale. This exercise will need very careful planning and execution. A method of checking that the appropriate training has taken place will need to be established. Methods of support are discussed in Chapter 14.

Large-scale ICT systems can be used across multiple small organisations, all of which carry out similar functions.

Reliability is particularly important with large-scale systems.

Extensive testing needs to be carried out.

User acceptance testing is done once the development team has completed functional testing.

There are additional aspects to testing network-based systems.

With large-scale systems, the need for systematic implementation planning is vital.

Producing good documentation is essential for any system; for a large-scale system, it is absolutely crucial.

System documentation is produced for the programmers who will maintain the system.

User documentation is designed to enable the users to operate the system.

Maintenance can account for up to 80 per cent of programming costs. Maintenance can be:

▶ adaptive

▶ corrective

▶ perfective.

Questions

1. Maintenance can take up to 80 per cent of the money allocated to the development of a system.

   Explain why this could be so and describe the measures that could be taken to reduce the cost of maintenance.

   (10)

2. Explain why user acceptance testing is such a vital stage in the development of a large-scale ICT system. (10)

3. A large multinational bank is about to install a new software system in offices located around the world. The project is managed by a team based in London. Discuss options for conversion from the current system to the new system. (6)

4. Discuss the different reasons for maintenance of an ICT system. (9)

5. Discuss the measures that a company should take to ensure that the installation of a large-scale system is successful. (10)

The corporate consequences of system failure ◄

Any business that loses its computer data will face serious financial losses. If the computer system is not working for any reason, they will not be able to process transactions which are at the heart of their business. For example, a supermarket will have to close its doors and stop trading if the POS terminals fail to function. This would lead to loss of trade as customers are forced to go elsewhere.

Serious, extensive or repeated failure is likely to lead to a company being forced to stop trading. Customers will lose confidence in the business and its image will be adversely affected. Any disruption to customers will lead to the loss of goodwill, resulting in the loss of existing trade on a permanent basis and potential new business. A high proportion of businesses never recover from serious failure to their information systems.

It is vital that businesses plan to avoid data loss and have a disaster recovery plan, also called a **contingency plan**. Two categories of loss need to be considered – the loss of data and the loss of the whole system, including hardware.

Potential threats to information systems ◄

The threats to an information system are far-ranging. Some of the major threats are described in Figure 12.1.

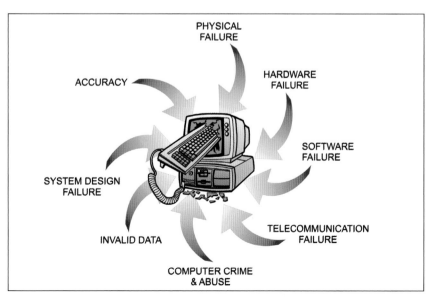

Figure 12.1 Threats to an information system

▶ Physical failure

Physical disasters caused by events such as fire, floods or earthquakes may be relatively rare, but when they do occur they can be devastating. The threat of terrorist attack has increased over the last few years and has to be taken seriously by all organisations. Less dramatic damage can be caused to cables whilst building works are being carried out or even by spilling a cup of coffee on a stand-alone computer.

As well as equipment, files containing vital data could be destroyed by such disasters. Without far-sighted disaster planning, many businesses would be unable to recover from the data loss. Many organisations employ specialist disaster recovery companies to manage their plans.

▶ Hardware failure

Hardware failure is a major cause of system breakdown. Failure can arise from events such as processor failure or disk head crash. Computers are dependent upon a constant supply of electricity. The failure of one hardware component can cause the whole system to crash. The growth in networks and distributed systems has in some ways made disaster recovery easier as it is possible for alternative sites to take over the functions of a site which has a hardware failure. On the other hand, as sites become more dependent on each other, a failure at one location could cause universal shutdown.

▶ Software failure

Software can contain errors which are only noticed when a particular combination of unusual events occur. Such bugs may not be detected in testing and can lead to system breakdown. They can be hard to locate and put right and can cause considerable damage to data as well as a delay in processing. Software can fail because it is unsuitable for the task, such as if the volume of data used in a system grows too large for the system to cope with.

▶ Telecommunications failure

As the use of telecommunications networks has grown, the potential for breakdown has increased. Causes of such failure include faulty cables or a gateway that is non-functioning, thus denying access from a LAN to the WAN or the corruption of data as it is transmitted.

▶ Computer crime and abuse

Data is very vulnerable to illegal access such as hacking. The company's ICT security policy should state exactly how to prevent problems occurring and what to do if they do occur.

Viruses can alter the way that programs function and lead to breakdown.

Wireless network hotspots may be subjected to abuse. If data sent by a wireless network is not encrypted it may be intercepted and read by a third party.

▶ Invalid data

Data can be invalid either due to user error on entry or through corruption that has gone uncorrected. Such errors can be copied from one backup version to the next without the corrupt data being detected.

▶ System design failure

Many failures arise as a result of poor system design which failed to build in appropriate measures to deal with all situations. Very often exceptional situations, or combinations of data, are missed by the designer.

Backup and recovery strategy ◀

You will have studied backup and recovery as part of your AS course (see *ICT for AS Level*, Chapter 21). Before continuing, it would be a good idea to re-read the chapter.

You will recall that the aim of producing file backups is to make sure that if data from a computer system is lost or corrupted for any reason, the files can be recovered and the computer system restored to its original state. As discussed above, the loss might occur due to:

- a hardware fault, such as a hard disk crash
- a file being accidentally deleted
- a natural disaster, such as a flood or an earthquake
- deliberate actions such as sabotage or terrorism.

An organisation's backup and recovery strategy will depend on the data involved and its use. The strategy will cover:

- the best time to back up
- how often to back up
- the type of backup to use
- whose responsibility it is to back up
- the media that will be used
- where the backup media will be kept
- a log of backups taken
- testing the recovery of backed up data.

Small-scale systems, such as a local newsagent's delivery system or a hairdresser's booking system, can use relatively simple backup procedures, such as nightly copying of files to an external hard disk together with a printed record of any bookings made to act as a transaction log.

Large-scale systems, such as a personal accounts system for an international bank or the stock and sales system for a large supermarket chain, will need extensive and more complex backup and recovery strategies.

▶ Drawing up the strategy

After carrying out a risk analysis (see page 168), a formal strategy should be established that ensures that regular backups of critical data are taken in a consistent and appropriate manner.

They need to be done in such a way that, if necessary, the system could be restored in a reasonable amount of time. What is considered reasonable will depend on the nature of the data being backed up. With many large systems, even very small periods of **outage** time can be unacceptable and very damaging to the business. The term **Recovery Time Objective (RTO)** is used; it is the period of time after an outage within which the systems and data must be restored.

It is important that the backup procedures should not affect the provision of service; ideally they should be invisible to the user.

Archiving data

Some people confuse backing up data and archiving data.

Backing up is the process of keeping a second copy of current data so that it can be restored in case of loss or corruption.

Archiving removes old, no longer used data and stores it on removable media. The data is unlikely to be needed so it is stored offline but can be accessed if required. Organisations should have a strategy for the archiving of old data that is no longer needed online. Archiving is a good idea as it frees up hard disk space and not so much data has to be backed up.

▶ When is the best time to back up?

Part of a backup strategy is to establish when backup should take place so that the process of backup is effectively managed. In many organisations, backup is planned to take place at night as many systems only run during working hours.

A person will be assigned the role to set up the software to carry out the backup automatically without human intervention. He will need to make sure that the backup tapes are changed every day. He will also maintain a backup log in which the details of all backups taken will be recorded, with details of time, date, and the medium used (identified by a volume number).

With an online sales system, suitable backup facilities must be in place to ensure that all lost transactions can be restored. The volume of data involved in the system and the importance of the speed required in restoring from backed up files must be taken into account. Arranging backup for systems which are online for 24 hours a day can be complicated.

When a network is used, the process of backing up can be centralised and all servers can be backed up from one place. In most cases, the user is responsible for the backup of any data that is stored on the hard drive of their own workstation.

The strategy will need to specify which files need to be backed up at what frequency. A backup strategy will ensure the backups are performed at the appropriate intervals. Most organisations back up at least daily but some backups may need to be performed more or less frequently. To use removable storage media it must be possible to allocate time when backup can take place without interfering with the normal running of the system. In many organisations, systems are not in use at night and so full backups can be taken then.

▶ Online backup

Managing the backup of the vast data warehouses that are stored by many large systems becomes a key activity. As we have seen, using taped backup is not a realistic option in such circumstances. As well as having very high volumes of data, the organisations running these huge systems cannot afford to lose even a small amount of data or lose operational time while data is being restored from a backup.

It is likely that an individual or a team will be assigned the task of managing methods that provide an alternative way of ensuring that the system keeps running with minimal time loss and no data loss when a failure occurs.

Techniques such as **disk mirroring** may be used to store identical data on two different disks. Whenever data is stored to disk, it is stored on both disks. If the main disk fails, identical data is available on the second disk. The mirror disk does not have to be located in the same place as the first disk. If it is in a different building, then the data is protected from disasters such as fire or terrorist attack.

RAID (Redundant Array of Inexpensive Disks) is a fault-tolerant system which uses a set of two or more disk drives instead of one disk to store data. By using two disks to store the same data, a fault in a disk is less likely to affect the system.

▶ Risk analysis

Risk analysis plays an important part in counteracting potential threats to ICT systems. The continuing operation of any organisation depends on its management's awareness of potential disasters and their ability to develop a plan that will minimise disruptions and ensure successful recovery. The process of risk analysis provides management with the basis for establishing a recovery plan.

Risk analysis involves:

1. identifying each element of an information system
2. placing a value on that element
3. identifying any threats to that element
4. assessing the likelihood (or probability) of such threats occurring.

The organisation should then take measures to protect data that are appropriate to the risk. For example, a very tall building in an area with a high incidence of thunder storms may be very likely to be struck by lightning. A lightning strike would probably damage electrical equipment, including computer systems. Installing a lightning conductor would be an appropriate counter measure. It may not be appropriate in a low building.

Businesses should consider the potential threats to the data, the vulnerability of the data and the value of the data to the business. Risk analysis compares the vulnerability to threats and the cost of potential losses with the cost of possible counter measures.

Every situation is unique. Managers may have statistical data on power failures, crime levels, and so on when making decisions, but the value of the data to the organisation will vary. Risks (see Figure 12.2) are calculated using:

■ the likelihood of an event occurring
■ the seriousness if an event does occur.

Where a particular system lies on the graph will influence the type of measures put in place. The criteria likely to be used in selecting appropriate measures are:

■ the cost of measures to protect against and recover from failure
■ the potential cost of the loss of data
■ the statistical likelihood of the problem occurring
■ the inconvenience to staff – security measures are useless if everyone bypasses them.

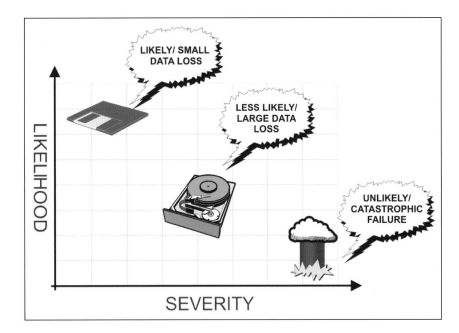

Figure 12.2 Graph of risks

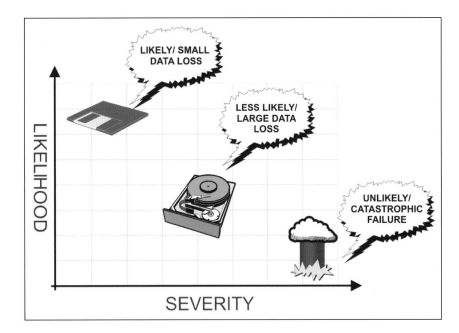

case study 1
▶ **Risk analysis**

A manufacturer has calculated that if a physical disaster such as a fire occurred at his computer facility and data was lost, the loss of trade could be around £1,000,000.

He uses a software package that provides a checklist of all recognised dangers for different types of installation. The software suggests that the probability of a physical disaster at this sort of building over 10 years is 1 in 50 or 0.02. The software calculates that it would be worth spending up to 0.02 times £1,000,000 (£20,000) to protect the data, for example by investing in a backup system based on magnetic tape.

1. What other methods of backup could be installed?

2. Describe other potential threats to the system.

▶ Backup of large-scale systems

For a large-scale system, the idea of taking a backup copy no longer fits the needs. With systems that deal with huge amounts of data that change very quickly, a standard regime of a weekly full backup augmented by nightly incremental backups is nowhere near adequate. Any such backup is likely to be substantially out of date hours or even minutes after its creation. In large **data warehouse** environments, backing up data that constantly changes is not a realistic possibilty.

Large-scale systems must use storage system mirrors: identical servers with the same amount of storage space. This is a method of data replication that provides a continuously updated copy of data at a remote site. Replicating data in this way minimises any data loss if failure of the main system occurs and recovery is needed.

Storing frequent data snapshots to an alternative site over a wide area network can form an effective form of backup. A **snapshot** is a copy of a defined collection of data that contains an image of the data as it appeared when the copy was made.

When deciding on the exact form of backup and recovery strategy, an organisation needs to decide how much data loss will be acceptable in the event of a failure and how fast the data must be recovered after a failure.

Why is tape backup just not good enough for many large-scale systems?

Traditionally, organisations backed up data onto tape and then transferred the tapes to an alternative location so that the data held on them would be available if a disaster such as a fire destroyed the main site.

However, as the size and complexity of systems have grown, tape backup is no longer appropriate in many situations. Backing up files to tape takes time, during which the normal system cannot run. This is known as a backup window – the system being backed up cannot be used during the backup process.

If tape backup is used a decision must be taken as to where the tapes are to be stored so that they can be accessed easily if needed, and not be vulnerable to disaster. If backup tapes are to be physically moved to another site, there might be a need to encrypt the data held on the tapes in case of theft.

It can take considerable time to recover a full system from backups held on tape. First, files need to be restored from the last full backup, then every subsequent partial backup must be used, in the correct order, to make the restored file fully up to date. Such a procedure can take days rather than hours for a very large system. For many large systems, restoring data from tape backup is just too slow.

Tape backup can be costly: backup hardware and software will be needed as well as staff assigned to set up and maintain them. Costs will be especially high if the organisation has many sites with backup being carried out at each site.

► Data recovery plan

The recovery plan is as important as the backup plan. Obviously the two are closely linked and neither can exist without the other. Several levels of recovery need to be considered:

- partial or full loss of data
- loss of data and applications software
- loss of data, applications software and operating system
- loss of everything including hardware.

A recovery plan needs to be in place for every level of failure.

Any recovery plan needs regular testing; failure of a plan at a time of crisis could prove disastrous for a company. A secretary in a company had been inserting tapes in the backup system every evening for over two years, not realising that the tapes were too worn to record the data properly. She had never thought to check the error logs.

Frequently, when an organisation has a data disaster there are multiple failures that have a knock-on effect. It is sensible therefore to have several different ways of restoring data as part of a recovery plan.

Disaster recovery and contingency planning ◄

► Disaster avoidance

There is much that can go wrong when using an ICT-based system, and it is important that any potential problems are identified before they occur and appropriate measures put in place to minimise their likely occurrence. This is known as disaster avoidance.

The use of fault-tolerant computer systems provides protection against hardware failure. A **fault-tolerant computer** has extra hardware, such as memory chips, processors and disk storage, in parallel. Special software routines or built-in self-checking logic detects any hardware failures and automatically switches to the backup device. Some systems automatically call in the maintenance engineers. Faulty parts can be removed and repaired without disruption to the running of the system.

The chances of damage from fire can be reduced by having detectors in the computer room with CO_2 extinguishers available and using fireproof safes for disks and backup tapes.

The chances of flooding can be minimised by placing the computer room on the upper floor of the building.

The chances of loss of power supply can be reduced by installing an **uninterruptible power supply (UPS)** and a standby generator.

The chances of malicious damage to the system can be reduced by having strict physical security methods, such as swipe-card-controlled access. Strict codes of conduct need to be enforced to protect data. For example, many companies ban the use of floppy disks as they are easily lost and data stored on them is easily accessed.

The chances of hacking and associated problems could be countered by software security measures such as checking all accesses to the system, and only allowing three attempts before shutting down a terminal. The encryption of all data sent along communication channels should be considered.

case study 2
▶ Disaster avoidance

Dawson and Mason Ltd is a medium-sized manufacturing company which, over the last few years, has become more and more dependent on ICT. The company has decided to adopt the following disaster avoidance plan, which consists mainly of commonsense practices – reasonable and inexpensive measures to avoid a disaster that could cost the company thousands of pounds in loss of revenue.

Hardware and software inventory

Each department of the company must keep a detailed inventory of all computer equipment; they must make sure the inventory is up to date. The inventory should cover all hardware, software, communications equipment, peripherals and backup media, including model and serial numbers.

Administrative procedures at ICT facilities

- All perimeter doors must be kept locked if the room is unattended.

- Windows and other access points should be kept locked if unattended.

- Access should be restricted to authorised personnel.

- Strangers seen entering office areas should be challenged and asked for identification.

Local area networks

- Backup of server files is automated on a nightly basis.

- A rotation schedule for backup tapes is used and several generations of backups kept.

- Two copies of the server backup tapes are generated. One backup copy is available on-site in case recovery is necessary. The other copy is stored off-site.

case study (contd.)

- Disk mirroring is used to duplicate data from one hard disk to another. Mirrored drives operate in tandem, constantly storing and updating the same files on each hard disk in case one disk fails.

- In the case of vital and sensitive data, hot backup is used. Two file servers operate in tandem and data is duplicated on the hard disks of both servers. If one server fails, the other server automatically takes over.

- A UPS has been installed for every LAN server. The batteries should be checked regularly to ensure that they are not drained and that they are charging properly.

Storage media

- Magnetic media must be kept away from sources of heat, radiation, and magnetism.

- Backup media should be stored in data safes.

- Vaults used for storing critical documents and backup media should meet appropriate security and fire standards.

Preventing theft

- If a computer is used to store sensitive data, the data should be encrypted so that the data cannot be accessed even if the equipment is stolen.

- Anchoring pads and security cables are used to prevent equipment from being stolen.

Employee awareness

Security and safety awareness is critical to any disaster avoidance program. Employees are trained to look out for conditions that can result in a disaster.

1. Disasters can be caused deliberately or be a natural disaster. Give one example of a disaster caused deliberately and one caused by accident.

2. Explain the reasons for keeping an inventory of hardware and software.

3. Dawson and Mason's plan does not mention computer viruses. Describe the actions that should be taken to prevent infection by a virus.

4. Describe the process of encryption.

5. Describe alternative methods that Dawson and Mason could use to back up their data.

▶ Planning for recovery from disaster

Although it is obviously best for a business to avoid disasters, sometimes these situations cannot be avoided despite the best security measures. In such cases, the organisation needs an appropriate plan in place so that it can recover from the failure and avoid disastrous consequences such as the organisation going out of business.

Many backup strategies involve data being stored off-site. However, there should be plans in place that allow for a second location to act as recovery site that can be used if the system's location becomes completely unavailable. This second site would need to have the hardware, operating system, applications software and network infrastructure of the original. After the attack on the World Trade Center in New York, a number of financial services companies who were located there did not lose a single transaction. This was because they had expensive duplicate systems running with identical hardware available at another site that was remote from New York. Immediately the attack destroyed the World Trade Center systems, the companies' powerful networks switched to the alternate sites.

A **contingency plan** or **disaster recovery plan** sets out what to do to recover from a failure. It is a planned set of actions that can be carried out if things go wrong so that disruption is minimised.

The contingency plan is likely to cover equipment, data, staff and business functions. It should take into account that the organisation will change over time, so reviews of the contingency plan must be built in.

Different organisations will have different contingency plans. The contingency plan chosen will depend on:

- the size of the organisation and its ICT systems
- the method of processing (e.g. online or batch)
- the length of time before the alternative system needs to be up and running
- the financial losses sustained while the computer system is down
- the costs of the various backup and recovery options
- the likelihood of disaster happening, based on risk analysis.

▶ Contents of a contingency plan

- **Alternative computer hardware:** The organisation will need to carry on if its hardware has broken down. Large organisations, such as supermarkets and banks, have more than one computer site in case of hardware problems. If a business has distributed processing facilities it may be possible to use them. Another option is the use of a disaster recovery company that will provide hardware until the organisation's own computers are back in action.

- **Backup procedures:** For successful recovery from disaster, data and software must have been backed up and the backup media stored safely. Tapes and disks must be clearly labelled and dated, so that they can be restored in the correct order. Staff also need to know where these tapes are stored and who has access to them.
- **Recovery procedures:** The plan must specify the order for restoring data.
- **Staff responsibilities:** The plan should state who is responsible for doing what if a disaster occurs. Personnel will need to be trained to follow the contingency plan correctly and a step-by-step course of action for implementing the plan must be drawn up.
- **Alternative working location:** If a total loss were to occur, for example if the company's premises were made unusable due to fire or flood, the employees would need somewhere to carry on their work straightaway. As customers would still need their enquiries answered and sales would still need to be processed, employees would need to have access to at least a desk, a phone and a computer. The payroll department would still need to ensure that pay cheques were created and distributed.

The whole contingency plan needs to be tested regularly to ensure that staff are fully aware of their responsibilities as well as to check that the plan actually works.

▶ Worked exam question

A travel company is reviewing the current disaster recovery plan for its computer-based booking system. Bookings come into the company by various means, including via post, over the telephone and via the Internet.

a) State, with a different reason for each one, **three** possible weak points in the booking system. (6)

b) Besides the frequency and content of the backups, and the media used, describe **two** other issues that should be considered when reviewing the backup strategy. (4)

ICT5 June 2003

▶ **EXAMINER'S GUIDANCE**   *a) One mark is for stating what is the weak point and one mark is for explaining why it is a weak point. Answers must also relate to the need for a disaster recovery plan and not just any weak points.*

▶ **SAMPLE ANSWER**   One possible weak point is the computer hardware which stores the bookings. If the computer crashed the bookings might be lost.

Another possible weak point is physical security. If physical security is not tight, unauthorised users may break in and delete valuable data.

A third possible weak point is if the company's website was unavailable for a period of time, the company would not be able to take bookings and valuable custom would be lost.

▶ EXAMINER'S GUIDANCE

b) *One mark here is for what should be considered, and the second mark is for why it needs to be considered.*

▶ SAMPLE ANSWER

The company must consider where the backup media should be stored. It needs to be stored in a safe place so that it is not destroyed by whatever knocks out the computer system.

The company must consider testing its recovery procedures so that if recovery is necessary the organisation can be sure that it can be carried out properly.

---

case study 3
▶ The scale of the problem

Almost a fifth of European organisations have no disaster recovery plan, and many of those that do would find them ineffective in an emergency. Research shows that 45 per cent of organisations have not tested their disaster recovery plan in the last 12 months. Figures show that some organisations put out of action by a disaster can lose more than $1,000,000 per hour – a bank could lose $250,000 per minute if systems are lost. An estimated 40 per cent of companies that suffer a disaster will cease to be around within five years.

1. Why do you think so many disaster recovery plans prove to be ineffective?

2. Why do you think so many organisations fail to test their disaster recovery plans?

Options for recovery ◀

Of course, it is not enough just to keep backup copies of data. Such backup is only useful if it allows a system to be restored after failure in a suitable timescale. A disaster such as fire or flood could result in hardware and software as well as data loss. Also, key personnel may have nowhere from which to work.

There are a range of options available to an organisation that will allow them to recover their systems in case of disaster:

■ in-house provision
■ subscription service
■ reciprocal arrangements.

▶ In-house provision

An organisation can duplicate hardware and software on a different site. This is often achieved when an organisation has a number of local ICT sites, each of which also mirrors another site. This makes each site more expensive to run day to day but with such an arrangement it is possible to provide almost full continuity of service in case of failure.

▶ Subscription service

Specialist companies offer an organisation a range of possible recovery services for which the organisation pays a regular subscription. They can offer hot-site recovery or cold-site recovery.

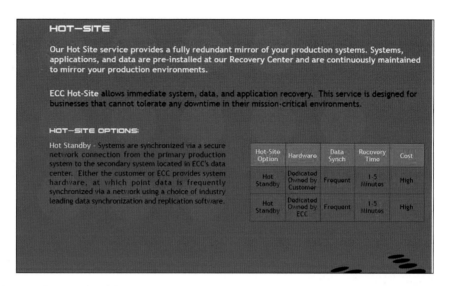

Figure 12.3 Hot-site recovery service

A **hot site** is a building with electricity and the hardware and software that the organisation uses. It is a duplicate of the original site of the subscribing organisation. Very often the organisation's current data is stored, using disk mirroring or other techniques. The site also has office space and furniture and telephone sockets so that, in the case of disaster, an organisation can quickly set up and carry on its business. In the case of a disaster, a hot site should be able to be up and running within a matter of hours. Key staff may have to be moved to the hot site.

The hot site is not owned by the organisation itself and may hold subscriptions from several different organisations, assuming that only one will need to run live at any time. The equipment at the hot site is maintained and managed by the leasing company. Subscribing organisations are given the opportunity to test their systems several times a year.

A subscription to a hot site is very expensive. Organisations that operate very large, critical online systems, such as banks and airlines, will subscribe to a hot site.

A **cold site** is a building with electricity and office space but no installed equipment. In case of disaster, an organisation will have to set up equipment, either salvaged or replaced, configure it, install software and restore data from backup copies. Systems can be restored, but it could take a number of

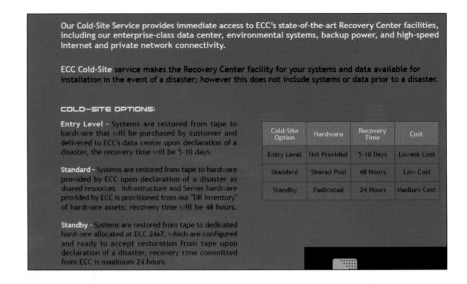

Our Cold-Site Service provides immediate access to ECC's state-of-the-art Recovery Center facilities, including our enterprise-class data center, environmental systems, backup power, and high-speed Internet and private network connectivity.

ECC Cold-Site service makes the Recovery Center facility for your systems and data available for installation in the event of a disaster; however this does not include systems or data prior to a disaster.

COLD-SITE OPTIONS:

Entry Level - Systems are restored from tape to hardware that will be purchased by customer and delivered to ECC's data center upon declaration of a disaster, the recovery time will be 5-10 days.

Standard - Systems are restored from tape to hardware provided by ECC upon declaration of a disaster as shared resources. Infrastructure and Server hardware provided by ECC is provisioned from our "DR Inventory" of hardware assets; recovery time will be 48 hours.

Standby - Systems are restored from tape to dedicated hardware allocated at ECC 24x7, which are configured and ready to accept restoration from tape upon declaration of a disaster, recovery time committed from ECC is maximum 24 hours.

Cold-Site Option	Hardware	Recovery Time	Cost
Entry Level	Not Provided	5-10 Days	Lowest Cost
Standard	Shared Pool	48 Hours	Low Cost
Standby	Dedicated	24 Hours	Medium Cost

Figure 12.4 Cold-site recovery service

days to do so. A cold site is less expensive than a hot one but it takes much longer to get a system fully operational.

Some leasing companies provide a **mobile service** which is operated from a large lorry. This can be driven near to a subscriber's site where some partial failure has occurred. The equipment in the lorry can be linked to any surviving equipment in the main building.

case study 4
▶ Fire

It was pay day at food manufacturer and retail group William Jackson, based in Hull. Anticipating her busiest time of the month, payroll administrator Diane Rush was at work by 7 a.m. preparing wages data to be transferred from the company's AS/400 computer to BACS, the system for paying wages directly into banks.

Diane noticed smoke billowing from the food factory next door and phoned Safetynet, the company's disaster recovery partner, at 7.45 a.m. All staff had to be evacuated from the offices as fire swept through neighbouring buildings.

Although the tapes had been recovered, the continuing blaze meant that the payroll could not be processed on site. Under protection from the fire brigade, Safetynet successfully rescued the AS/400 from the ashes and installed the charred machine alongside their own mobile unit. Using a parallel recovery process, the payroll was successfully relayed to BACS and all 2500 staff were paid on time.

■ List features from the William Jackson contingency plan.

▶ Reciprocal arrangements

A reciprocal agreement is an arrangement between two organisations that each will support the other in case of disruption to the running of a system. Such agreements are usually made between two organisations that have similar processing requirements; for a reciprocal agreement to be effective, hardware and software at the two sites must be compatible. It is a relatively cheap option; however, care must be taken to ensure that a reciprocal site has adequate capacity to run a second organisation's systems if disaster strikes.

Reciprocal arrangements are particularly suitable when organisations use unusual, specialist equipment.

| case study 5 ▶ Data recovery specialists | A company of automotive engineers archived their important drawings and documents in a locked fireproof safe in their basement.

Sadly, although they were prepared for fire, a flood filled the basement with water and fine silt. Over 40 tape cartridges of archives and backups were soaked through and the tapes were coated inside and out with a thin layer of sediment.

The engineers contacted data recovery experts Authentec International, who were able to extract each tape from its cartridge, remove the sediment and then place the tapes in brand new cartridges so that the data could be read. Within a few hours, the engineers had their data back. |
|---|---|

It is most important that adequate training is given to staff so that, in the case of failure or disaster, they are able to carry out their allotted tasks quickly and efficiently. (See Chapter 13 for more about training.)

SUMMARY

There are a number of threats to information systems:

▶ physical failure

▶ hardware failure

▶ software failure

▶ telecommunications failure

▶ computer crime and abuse

▶ invalid data

▶ system design failure.

Every organisation requires a backup strategy that lays down the way in which backup is managed. The strategy will cover:

▶ the best time to back up

▶ how often to back up

▶ what type of backup will be used

▶ whose responsibility it is

▶ what media will be used

▶ where the backup media will be kept

▶ a log of backups taken

▶ testing the recovery of backed up data.

Risk analysis involves:

▶ identifying each element of an information system

▶ placing a value on that element

▶ identifying any threats to that element

▶ assessing the likelihood of such threats occurring.

The recovery plan is as important as the backup plan.

Disaster avoidance is the process of identifying potential problems before they occur and putting in place appropriate measures to minimise their occurrence.

A contingency or disaster recovery plan sets out a planned set of actions that can be carried out to recover from a failure.

A contingency plan should contain the following considerations:

▶ alternative computer hardware

▶ backup procedures

▶ recovery procedures

▶ staff responsibilities

▶ an alternative working location.

The whole contingency plan needs to be tested regularly.

There are a range of options available to an organisation that will allow them to recover their systems in case of disaster:

▶ in-house provision

▶ subscription service

▶ reciprocal arrangements.

Questions ◀

1. A computer repair service uses different information systems to keep records of clients, current jobs and parts held in stock. These are accessible from a number of workstations, on a local area network, which are used by several employees.

   Describe **four** factors that need to be addressed in forming a suitable backup strategy that the company can use. (8)

   ICT5 June 2004

2. A local college with over 5000 students has classes from 9 a.m. until 9 p.m. Monday to Friday. Software installation and management of network users on the college's computer network are generally carried out during the holidays. Student files however are changing every day.
   a) Describe a suitable backup strategy for this system. (6)
   b) Describe suitable recovery procedures for the college system. (4)

   June 2004 AQA ICT 5

3. A local council has a local area network at the town hall that is connected to the Internet so that residents can pay their council tax online. Files are created, deleted and amended every day.

   The council has a backup strategy. Every evening from Monday to Friday at 6 p.m. the network is shut down and a global backup is made of every file stored on the file server.

   The council has five backup tapes named Monday, Tuesday, Wednesday, Thursday and Friday. The Monday tape is used on Mondays, and so on. The town hall is closed on Saturdays and Sundays.

   State, with a reason for each, **four** improvements that could be made to the backup strategy. (8)

4. A bank uses batch processing to update bank accounts following transactions. A new transaction file is created every day and used to update the files every evening. The transaction file tapes are clearly labelled and kept for a week before being reused.
   a) Why is it important to label the tapes? (1)
   b) Explain why the tapes are not used until the following week. (2)
   c) The bank decides to replace the batch system with an online system. Describe the implications this would have for backups. (4)

5. a) Define the term "risk analysis". (1)
   b) Describe how such an analysis is carried out. (6)

6. A dental practice has a LAN with workstations in each dentist's surgery as well as several at the reception desk. Data on all patient bookings and treatment is held on the system as well as employee data, a supplies database and statistical information.

   The practice has a contingency plan in case of a disaster occurring.
   a) Describe the possible occurrences that may require the plan to be put into action. (6)
   b) Describe the likely contents of a suitable contingency plan. (12)

Training users

AQA Unit 3 Section 11 (Part 1) ◀

Training is "the acquisition of a body of knowledge and skills that can be applied to a particular job."

Today the job market is very flexible. People do not stay in one single job for the whole of their working life, but are likely to make one or more major career changes. As well as this, the nature of a particular job changes as new technological advances are made. This is particularly true for ICT users. New hardware is appearing every few months. New versions of software appear every few years. Employers need to give ICT training to their workforce on a regular basis. Training should consider both the needs of the company and the needs of the individual.

Training needs ◀

Different users have different training needs, depending on their previous experience, their knowledge and their job and its requirements. Some jobs involve ICT tasks that are repetitive and specific; other jobs call for a more open-ended use. It is crucial that the level and pace of the training fits the user and the task.

Someone who has not used a computer before will need initial training. A more experienced user may need training in higher level skills. Users of specialised equipment (for example, a bar-code scanner) or software (for example, an accounting package) will need specific training.

Different levels of staff need to learn different functionality of systems to match their job and role requirements. Consider a supermarket chain that is installing a new sales and ordering system that:

- collects data on sales using POS at the checkouts
- collects stock levels from hand-held devices used by shop-floor staff
- provides store managers with information that will influence product ordering
- produces statistical reports on performance for senior management at head office.

Staff will require training in the new system. Those who work on the checkouts will need training in the use of the new POS tills. The store managers will need training in using the system to reorder products and in interpreting the information given to determine the reorder quantity of a product. The senior executives will need to learn how to extract and interpret the information that they need to make strategic decisions.

A database management system (DBMS), such as Microsoft Access, can be used at a number of different levels. Training needs to be available which meets these differing needs:

- An operator whose job is to enter data may only need to be taught how to access an existing database, add and modify records.
- A manager who uses information from the database as a tool in decision making may need to be taught how to produce standard reports and carry out a range of queries.
- A database programmer will need to learn much more about the package. She must know how to set up a new database and amend an existing one, how to write reports and macros, and much more besides.

It would be inappropriate for all the above users to attend the same course.

case study 1
▶ Training college staff

A college uses an electronic attendance registration system that allows teachers to enter the details of attendance in each class using a hand-held device.

A member of the tutorial staff can access the system, on his office computer, to view the information collected in classes. He is able to produce a variety of reports relating to the attendance of an individual or a whole class over a selected time period.

The college information department manages the system. They maintain the interface between the registration system and the college MIS. They have to write new reports when requested and they troubleshoot the system. From time to time they need to contact the developers of the registration system.

Different training is needed by different groups of staff.

1. Outline the training needs for:

- teachers

- tutorial staff

- information department personnel.

2. State two occasions when training would be required.

Training for external users

Users of ICT systems can be internal or external to the organisation. The training and support requirements may be different. Examples of external users are online customers or suppliers. Such external users will require specific methods of training. It is not possible to expect customers or people working for another organisation to go on a training course. The training material for such users would need to be supplied – perhaps in the form of downloadable manuals, training programmes and materials.

Types of training

▶ Skills-based training

Some training is based on learning a skill, such as typing on a keyboard or using Microsoft Windows, Microsoft Word or Microsoft Access. These skills are often used so this type of training is commonly offered in standard courses that teach participants how to use a range of facilities according to their current skills level. Such training can be fairly open-ended, leaving the trainee to decide exactly how to incorporate the skills learned into the current job.

This type of training provides an individual with skills that are transferable and can be used in other jobs and organisations as they can lead to qualifications that are well known and highly regarded. Such a method can provide an employee with a thorough understanding of a system and skills that may enable them to problem solve if things go wrong or need modifying in the workplace. This could be of value to the organisation: the employee would be able to cascade their knowledge to other members of staff.

▶ Task-based training

Other training is based on learning how to do a particular task. Examples of this could be: how to use a PDA to record electricity-meter readings; how to process a sale with a Visa card; or how to load transaction and master file tapes in a batch-processing system. Because this training is designed specifically for the occasion, it is more likely to take place in-house. Skills acquired are very specific and are often not transferable into other situations.

When training to use a software application such as a sales database management system, different personnel will require different training based upon the tasks that they are required by their job to carry out on the database.

A telesales person is likely to need training in data entry. They might need to know:

- what data has to be entered and what is optional
- in what order to work the data entry process
- how to deal with errors and unusual data
- how to answer enquiries.

A sales manager using the same database package might need training in how to produce a range of reports and how to "drill down" from summarised information to find more detailed information when searching for explanations.

The database administrator will need a more technical and complex training course that provides an in-depth knowledge of the software. The administrator will need the skills to carry out a wide range of tasks, including writing new reports, modifying the database structure to meet changing needs and troubleshooting when problems occur.

▶ Skills updating and refreshing

For employees in many jobs, keeping ICT skills up to date is a nearly constant need as job requirements and facilities change. Employees will need to update their skills on a regular basis, particularly as new or updated versions of software or hardware are installed. Old skills may be superseded when new systems are installed.

Employees may also need to refresh old skills, if they have not used some piece of hardware or software for some time. Some activities are only carried out at irregular intervals and it is easy to forget how to use features of software if they are not constantly being practised.

When an employee changes job within an organisation, either because of promotion or as a result of changes in the structure of the organisation, he or she might need to be trained in new ICT skills that are needed in the new role.

Training methods ◀

There is a wide range of training options available. It is important that the method is carefully chosen to meet the specific needs of an individual.

▶ Face-to-face or instructor-led training

Formal training with an instructor training a group of trainees is a popular but expensive option. However, this method has the advantage that the trainer can answer questions and provide immediate help and feedback. Face-to-face training may take the form of on-the-job training or may be delivered through in-house or external classroom courses.

Instructor-led training remains very popular as students are able to interact with each other and their tutor, sharing ideas and information.

A disadvantage of instructor-led training is that it is usually planned some time in advance, which might not coincide exactly with the time the trainee actually requires instruction; in this way it lacks flexibility. If the training is not followed up by immediate practice, much of what has been learned is quite likely to be forgotten.

On-the-job training

This, as the name implies, involves learning while at work. A trainer from inside or outside the company may come and give instructions to a trainee. The trainee may spend time observing a colleague or a mentor complete a task and then carry out similar tasks under supervision. Staff working on a telephone, such as help-desk operators, may have calls recorded to monitor that they are giving correct advice in the right manner.

Although on-the-job training has the advantage of providing training in a realistic setting, it is often difficult for the employee to learn while still dealing with the day-to-day stresses of the job.

In-house courses

In-house courses are specially organised for a group of employees. They are normally held on-site using an internal or an external trainer. The trainees may all have the same needs, for example, if the software used by the company has recently been replaced or upgraded. The biggest advantage of providing training in-house, run by employees of the organisation, is the cost. Outside trainers are usually very expensive. In-house trainers will have a very good understanding of the organisation itself, its procedures and structures, and will be able to tailor the training to meet exactly the needs of the employees.

When electronic registration of students using Bromcom's EARS system was introduced at a college, the ICT department undertook to train all teaching staff. A number of sessions were put on and teachers were invited to join a session at a time suitable to them. During the training session the teachers were each given their own EARS hand-held device and were shown the different functions that the system offered. They were also handed an A4 sheet of hints to remind them what to do. The ICT staff were then available at the end of a phone to deal with problems and queries. As the only way to get a device was to attend the training session, everyone attended!

This approach has the merit of allowing the organisation to tailor the content of the course to meet the specific needs of the organisation. An individual does not have to travel for the course, which can take place during normal working hours. The training can take place at a time suitable for the individual employee; the amount of help and support required can be easily monitored.

External courses

Many local colleges offer training courses in various aspects of ICT. A company may send employees to the college for a course that is offered there regularly. As the trainees could include employees of different companies, the costs will be shared and so reduced.

A college may also put on courses especially for a group of employees of a company, either in the college or at the company.

Commercial companies also put on training courses. These are often very specialised and can be very expensive. However, many companies offer a wide range of courses that can meet the specialist skills needed for certain roles such as an IT technician. Such courses allow an individual to meet and exchange ideas with people in different organisations; they can provide them with contacts that are useful both within their job and in career advancement.

▶ E-learning

E-learning means using electronic methods to teach the trainee. These methods include online tutorials, on-screen help and interactive videos and DVDs. A few years ago some people felt that e-learning would quickly take over all other forms of learning, but change has not been as rapid as these people predicted. However, e-learning is growing in popularity; its big advantage is that a person can learn when and where he

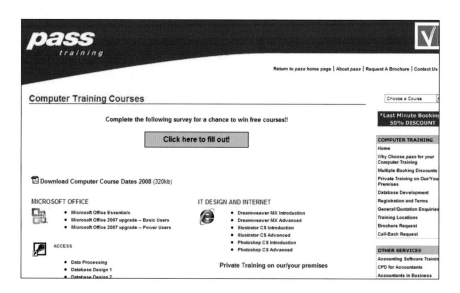

Figure 13.1 Training courses

wants. If someone needs a particular skill for a project, then e-learning allows him to gain it straightaway without having to wait for a relevant course to be run. So training can be provided at the convenience of the individual, to meet his or her specific work needs. Using e-learning, an organisation can provide relatively inexpensive training, which does not disrupt the day-to-day working, to large numbers of the workforce.

A factor that has held back the growth of e-learning is the lack of enthusiasm from many employees to learn in this way.

E-learning, which is often very heavily graphics-based, is demanding on computer and network resources (such as memory, processor time and bandwidth) so its use will only be feasible in organisations that support a good ICT infrastructure.

A company can upload e-learning materials to the Internet or the company intranet for use at work. Password protection can be used so that only their employees can benefit. They can then take their training course at home at a convenient time.

case study 2 ▶ Reuters using e-learning	Reuters, the news agency, is planning a change from classroom-based training to e-learning that could save them up to £1 million. The move is an attempt to integrate learning within normal working life. The head of training sees classroom-based training as an inefficient way of transferring knowledge. He is aiming for 25 per cent of all company training to be delivered online. ■ Suggest four issues that Reuters will have to consider to ensure that the move to e-learning is successful.

Online tutorials

There are many tutorials available online via the Internet. Some are free; others are available cheaply. For example, there are lots of courses available at www.freeskills.com. For an annual membership fee of £99, the trainee has access to every training course. Trainees can study what they choose, when they choose, at their own pace and within a small budget.

The database courses available include: Access 2002 (XP), Access 2000, Access 97 and other programs such as FoxPro, SQL Server, Oracle, Lotus Notes, Informix, Paradox and Approach.

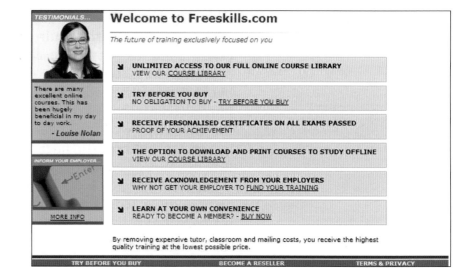

Figure 13.2 Freeskills' website

On-screen help

Most software packages offer on-screen help simply by pressing the F1 key. On-screen help is commonly used as it is free and immediately available.

On-screen help allows you to search on keywords or to type in your question in a natural language and be given an explanation as well as examples of use. Sometimes animated demonstrations and cue cards (small windows that appear over the application screen) are also available.

Sometimes an error message will include a help button that takes you to the correct page of the help file.

On-screen help has the advantage of being always available while the software is in use; it is quick to use, free and fairly user-friendly.

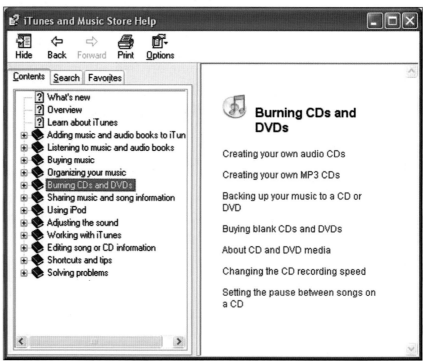

Figure 13.3 On-screen help

Interactive video

Interactive video can provide professional training at your computer. Interactive video normally makes use of the facilities of a DVD system. It is interactive in that users can choose which sections to cover, miss out sections or go back over sections. The video may require the user to make responses which will reinforce their understanding and determine how quickly the trainee progresses through the course.

Interactive video is a low-stress learning environment and the videos can be navigated in a logical way using an easy-to-use interface.

▶ Paper-based materials

Paper-based materials offer a traditional method of learning from user manuals, books and training manuals.

Software manuals are widely available even though today they rarely come free with the software. They have been removed to reduce costs. Manuals claim to teach you all you need to know, but they vary in quality and are not always very easy to follow. A manual can prove to be a good reference if you have a problem. Manuals can be used when and where the user wants and progress can be made at the individual's own pace.

Books are commonly available for popular software packages from bookshops. Many books are available at an introductory level. Titles that teach about Microsoft Access include *Access for Dummies*, *Field Guide to Access* and *Ten-Minute Guide to Access*. These books take the reader step-by-step through the basic functions of the program but don't include much depth.

Books can be dipped into from time to time when a particular problem is met and can be read anywhere: in the work place, on the train going to work or at home. Alternatively, they can form part of a structured training programme. The programme will have several objectives such as teaching key features of software. These features should be covered by the books in a logical order.

Training manuals give the user an opportunity to work at their own pace and refer quickly to the appropriate section.

Activity 1

1. Use the Internet to find the details of courses that teach the advanced features of Microsoft Access or another software application of your choice. A good starting point is to use a search engine such as Google to search UK pages for "Advanced Access training course".

2. Draw up a table comparing the location, duration and cost of courses offered by five different companies.

3. Produce a second table showing details of five e-learning courses.

4. Discuss the costs and benefits of the different types of course you have found.

5. Discuss the relative merits of these two methods of learning for an organisation.

6. Describe other methods that could be used by individuals to acquire advanced skills in a software package.

Activity 2

Prepare a table showing the advantages and disadvantages of each training method.

▶ Worked exam question

A building society is installing a new database management system to store details of all customers' accounts. The counter clerks will need to be trained in using the new system.

a) Other than the counter clerks, suggest one category of user that will also need to be trained in using the new system. (1)

b) Explain why these users need different training from the counter clerks. (2)

c) The building society is considering whether to offer counter clerks on-the-job training or off-the-job training.
   i) Describe one benefit of on-the-job training. (2)
   ii) Describe one benefit of off-the-job training. (2)

▶ SAMPLE ANSWER

a) One possible category of user that will also need to be trained in using the new system could be the branch managers.

b) These users need different training because their jobs are different and the tasks that they will perform on the computer are different.

c) i) On-the-job training takes place in the office and so is in a realistic situation with real data.

   ii) Off-the-job training takes place away from the stresses of the office and so there are no distractions.

SUMMARY

Training is vital in a highly skilled area of business like **ICT**. The rapid pace of change means that training is not something that only happens when you start a new job but is continuous.

Training can be skills-based or task-based.

Different levels of training are required for different situations, for example beginner, intermediate, or refresher courses.

Training courses may be:

▶ on-the-job

▶ in-house

▶ external.

Other methods of training include:

▶ reading user manuals

▶ online tutorials

▶ on-screen help

▶ interactive video or **DVD**.

Users of **ICT** systems can be internal or external to the organisation. The training and support requirements may be different.

An organisation needs to have an **ICT** training strategy to ensure that employees have the skills necessary to carry out their jobs.

Questions

◄

1. Describe **three** ways in which training may be provided for users of ICT systems. (6)

January 2005 AQA ICT 4

2. A small legal firm is about to replace stand-alone computers with a new computer network. Industry-standard software will be installed. As new users of both the equipment and the software, the firm is concerned about the levels of support and training that will be needed. There are three levels of system user: the solicitors themselves, the practice management and the administrative staff.

   a) Explain **two** factors that need to be taken into account when planning the training. (4)

   b) State **two** means of providing the training material and give an advantage of each. (4)

June 2002 AQA ICT 4

3. A large Insurance company with many branches delivers its training and assessment across their entire organisation using Internet technologies.

   Discuss the possible benefits to the company and their employees. (12)

4. Jane works in a call centre for a bank dealing with questions and instructions from customers. Although Jane underwent task-based training related to her job last year, she must undertake more training shortly.

   a) State **two** reasons why Jane may need to undergo further training. (2)

   b) Describe what is meant by "task-based training". (2)

   c) Describe other options for training that might be available to Jane. (6)

Support options for application software ◀

Most software producers provide some form of support for users in case they have difficulty in installing or using their software. Support is sometimes provided free under the product warranty or an entitlement to help can be bought for a fixed period of time. Large organisations will have an ICT support team whose members will provide hardware and software support for users in-house.

Users may also need access to help from time to time. The software package may offer many features, not all of which the user makes use of on a regular basis. There needs to be a suitable way for the user to find out what he or she needs to know at the appropriate time.

▶ On-site help

When a software house supplies and installs a large, new, bespoke system for an organisation, considerable support is likely to be needed for the first few weeks or months. New users will be unfamiliar with the package and may need guidance from members of the software house's development team in its use. At this stage, unforeseen errors may occur in the software and modifications may need to be made. For this reason the software house is likely to supply on-site technical support during the early stages of the software's use. This is the most expensive support option for a software house.

▶ Call-out support

This is a less wide-ranging, but cheaper, method of support than having software house personnel working on the site of the user company. A call-out support service will make a technician available to go on-site to a user organisation to provide specific support. Such support might particularly be used after the phase of on-site support has come to an end, when new features have been added to the software or when users within the organisation are extending the use they make of the package and thus need to know how to use different features. It can be expensive for a software house to provide call-out support but it is crucial that a customer does not have to wait too long for the help to arrive, otherwise the customer will lose confidence in the product. Indeed, suppliers may guarantee response times.

▶ **Telephone help desks**

In addition, many software suppliers offer telephone support for immediate help and advice. It provides someone with technical skills to guide the customer.

This help may be available during business hours. For some widely-used general-purpose software, the help is available 24 hours a day. The user phones the help desk (or call centre) when they have a problem. Help-desk operators are trouble-shooters who provide technical assistance, support, and advice to customers and end-users. They are experts in the software package and are likely to have a computer on the desk in front of them, which they use to try to replicate and solve users' problems. Alternatively, it is possible for the expert to take remote control of the user's computer and carry out tasks on behalf of the user.

When a help desk is provided for a widely-used software package, it is likely that a high number of requests for help will be received. The help-desk provider will need to establish procedures for logging and tracking the requests for help and the advice given. This is to ensure that all requests are dealt with in a fair and timely manner to maintain customer satisfaction.

When a call is taken, the user will need to give some information to the help-desk operator. This should include:

- their name and telephone number
- the nature of the problem
- the name and version number of the software
- the specification of the computer it is being run on (the type and speed of processor and the size of memory)
- the operating system in use
- any error messages being displayed
- the licence number of the software so that the help desk can check that the software is being used legally.

The help-desk operator will record this information with the date and time.

Monitoring the help desk

A help desk is likely to use a computerised call logging system giving a unique call reference number for each user query. This allows the performance of the help-desk operator to be monitored as well as providing a reference for follow-up calls. Different levels of support are provided; the level can determine the number of calls a user is entitled to make to the help desk. Logging calls enables the help desk to keep a count of all the calls made.

Help-desk employees should have access to a file of registered users to enable them to check that the caller is entitled to help whenever a phone call is received. A computerised database of known errors and their solutions, together with answers to frequently asked questions should be available. This could take the form of an expert system.

The performance of the help desk should be monitored to ensure that it provides a high level of service. Performance indicators could include:

- the number of calls logged daily or per hour
- the response time to the initial call
- the time taken to resolve the problem
- the number of repeat calls on the same problem for a particular user.

It may also be possible to record the level of the user's satisfaction with the problem resolution using a qualitative code.

The manager responsible for the provision of help-desk facilities would review the performance indicators on a regular basis and make necessary changes to staffing levels and procedures. It might prove necessary to provide extra training for help-desk operators.

A number of problems can arise when using a manufacturer's telephone help desk. The waiting time on the phone can be considerable at certain times of day. Many of these services are popular and it is not unusual to spend a lot of time listening to "music" while a call is queued. There have also been considerable problems when help desks have been outsourced.

Very often, the company employees in a help desk for clients that is based in-house will have an intimate knowledge of the products as well as access to a range of experts within the organisation. For employees working at an outsourced help desk, the information will have been entered into a knowledge database; however the information is not always kept up to date and may not be understood by the help-desk employee.

Help desks that are outsourced to other countries (see Chapter 15) can encounter further problems with cultural differences or language and dialect difficulties. Sometimes the rather formal English used by many employees of India-based help desks can confuse users who are seeking help.

Some problems are common and are easy to answer but other, complex, ones will not be able to be answered on the spot, as several experts may need to confer. In these circumstances, it will be necessary for the help-desk operator to phone back to the customer at a later time.

case study 1
▶ Helpdesk

(From an article by Angelique Chrisafis, *Guardian*, 20 March 2003, http://www.guardian.co.uk/society/2003/mar/20/publicvoices60)

Computer help-desk operator, salary: £24,500

I went straight from A Levels to work when I joined UMIST (University of Manchester Institute of Science and Technology) at 19 as a receptionist in the computer department. Now, two years later, I work as a computer help-desk operator. I work from 8.45 a.m. until 5 p.m. I don't suffer from stress, I feel valued and everyone in my department treats me as an equal.

In the morning I organise computer training courses. In the afternoon, I staff the walk-in help desk. I deal with staff and students complaining they can't log in, print or set up an account.

We get around 60 calls a day. People turn up saying, "You're the help desk, it says on this leaflet you'll fix it." They expect instant results and the high-ranking professors tend to get more hysterical on the phone than the students. I tend to keep calm when people lose their temper.

At the beginning, I was amazed that so many students in a place specialising in technology needed help with logging in.

1. Describe any help-desk facilities available at your school or college.

2. Find out the five most frequent problems taken at this help desk.

▶ **Email support**

If a problem is not time-critical, then email could be used as an alternative to the telephone. This has the advantage of smoothing out the demand, so that the operator can answer queries in order throughout the day. A priority system could be used which would ensure that more critical enquiries were answered first. Operators will be able to spend all their time finding solutions to problems without being interrupted by a ringing telephone.

From the user's point of view, the use of email avoids wasted time on the telephone. However, instant answers to simple problems are not possible. Email lacks the opportunity for human interaction offered by a telephone conversation.

Many suppliers now offer **instant messaging** support, as one operator can deal with several sets of instant messages at the same time. Answers are given as soon as the question is asked and it is very easy for a user to follow a problem through by asking follow-up questions.

▶ User guides

A software house will usually provide written instructions in using a package. These are typically provided free with the software. This user guide may come in hard copy form as a book or in a soft copy format that can be stored on the user's hard disk so it can be accessed whenever required. The user guide will describe how to install and use the software. For complex packages, there can be a number of different guides: perhaps one aimed at a first-time user, in the form of a tutorial, and another involving a complete description of all functions to serve as a reference document. Software user guides allow users to work at their own pace with the instructions beside them so they can find out how to use the software functions for themselves.

In an organisation, some people, perhaps senior managers, may not directly use a software package themselves. However, the software may produce reports that will provide them with information that they need to make appropriate decisions. They need to know what reports the software is capable of producing and how to interpret them. These managers would require a written manual that provides instructions for using the reports from the package, together with samples of the report so that they can determine which reports will aid them in their decision making.

▶ On-screen help

Help facilities can be installed with a package so that immediate guidance can be given in the use of the package. **Wizards** can be provided to make complex procedures within the package easier for the user to utilise by breaking down a task into manageable steps, each step having a clear explanation of what data the user needs to enter. Such help is particularly appropriate when a user wants to use a feature of the software that they have not used before, or needs to be reminded of an infrequently used operation. A user may wish to check how certain data that has to be entered needs to be formatted.

For infrequent or inexperienced users, detailed explanations can appear on the screen when data is being entered to ensure that data entry mistakes are avoided. For example, the format in which a date is to be entered can be shown.

▶ Online support

A popular way of making support available to the user is to use the Internet and store help facilities on the Web. Information can be kept very up to date. Users can access patches to update software or fix errors. Such a site would offer the facility to email a package expert for advice on a specific problem.

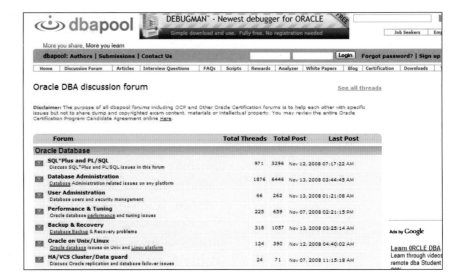

Figure 14.1 dbapool forum

Online self-help groups run on bulletin boards are available for many popular software packages. A **bulletin board** is an Internet service that makes multiple discussion groups (or forums) available. A **discussion forum** allows users to pose questions to other users and provides the opportunity for the sharing of problems and ideas. These are particularly useful when a user of a complicated software package encounters a problem that no one else in their organisation can help them with. A forum offers a number of topic areas where related problems and questions can be grouped together (see Figure 14.1).

Each topic area will have a number of questions known as **threads**. Each thread consists of the original user question or comment together with all the responses made by other users (see Figure 14.2).

Topics: System Administration

Topic	Replies	Views	Last Post
manually create oem in oracle 10g -By: sam on Sep 07, 2008 03:46:40 PM	2	68	Sep 08, 2008 08:13:26 AM
not able to run rcp -By: shekhar on Aug 26, 2008 07:23:13 AM	0	60	Not yet replied
what is dot (.) and double dot (..) in linux, when we use ls -a -By: Monu on May 21, 2008 12:53:11 AM	4	197	May 21, 2008 02:02:56 AM
how to solve service error -By: sam on May 16, 2008 05:38:44 AM	2	157	May 16, 2008 05:42:56 AM
how to sove service error -By: sam on May 16, 2008 05:34:38 AM	5	185	May 16, 2008 06:34:35 AM
How to recover passwd of a user in Sun Solaris 5.10 -By: Monu on Mar 15, 2008 03:58:17 PM	4	198	May 01, 2008 07:14:25 AM
LINUX & Sun Solaris server Health Check -By: Monu on Mar 03, 2008 11:17:26 AM	2	562	Mar 03, 2008 11:17:58 PM
accessing oracle -By: Duchi on Feb 24, 2008 02:36:16 PM	3	206	Jun 29, 2008 03:20:45 PM
LINUX FOR DBA -By: Monu on Feb 23, 2008 07:14:37 PM	3	282	Feb 25, 2008 12:37:14 AM
ODBC error 3146 -By: abhi on Feb 12, 2008 06:36:12 AM	0	263	Not yet replied

Figure 14.2 dbapool forum threads

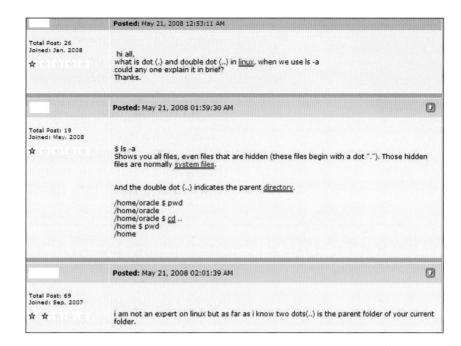

Figure 14.3 dbapool forum posts

case study 2
▶ **Thomas Cook support for travel agents**

The travel company Thomas Cook Group has implemented an agent support system across 17,000 users in 800 high street stores and third-party travel agents. The system provides in-depth information to staff as they serve customers in stores.

Previously, an agent had to call up a member of Thomas Cook's agent support team by telephone to get any extra information they needed, while the customer waited in the store or on the telephone. With the new system, agents will have more product details at their fingertips, including details of how to book twin-centre holidays and information on paying deposits.

In addition, the new system gives more than 200 call-centre and home-based agents access to a separate data repository to help them field remote enquiries, with information on a range of subjects from flight details to how to handle a refund.

1. What are the advantages of the new system to the personnel in the store?

2. What are the advantages to the management of Thomas Cook Group of the new system?

▶ **Package credibility**

It is not cheap for software companies to provide and staff a customer help desk. Of course the support is not free. Someone has to pay for it and it is likely that the price of the software reflects the provision of user support. Despite its cost, user support is necessary and is a major factor in determining the credibility of the software.

The provision of user support reassures the customer when they buy the product. They are more likely to buy the product if they know that an appropriate level of support at a reasonable cost is available. If user support is not available, business users are unlikely to risk using the software.

User support shows the customer that the software company has confidence in its product. A poor-quality product could result in thousands of help-desk calls and would be expensive for the company.

If the user suffered a problem and no support was available, they would be unlikely to buy a product from the same company again. A help desk helps retain customers.

Support options for industry-standard packages ◀

Many industry-standard packages, such as Microsoft Office or Adobe Photoshop, have a very large user base. Between them, the users need to know all aspects of the software's functionality, although each individual user is likely to use only a part of the range of options a software package offers. Support is provided in a variety of ways.

Help is now usually available over the **Internet** where up-to-date advice on common problems can be stored.

Books about using popular software are produced independently by publishers and sold in most bookshops or over the Internet. For the most popular packages, there is a very large number of titles available. A user needs to ensure that any book purchased is designed for a user of their skill level as books will vary from those suitable for absolute beginners to those designed for the most advanced user. Publishers of widely used software may send **newsletters** to all registered users, including **support articles** on tips, solutions to common problems and advanced functions. These newsletters provide a forum for users to share ideas and problems.

Software houses provide a considerable amount of information on packages via specialist **bulletin boards** on the Internet, often in the form of **Frequently Asked Questions (FAQs)**. Users can search through questions that other people have asked and are likely to find a solution that resolves their own current problem. The software house provides websites with information about the packages that give email access to experts. It is often helpful for the user to print out a version of the advice for use at a later time when the same information is needed. Such facilities are particularly useful for more able users who can help themselves by reading the information provided.

For complex software, **user groups** are set up, where users can get together to share problems and ideas. Such groups can meet physically or, more often these days, via bulletin boards on the Internet.

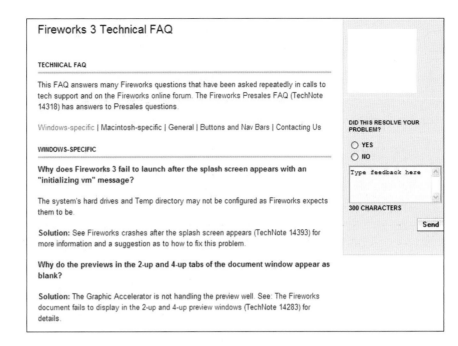

Figure 14.4 FAQ for Fireworks 3

Many of these facilities are of most use to the experienced user who, given access to the appropriate information, can work out the solution to a problem for themselves.

Very often, the help that a less experienced user needs is closer to hand. It is possible that a colleague or friend who is familiar with the software can help with their problem.

A company that provides IT hardware or software will need to provide forms of support for its customers. The interfaces available have been discussed above from the customer's viewpoint. Access to support can be sold with software products. Most software companies provide customers with websites that contain a wide range of support materials. These are often only available upon the registration of software.

Activity

Adobe offers a range of help and support to its customers.

1. Access the website http://www.adobe.com/support/photoshop/ and list the different kinds of help and support available for Photoshop.

2. Describe any uses that you have made of online help or support for software packages.

Figure 14.5 Online support for Photoshop

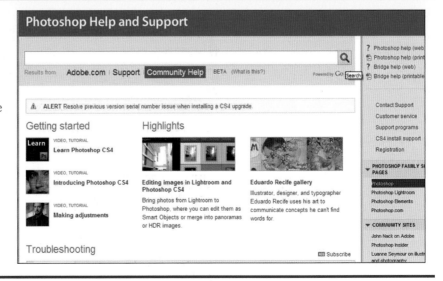

Documentation ◀

Documentation consists of written material that provides information on how to use a software package. All types of software should be supported with appropriate documentation. In fact, the quality of the documentation will be one of the criteria considered when choosing software.

Different types of user will have differing documentation needs. The technical support team will need documentation that provides installation instructions including disk, peripheral devices and memory requirements. They will need to have documentation of backup routines and recovery procedures. An explanation of all technical error messages, together with the necessary action to correct them, will be required.

A data entry clerk, using the same system, will need clear instructions on how to use functions. Details of appropriate error messages due to incorrect data entry should be included, together with a list of useful keyboard shortcuts.

End-users who will receive reports, perhaps in printed form, will need to have documentation that explains how to interpret and make use of the reports.

Documentation is not always produced in book form. It can usually be accessed online or may be produced and distributed as documents saved on a CD-ROM.

Factors to consider when selecting a support ◀ option

The support options chosen for a system by an organisation will depend on a number of factors. Different methods are likely to be chosen for different systems. The choice of option will depend on the cost of the different options and various other factors:

- The skill level of the employees: experienced users who have used a great number of different software packages are less likely to need help with everyday functions as they will be able to use their previous knowledge to work through problems for themselves. They may be able to make use of complex manuals and online support methods, such as discussion groups. Inexperienced users are likely to benefit from one-to-one help, either from a colleague or a help desk.

- Whether the new system is very different from the one that it replaces: if it is similar, some level of call-out help may be sufficient but if it is very different it may be best to provide on-site support for a time after the system first goes live.
- How critical the system is (how bad would it be if the system were not working?): the more critical the system, the more necessary it is to have very fast access to expertise so that if problems are encountered with the system, they can be resolved very quickly.
- The number of employees: if only one or two employees use a particular system, access to external help desks and online forums might be the most appropriate option. If there are many users of the system within the organisation then establishing in-house support could be the best option.
- The patterns of work: for example, users on a night shift may not have call-out support available; they will require other means of gaining the help they need.

Which of the available options that an employee will choose to use in any particular instance will depend on the nature of the problem and the skills and circumstances of the employee.

Many users rarely look in a manual, preferring to find out the answer for themselves, although this is not always the most efficient way of operating. The first point of call is usually the on-screen help as it is always available. On-screen help can usually be easily accessed from a simple menu choice so that a user who, for example, is not clear of the format required for entry of a particular piece of data can get immediate clarification.

If the on-screen help is not sufficient to solve the user's problem, a colleague may know the software well enough to solve the problem. Many employers rely on skilled colleagues to provide support to more inexperienced users together with reassurance that the right approach is being used.

Checking the Internet for a bulletin board may be more convenient for an office worker than buying a book. The information given may also be more up to date. Using a telephone help desk is often the last resort for a user; it can be time-consuming and require great patience.

case study 3
▶ Online class registration

A school makes use of an online registration system that allows teachers to take class registers in the classroom on a computer (see Chapter 13, Case study 1). Each teacher enters a unique identification code supported by a password. The attendance data is stored centrally and links to the student database.

The ICT support department manages the system carrying out tasks such as adding new teachers and pupils, entering details of classes and the pupils in those classes to the system and making modifications.

Class tutors and senior managers receive regular reports on attendance. These include weekly attendance lists for each tutor group or form as well as statistical summaries.

Pupils and their parents are able to access a summary of their own attendance online through the school's intranet.

Each user needs the facility to gain help when necessary so that they can make good use of the features of the software.

Teachers have access to on-screen help that relates to the stages they go through to enter the attendance for a class. Teachers quickly become familiar with the day-to-day functions that they need. There are, however, some other functions, such as registering an absent colleague's class, that teachers only use occasionally. On-screen instructions that remind them of the data that has to be entered help them use the software in this situation. Every teacher has a printed instruction sheet highlighting the main procedures of the system for use after long school holidays!

The members of the ICT support department have technical manuals that include the details of all functions in the system. They set up and maintain the appropriate data on an annual basis. From time to time, they need to phone the help desk of the software house when a problem occurs that they cannot solve for themselves. An online user group has been set up where those supplying technical support to different schools and colleges share their problems through a bulletin board.

The tutors and managers are provided with a printed guide showing the reports that the system can produce and how to interpret each one. The guide includes sample reports.

The pupil or his parent is given simple online instructions via the Internet, explaining how to access and interpret the information relating to their own attendance. A step-by-step guide is provided, helping the user complete all the actions required, showing exactly what data needs to be entered in every field. There are explicit instructions displayed on the screen to make data entry as simple as possible.

case study (contd.)

■ Copy and complete the table below. Include further ideas of your own as well as those given in the case study.

User	Use of software	Typical help needs	Appropriate sources of help
Teacher	Entering class attendance data		
Form tutor			
ICT support			
Pupil			

case study 4
▶ Cinema bookings

A software house has produced a seat-booking software package for sale to theatres and cinemas. The system allows front of house staff to receive seat bookings over the telephone and face-to-face before a performance. The tickets produced list the title of the film or play, the date and time of the performance, the seat number and the price.

Customers can also book online through a website.

1. What forms of support would a new member of staff need to enable them to ensure that they can deal with any problems that may arise when using the booking system?

2. What form of help would be appropriate for customers booking tickets online?

SUMMARY

Software houses provide a range of support options to customers:

► **on-site help**

► **call-out support**

► **help desks**

► **email support**

► **user manuals**

► **on-screen help**

► **online support.**

Much support is expensive to provide. However, a software package needs support if it is to maintain credibility with the public.

Industry-standard packages have a very large number of users. Other methods of obtaining help are available to users of these packages:

► **books**

► **newsletters**

► **bulletin boards on the Internet**

► **frequently asked questions (FAQs)**

► **user groups.**

Documentation consists of written material that provides information on how to use a software package. Different forms are available for different categories of user.

Factors an organisation might consider when selecting a suitable support option include:

► **cost**

► **skill level of the employees**

► **how critical the system is to the business**

► **number of employees**

► **patterns of work.**

1. Many industry-standard packages have a very large number of users. For such packages, help might be available from other sources than the manufacturer.

Describe other methods of gaining support from sources other than the software's manufacturer. (8)

2. Describe **three** ways in which support may be provided for users of ICT systems. (6)

January 2005 AQA ICT 4

3. "Now that all software has extensive online help facilities, there is no longer any need for other forms of help."

Discuss the above statement. (12)

4. A software company that maintains a help desk logs the calls that are received from users.

a) State the meaning of the term "help desk". (1)

b) State **four** items, other than date and time, that might be entered into the log when a user call is received by the help desk. (4)

c) The manager in charge of the help desk needs to have information relating to the effectiveness of the service provided. Describe **three** measures that could be used to assess the effectiveness of the service. (6)

5. When introducing new or improved ICT systems, successful organisations know that, in order to achieve a successful transition, they must provide both initial training and ongoing support.

A national supermarket chain relies heavily on various information systems. It employs both full-time and part-time staff working in stores and warehouses sited around the country or at the head office.

Discuss the options available for both training and support. Make suitable recommendations for this particular company for the training and support of the following groups of staff:

- part-time store staff
- full-time store staff
- warehouse and home-delivery staff
- head-office staff
- managers at all levels.

The quality of written communication will be assessed in your answer. (20)

June 2005 AQA ICT 4

(This question also relates to topics covered in Chapter 13).

15

External and internal resources

AQA Unit 3 Section 12 ◄

There are many different kinds of resources involved in the development, running and maintenance of ICT systems within an organisation. These include:

- hardware
- software
- communications
- people
- consumables
- facilities and power.

Many resources are **internal** to the organisation. For example, employees, buildings and hardware owned by the organisation can all be considered to be internal resources. However many organisations also make use of resources that are **external**, such as ICT professionals from an agency working for the organisation under a contract. Certain services, such as the payroll function, may be carried out by an external agency.

Using external ICT services and business support ◄

▶ Outsourcing

Some companies specialise in providing ICT-related support services to other organisations. When an organisation makes use of such a company's specialist services, it is known as outsourcing. **Outsourcing** is the subcontracting of aspects of a business to an external agency. An organisation might outsource functions such as payroll, ICT support or backup.

An organisation may decide to outsource a function for a number of reasons. An important factor is cost. It can be cheaper to buy in the service than provide it in-house. In most industries, ICT executives are under pressure to reduce spending while providing more accurate and timely information as well as developing more innovative services, such as online sales systems. Thus any ways of reducing costs are being explored. Apart from costs of equipment, people with strong ICT skills can be expensive to employ. In addition to the cost of a salary, there are added costs of pensions, training and management for every employee.

To carry out a payroll function internally could take up considerable amounts of management time. Specialist software will be needed. Someone will need to be employed in the Human Resources department with specialist knowledge of payroll, tax, salary and legal requirements; they will need to be provided with office space and ICT equipment. Computer resources will be needed to run the payroll software. The cost of outsourcing the payroll function could be considerably less than performing the function internally.

Companies also outsource to improve performance. ICT support for an organisation is frequently outsourced. Using the expertise of hardware or software suppliers or external experts means that people within an organisation have access to a much wider range of expertise than could be supplied internally. An external company can provide higher levels of service, providing help whenever it is needed whatever the time of day or night. When services are provided internally, continuity of service can be jeopardised when employees are absent due to illness or holiday. A specialist company to which a function has been outsourced should have additional resources available at short notice. This will enable them to cope with peak workloads or specific IT projects requiring specialist skills.

The management of backup and recovery processes are often outsourced by organisations. This is explored in Chapter 7.

case study 1
▶ Everton Football Club outsourcing

Figure 15.1 Everton FC

Everton FC has recently outsourced its payment-processing system. All transactions or payments from ticket sales and other sources are transferred from the club to the outsourcing company's computers from where they are sent to the appropriate bank.

case study (contd.)

Before the function was outsourced, someone in Everton's ICT department had to transfer payment files to the banks at the end of each day in a manual process. With the outsourced system, it is all done automatically. The outsourcing company has full responsibility for payment transactions.

The importance of a reliable and efficient way of processing payments is clear: the club takes more than £10 m per year in ticket revenue alone, with three club shops and the hiring of executive boxes bringing in around 16 per cent of annual revenue.

There are a number of benefits to Everton's ICT department as a result of the outsourcing. They no longer need to train new staff in the payments process nor do they need to look after so much hardware. In fact, as they no longer need a dedicated server to process payments, they have been able to create space in their server room that can be used for future upgrades in ICT. Everton is saving about £180,000 a year by outsourcing the payments system.

1. Explain what is meant by "outsourcing".

2. List the benefits to Everton Football Club of outsourcing the payments system.

3. Describe any disadvantages of outsourcing that you can think of.

Another benefit for an organisation of outsourcing ICT functions is that outsourcing can lead to more predictable ICT spending.

Activity 1

Another function that is commonly outsourced is data entry.

Research the Web to find examples of the outsourcing of data entry.

1. Write a brief summary of your findings.
2. What are the benefits of outsourcing data entry?
3. What are the drawbacks of outsourcing data entry?

case study 2
▶ **WHSmith outsourcing core ICT functions**

Figure 15.2 WHSmith

WHSmith is a major retailer selling books, stationery, magazines and a range of other products. WHSmith has outsourced the management of its ICT hardware, software and help desk.

Fujitsu has a contract to provide IT hardware and operational support 24/7 for WHSmith's retail headquarters and its high-street shops throughout the UK. The hardware includes the company's mainframes, point of sale terminals, over 1000 desktops and laptops as well as office and network servers.

WHSmith used to have a number of separate help desks. Fujitsu provides a single help desk that handles service requests electronically and by phone or fax. Service response times and productivity for WHSmith have both been improved.

Since it has outsourced its ICT operations to Fujitsu, WHSmith has been able to focus on its core business activities and the achievement of business targets. As less of the time of the store staff has been spent on IT problems, customer service has improved. WHSmith no longer has to pay to train their own ICT employees in the skills needed to maintain the hardware and staff an ICT help desk.

1. List the benefits to WHSmith of outsourcing; include any potential benefts that have not been described.

2. Discuss other functions that WHSmith could outsource.

3. Under what circumstances might the decision to outsource key functions result in a less successful outcome?

▶ Offshoring

When an organisation purchases services in one country to be provided in a different country, it is called **offshoring**. At present, most offshoring for UK organisations takes place in India, but other offshore locations include South Africa, Ireland and China. Some organisations have moved services offshore because the services had become unprofitable at existing operating costs in the UK.

Offshoring can take one of three forms. Firstly, a UK firm can set up its own offshore operation. The bank HSBC has set up a section in India where it has 2000 employees working on back-office operations. Offshoring in this way has reduced HSBC's costs considerably whilst still maintaining close managerial control. Alternatively, offshoring can be achieved by outsourcing to a company that has a history of providing services, such as IBM, which has its own offshore facilities. A third option is to use a company that is based in the country involved.

For an offshoring operation to be successful, the provider must be well established and employ experienced and technically-capable personnel. The organisation must have strong management and must be flexible and adaptive to the needs of the client company. Strict standards must be set by the company obtaining the services. A **service level agreement** should be set up.

> A service level agreement is a contract that is made between a company obtaining a service and the company providing the service. It specifies the nature, scope and quality of the service that is to be provided.

There has been a growth in the use of offshoring for website and Internet development projects, as well as for programming other applications.

case study 3
▶ Development India offshore web design

Development India "offers **turnkey** website design and development centres from India. Our services span from development of your corporate identity to web development services for both offline and online media.

Development India excels in custom website solutions, web programming, web application development using Web 2.0, e-commerce design and development across various industries including but not limited to publishing, travel, real estate, television, entertainment and education."

Development India offers:

- web design

- web development

- e-commerce

- flash design and development

- web maintenance services

- web hosting.

case study (contd.)

1. Define the term "offshoring".

2. Find out what is meant by the term "turnkey".

3. Discuss any problems that might arise if a company contracts the development and maintenance of its website to Development India.

4. Describe any safeguards that a company using the services of Development India should put in place to ensure a successful venture.

IT support and help desks are often provided offshore. IT support is the second most likely activity to be offshored by UK businesses.

The supermarket chain, Somerfield, has transferred its IT help desk to India to be run by an outsourcing company, Tata. They see offshore outsourcing as a way of improving business efficiency and cutting costs. Before the system went live, Tata provided a trial when all the IT help-desk functions were provided by the outsourcer's employees working in the UK.

There have been some problems with offshoring help-desk functions and a growing number of people believe that functions that require extensive client interaction are better carried out in the UK. This is because cultural and language differences between clients and offshore help-desk workers can cause frustration and misunderstanding that leads to dissatisfaction and complaints.

Perhaps the best functions for offshoring are those that are mainly technical, for example development and testing. With such functions, the majority of the work is carried out by technical experts; client interaction can be carried out by project managers who are specifically trained to do it.

case study 4
▶ Thames Water offshoring

Xansa is a UK-based outsourcing and technology company with over 8000 people in the UK and India. Thames Water has a contract with Xansa for some of its billing operations to be handled in India.

Xansa deals with metered-billing exceptions and customer correspondence for Thames Water. It accesses Thames Water's UK-based customer services systems remotely from India.

The offshore system processes and resolves about half a million metered-billing exceptions annually. There are over 70 different causes of these exceptions. The system has to work out the reason for the exception and instigate the appropriate action so that any discrepancy is resolved. This results in correct billing for the customer and fast payment for Thames Water.

Xansa has worked with Thames Water for a number of years and has built up a detailed knowledge of its back-office processes. The relatively low operating costs in India are important to Thames Water.

As part of its service-level agreement with Thames Water, Xansa has to deal with customer correspondence within four days. 90 per cent of metered billing exceptions must be processed by day one and 100 per cent by day three.

1. Why do you think that the project described has been successful?

2. Find out about other companies that provide offshoring to UK companies.

▶ Bulk printing

Specialist companies provide a service to carry out bulk printing, for example for payroll and billing systems. These companies have high-speed, high-quality printers that enable them to print at much higher speeds than normal business printers. They also have equipment that allows them to fold documents and place them in envelopes at high speed. By using such a service, a company will save:

- the cost of having their own equipment
- time
- space.

▶ Ways of obtaining ICT services from suppliers

An organisation can hire an employee on a permanent contract, they can buy equipment to own outright, they can purchase buildings and set up their own network infrastructure both locally and over a wide area. However, there are alternative ways of acquiring the goods and services that they need.

Contracting

Contracting is a way of acquiring human resources, space or equipment. Individuals who work freelance can be hired on a short-term contract to carry out a specific task. Contractors are often used to take a role in developing a new system or in testing. Such individuals may be employed because they have skills that are not to be found within the current employees of the organisation, or the organisation may need extra manpower for a short period to fulfil a particular project. Such freelance workers may be committed to work solely for the organisation for a fixed time or may work on several projects

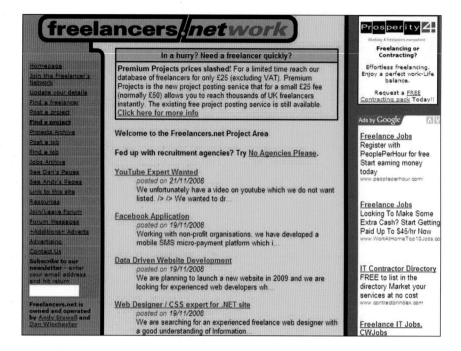

Figure 15.3 Freelancers network website

for different organisations concurrently. Many such freelancers will work from home. A number of websites exist that enable organisations and freelancers to find each other.

Alternatively, a contract for carrying out specific tasks may be agreed with another company that employs a number of professionals. This company will be responsible for ensuring that the work is done by appropriate personnel.

The benefit to an organisation of employing a freelancer directly for a specified project is that they have control over the choice of person; they are able to assess their skills and whether they will fit in with the existing team. However, if the freelancer is ill or does not complete the assigned tasks satisfactorily, the organisation will have to find an alternative person to complete the work. If the work is contracted from a company this would become the responsibility of that company.

A contractor can provide the office space for a company as part of the contract rather than the staff and equipment being housed on their own premises. This can save an organisation money as a large amount of capital can be needed to purchase offices. Some companies also arrange offices for organisations (see Case Study 5).

case study 5
▶ **Office solutions**

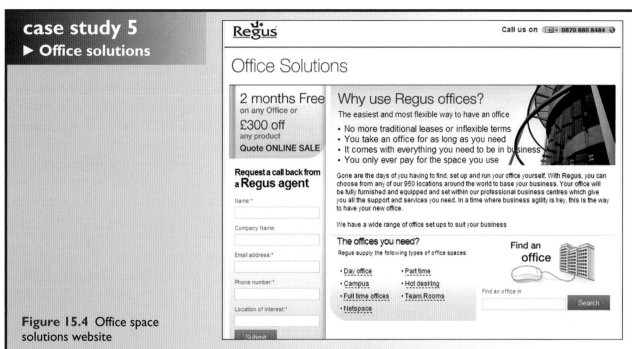

Figure 15.4 Office space solutions website

Figure 15.4 shows the services offered by Regus, a company that rents out office space. The site can be found at http://www.regus.co.uk. Regus states:

"You're free to run your business without the financial or management burden that comes with traditional office rental. That's because we take care of everything – your office is equipped and ready to go. All you need to do is choose the right location and move in."

1. Explore the Regus website.

2. Explain the meaning of "hot desking", "team rooms" and "day office".

3. Discuss other office rental options that Regus offers.

4. Discuss the benefits to a company of contracting office space rather than buying it.

An organisation can acquire IT equipment from a manufacturer through a contract.

Leasing

A **lease** is an agreement whereby one person or organisation hires a particular asset such as ICT equipment or office space. Hiring equipment or office space avoids the capital cost that is involved in owning it. For many organisations it is better to use capital for other purposes and to lease some equipment. The hire costs require regular payments from income. The decision to lease ICT equipment rather than to purchase it is often made because the equipment is likely to go out of date quickly.

There are some advantages to small businesses of purchasing ICT hardware outright as they are able to deduct a percentage of the value of their hardware purchases from their taxable income. A further advantage of buying hardware outright is that an organisation is not committed to medium- or long-term agreements that might become inappropriate if the needs of the organisation change. The overall cost of the hardware is likely to be less if purchased outright. Once the hardware is purchased there is no further administration involved.

However, purchasing outright means that the organisation has to pay the full cost at the time of purchase. This may cause cash-flow problems. Leasing IT equipment gives an organisation financial flexibility as the cost of equipment can be spread over a period of time. Often, a leasing contract for equipment includes a maintenance contract and an undertaking from the leasing company to replace any hardware in the event of total failure. Leasing companies may also offer the possibility of an upgrade or replacement with new equipment after a period of time so that the organisation can maintain up-to-date technology.

Standard software too can be purchased by paying a leasing company monthly payments spread over the useful life of the application. The payments made will cover all costs, including installation, training, maintenance and any upgrades that become available. It is usually possible to add extra licences when needed by increasing the monthly payments.

An alternative form of lease can be used to acquire software. A software house can develop bespoke software for an organisation. When the work is completed, the software house will be paid by a finance company. The organisation will then make monthly payments to the finance company for the term of the lease (typically 24 to 60 months). At the end of the lease, the software is theirs. A similar form of lease can be used when acquiring equipment.

While some large organisations install their own communication links, most will lease them. Many organisations use existing external infrastructures to allow for home working and outsourcing, both in the UK and offshore. Communication services can be maintained, expanded and updated by specialist companies as most organisations would not have the expertise to do it themselves.

Managing internal resources ◄

So far, we have considered external resources. An organisation is likely to have many internal resources and systems should be in place to manage these resources so that they are used to very best effect.

When a new ICT project is being developed, a range of resources is involved, including hardware, software and human resources. The use of project management software should help to make sure that resources are used effectively. This topic is covered in Chapter 9.

► Hardware resources

An organisation should have a procurement policy (see Chapter 6) that specifies how decisions concerning hardware acquisition should be decided. As discussed, hardware can be purchased outright or leased.

Once hardware arrives on site, details should be entered into an inventory. An inventory is an itemised catalogue of all hardware held by an organisation. It is likely to be held in database management software and it is very important that inventories are kept up to date. Data recorded for each item of hardware is likely to include:

- serial number
- description
- supplier
- date of purchase
- purchase price
- location in the organisation
- maintenance arrangements.

Hardware will need regular maintenance and repair. An organisation can provide all maintenance services in-house, outsource all services or, most commonly, provide some services in-house and outsource the rest. Regular checks need to be made that all equipment is working correctly; in all but the smallest organisations, a system of reporting and logging hardware problems and solutions will be needed. All electrical equipment needs an annual safety check. These tasks need to be allocated to specific employees; a system may be needed to monitor that regular checking and maintenance is taking place.

► Software resources

Considerable work is involved in managing software within an organisation. If bespoke software is used, very careful management of the software development will be needed (see Chapter 9). Training and reference materials need to be kept up to date whenever changes to the software are made.

When off-the-shelf software is used, careful records need to be kept of licence agreements. As with hardware, an inventory should be maintained. The job of keeping the inventory up to date should be allocated to a specific person or team. It should be part of someone's job to be accountable for ensuring that all licences are kept up to date and that no unlicensed software is installed on any of the organisation's computers.

Activity 2

Produce a list of the fields that would be needed for a record in a database of software licences.

When updates are issued for off-the-shelf software applications, they need to be installed on the hardware and the relevant people will need to be informed of any changes in use.

▶ Communications resources

An organisation may have dedicated WAN lines, leased lines or may access a WAN via the Internet. The hardware that is required for a network infrastructure will need to be set up and then maintained.

The type of communications link that an organisation uses in a particular location depends on where they are and how important the quality and speed of communications are to the business. For example, the bandwidth may need to be reviewed regularly if distributed databases and backups are to be kept in step. It may be necessary to have duplicate communications services if they are critical to a system, so that failure does not result in disastrous consequences.

▶ Consumables

Consumables are the regular minor items which need to be purchased for an ICT system, such as paper and ink or toner for a printer, CD-ROM disks or staples. Although such items are relatively cheap, they are vital in the running of a system. A variety of types of paper may be required, in different colours and weights; special stationery might be required for certain processes, such as producing payslips.

An organisation will need to manage the ordering and distribution of consumables. They may have a supplies department that carries out these functions. They will need to establish reliable suppliers who can provide the items they want at the best price, ensure that there is always sufficient of a particular type of stock available for use without over stocking, which would use up too much storage space.

Networking software should be installed that can advise the technical support team about the level of toner in the printers and also advise when the paper trays need topping up for larger printers that take huge print runs.

A system is needed for employees in the organisation to request and be provided with supplies. Employees need to be encouraged to return empty printer toner cartridges so that they can be recycled.

▶ Facilities and power

Organisations need buildings to house their computer hardware and provide office space for their employees. As discussed, buildings can be owned or leased by the company.

Rooms that house a lot of electronic equipment, such as a server room, may need to have air conditioning installed. Wherever there are computers there will be cabling. Computers need a power supply and, if they are part of a network may be physically linked to other hardware. It is essential that the layout of computers in a room and the position of cabling are planned before installation so that danger to employees – through tripping over a loose cable, perhaps – and to the equipment is minimised. There needs to be enough space and sufficient power sockets so that all employees can make safe and appropriate use of the hardware that they need to do their job.

The positioning of workstations in offices and the furniture to be used needs careful planning too so that the health of employees is not jeopardised.

All hardware needs a supply of electricity. When setting up a new office or computer suite, the supply of electricity needs to be checked so that sufficient power lines are provided to allow the safe running of the volume of equipment to be used. Computers used for critical systems will need an uninterruptible power supply (UPS); the organisation might need to install a backup generator in case of cuts in the power supply.

▶ People

A resource that must not be forgotten is the people who work in ICT. While most people use ICT as part of their job, there are some roles that are specifically related to ICT systems. A large organisation will have its own ICT support team of technicians who will manage the network, organise backups, install and monitor use of software and hardware, carry out some repairs and provide help and support to users. There is likely to be a staffing structure with specific areas of responsibility and chain of command.

ICT support staff will need to be provided with appropriate training on a regular basis.

SUMMARY

There are many different kinds of resources involved in the development, running and maintenance of ICT systems within an organisation:

▶ hardware

▶ software

▶ communications

▶ consumables

▶ facilities and power

▶ people.

Resources can be internal or external to the organisation.

Outsourcing is the subcontracting of aspects of a business to an external agency. An organisation might outsource functions such as payroll, ICT support or backup.

Offshoring is a term used to describe the purchasing of services by an organisation when the services are provided in a different country.

Specialist companies provide a service to carry out bulk printing, for example for payroll and billing systems.

Many resources, such as hardware and buildings, can be bought outright by an organisation.

Contracting is a way of acquiring human resources, space or equipment.

A lease is an agreement whereby a person or organisation hires an asset.

Software, communications links and equipment can be leased.

Internal resources need careful management.

Questions

1. The ICT policy of a large FE college states that an inventory of software licences should be maintained.
   a) Define "inventory". (1)
   b) Explain the importance of keeping an up-to-date inventory of software licences. (2)
   c) List the data fields that you would include in such an inventory. (3)

2. All the bills for Westric, an electrical supply company, are produced by an external company. Discuss the advantages to Westric. (6)

3. A company decides to outsource its payroll function.
   a) Explain what is involved in a payroll system. (4)
   b) Define "outsourcing". (2)
   c) Discuss the benefits and drawbacks to a company of outsourcing this function. (6)

4. The internal ICT resources of an organisation need to be carefully managed. Discuss the resources involved and the ways in which they need to be controlled. (12)

5. A travel agency decides to implement a new e-commerce system. Discuss the resources that will be required and the ways in which the agency could acquire them. (20)

16

Practical issues involved in the use of ICT in the digital world

AQA Unit 4 Introduction

What this unit is about

This is a coursework unit over an extended period of time, that will take up much of your A2 year. The unit concerns the use of ICT in the real world.

The marks available for this unit make up 20 per cent of the total marks for the A Level.

You will apply your skills, knowledge and understanding of ICT to solve a problem for a real client in an organisation such as a local company, a retailer, a school or college, a charity, a club or society, or just a group of people coming together to organise an event.

You will work with a client. You may work with other students in a team for the same client. Different members of the team should tackle different aspects or areas of work. For example, one team member may work on a website, another on backup and recovery strategies, another on a training package for some new software, etc. The work you hand in must be your own.

It is likely that you will use sources of information such as websites, textbooks, magazines, etc. This is an important part of your research and is perfectly acceptable but you must list all the sources that you have used.

You must produce a detailed report which you will hand in to your teacher when finished.

What you have to do

Your final report (see Chapter 22) will comprise the following:

- Background and investigation – who the client is, the organisation that they work for or represent and what exactly their requirements are (see Chapter 17).
- Analysis and deliverables – what the proposed system will do (see Chapter 18).
- Design and planning for implementation – designs for your system (see Chapter 19).
- Testing and documentation of implementation (see Chapter 20).
- Evaluation of the implemented solution (see Chapter 21).

Do I need a real client? ◄

This is a common question among students.

You should remember that the emphasis of this unit is to create a solution for a client, not to create a solution. The client will be involved throughout the project:

- You will interview the client to find out their needs.
- You will involve the client in producing evaluation criteria.
- The client will be involved in the design stage.
- The client will be involved in the testing and the evaluation.

Only a real client can do this. If you make up a client, you are likely to miss out on many of the marks available.

If you can't find a client, talk to your teacher who may be able to suggest a possible client from within your school or college.

Planning your work ◄

When a project is going to take several months to complete, you must break it down into sub-tasks and produce an estimate of by when each sub-task should be completed.

It is vital that you plan ahead and produce a timetable for your project. This could be in the form of:

- a word-processed list of dates and milestones
- a word-processed table
- a table created in spreadsheet software
- a Gantt chart created in spreadsheet software
- a timetable created in project management software
- an electronic diary.

Failure to produce plans like this will inevitably lead to too much work in the closing weeks of the project. As deadlines approach, stress levels will rise and you are unlikely to do yourself justice.

- Break the task down into sub-tasks.
- Estimate the time for each sub-task.
- Have a complete timetable for the whole of the project, including milestones along the way.
- Compare your actual progress with the original time plan.

If you get behind, take immediate steps to catch up – don't leave it to the last week.

What you will hand in ◄

At the end of the work, you will hand in a project report. This report will include all the sections listed in 'What you will have to do'. The report will be word-processed and include screenshots and print-outs of your work as evidence of what you have achieved.

Project ideas ◄

There are two main types of project that you could tackle:

- a software solution using generic software, such as database software or animation software, to create a system for a client
- information for the client's organisation on an ICT issue, such as producing and testing a disaster recovery plan for a small business or an ICT security policy for a junior school.

For either type of system, you will need to investigate exactly what the client needs, design and create the system to meet these needs and test the system you have created. If you produce a software solution, you must produce user and technical documentation for the system. You must also produce an evaluation.

Both types of project are sufficiently complex to need several months to complete. Neither type of project is an easier option. Choose the type of project that motivates you.

The right choice of project is vital to your success. You need a project with a real client which enables you to meet all the requirements of this unit. Your chosen project must allow you to include the following in your final report:

- background and investigation
- analysis and deliverables
- design and planning for implementation
- testing and documentation of implementation
- evaluation of the implemented solution.

▶ Software solution project ideas

If you choose to undertake a software solution, you will need to be very familiar with the chosen software. You will need to practise the skills needed before starting on this part of your project. The following list gives suggestions for suitable systems:

- a user-support database system for a help desk in a company, school or college, which logs faults and actions taken to rectify them
- a website, intranet site or extranet site for an organisation or an event

- a system to record purchases of books, stationery and other materials for the English faculty of a further education college
- an invoicing system to create invoices for a supplier of camping equipment
- an animation that could be used to enhance or add a function to a web page or pages
- managing relationships with customers by collecting and storing customer feedback via a website and a back-office system that can collect, store and classify responses, plus a system that results can be fed into for statistical analysis
- a booking system for a small country hotel
- a multimedia interactive map for a tourist information office, where users can choose what features are displayed. For example, the map might display details of tourist attractions, hotels, sporting venues, night clubs, etc.
- a spreadsheet system to store the accounts of a small organisation
- a stock control system that will record stock levels for a seller of cosmetics.

▶ ICT issue project ideas

- ICT training materials that provide information for users concerning all aspects of the client's computer system.
- A review of the security of an organisation's ICT systems, which could include laptop computers, PDAs and other mobile devices.
- A communication policy including what communication methods to use and a communal electronic diary system.
- A system for evaluating new hardware to be purchased for a replacement system including software, communications, consumables and services.
- A backup and recovery system and a disaster recovery plan for an organisation.
- An ICT equipment replacement policy for a school or other organisation, looking at costs of purchase, leasing costs, alternative hardware, bulk purchase costs, etc.
- Software training materials for an internal training course for employees of a company, covering one or more software applications in a variety of formats.
- Training, in a variety of formats, in ICT security, including physical security, software security and security procedures.
- Health and safety policies within an organisation: how they inform staff of requirements of legislation, including new laws, and how they ensure that employees follow the legal requirements.
- Environmental ICT policies for a company, including purchase, use, reuse, minimising the use of energy and disposal of equipment.

Finding a client

This is often not as difficult as it sounds. Nearly all organisations, such as a sports club or small shop, store data. If they store it on paper, would it be better to store it electronically? If they store this information electronically at present, could their system be improved?

Many organisations would like a website to promote their activities or to sell goods. Perhaps they already have a website but would like an animation to enhance the site. Could you create a website or an animation for an organisation?

All organisations, such as a youth club, need to keep financial records of income and expenditure. Could you set up a spreadsheet to help such an organisation?

Businesses also need policies on issues, such as security or backup. It is vital that important data is not lost and that no unauthorised people can get access to this data. They will need advice on what to include in these policies. They will also need practical help in setting up the policies and testing that they work. You will need to investigate what information is stored, how it is used and who has access to it.

These are just a few examples of the sorts of organisations that you could use as a client. You are likely to know someone, a parent, a friend, a neighbour, a teacher or a relation who would welcome your help and would be prepared to act as your client.

The client must be someone that you can communicate with as your project develops. This communication could be face-to-face but you could contact your client by telephone, email or online chat.

▼

SUMMARY

This is a considerable piece of coursework that will take some months. You will be creating a solution for a client.

You can choose either a software solution or a written solution. You will need to analyse the problem in depth, then design and create a solution. The solution will be documented, tested and evaluated. You must list all the sources that you use.

You will need to find a client – someone you can contact for their opinions throughout the project period. You will involve the client throughout the process. You will need to produce a time plan and monitor it closely so that you don't get behind.

17

Background and investigation

AQA Unit 4 Section 1

In this chapter, we look at how to use a variety of techniques to investigate situations and present your findings. The background and investigation section of your final report is worth up to 14 marks.

Background

The first section of your report should be an introduction in which you describe the organisation to which your client belongs. You should describe:

- the organisation – what is its name?
- its function or functions – what does it do?
- the client – what is their name? what is their job title? what does this involve?
- technical users of the proposed system, if appropriate – what are their names? what are their roles within the organisation?
- non-technical users of the proposed system – what are their names? what are their roles within the organisation? (the client and the users may be different people)
- the audience if there is one, e.g. for a website
- the current system, the people involved and their roles
- the problem that you will be trying to solve
- a business case for change.

However obvious it may seem, you must describe the functions of the organisation. If you are setting up a system for a boys' football club, you'd have to say that the club is member of a particular league, that it plays home and away matches against other clubs in the league and that it also participates in cup competitions. You would go on to describe how many players are members of the club, how they register, what subscriptions they have to pay, and so on.

You must demonstrate a good understanding of the organisation and how it operates at present.

You should describe briefly the problem that you are trying to solve. The business case for change means explaining why the organisation should adopt your system. There are normally only two main reasons for a business introducing a new system:

- introducing efficiencies and saving money
- improving service to attract more customers, thereby increasing income.

Within a non-commercial organisation, a system that makes work easier for staff may provide a case for change.

Example background

The Gladstone Arms Hotel, just outside the town of Wellford, is one of a handful of quality hotels in the local area. The hotel was converted from an old farmhouse in 1976 and is set in a country garden in the village of Hillbury.

Business people often hold important meetings and have lunch with clients in the restaurant. Often, they might also stay the night at the Gladstone Arms Hotel, attracted by its good facilities. The Gladstone Arms Hotel also offers the facility of holding wedding receptions, which attracts more business.

There are 19 individually-styled bedrooms, which all have a TV and en-suite facilities. Being situated in a small village, the hotel has quiet surroundings, which makes the place even more attractive. There are also three conference rooms for meetings, each equipped with a digital projector.

There are 35 members of staff at the Gladstone Arms Hotel, eight of whom deal with the hotel side of the business – the other members of staff work in the restaurant. Some staff are very computer-literate while others have never used a computer.

The Gladstone Arms Hotel uses a manual system to record bookings of hotel rooms and tables in the restaurant. When a customer phones to book a bedroom or a conference room at the hotel, the reservation is written in the diary. If they wish to book a table in the restaurant, they are put through to the restaurant and the booking is recorded in a second diary. This procedure has been used since the hotel has been running.

My client is the manager of the Gladstone Arms Hotel, Mrs Karen Anslow. Karen has been manager of the hotel for four years. Before that she managed a smaller hotel in the Cotswolds. She uses the manual system because all employees can take bookings and little training is required.

However, she thinks that an electronic reservation system could lead to a better service, efficiencies and save money. One system may be able to record reservations for both the rooms and the restaurant. This could save time and possibly reduce the number of staff needed.

The users of the proposed system would be all 35 members of staff. None of them are technical users or computer experts. If the system fails for any reason, they will need outside help. For this reason, the new system needs to be reliable and easy to understand with an effective user guide.

Investigation ◄

In this section of your report, you need to investigate the organisation and its requirements in more depth. There are various techniques that you can use, in particular:

- personally observing the current system in action
- examination of existing documents used in the current system
- a questionnaire to staff
- interviewing staff.

You need to use at least two of these techniques. The ones you use will depend on the proposed system.

Looking at existing documents, such as forms, is important. You can see what data is stored at present. You an also design the new documents to be as similar as possible to the old documents so that users are immediately familiar with the new documents. Figures 17.1 and 17.2 show documents from the Gladstone Arms Hotel.

If you need to get feedback from a large number of employees, a questionnaire is likely to be most appropriate.

If you have to get feedback from one or two users, you might want to interview them. You could use an interview to get feedback from your client and a questionnaire for other members of staff.

If you interview your client, remember that they are likely to be a busy person. You will not have much time. Prepare the questions beforehand. This will mean that you save time and don't forget anything. When the interview takes place keep a written record of what is said (see example transcript). You may find it easier, and your client may prefer it, if you send a list of questions by email.

Example of accommodation book

Date: September 2007

Monday 10th → Sunday 16th

Room Number.	Monday 10th September	Tuesday 11th September	Wednesday 12 September	Thursday 13th September	Friday 14th September	Saturday 15th September	Sunday 16th September
1		Ben Smith 01283 414228	→	→			
2	////	////	////	////	////	////	////
3		Pat Moore 01645 292016	→	Sam Rabbit 07922417811	→		
4							
5	Beth Small 01645 242526		Karen White 04543 290273	→	→	→	→
↓ 19							

This indicates when a customer stays for longer then a day

The rooms listed show when and where they are available for booking. The layout easily shows this. The blank spaces

(This is a hand drawn example of what the Brook House Hotel is currently using to book hotel rooms for guests)

//// This represents when a room is unavailable (eg redecorating) such as room 2

In each slot would consist of name, address, and telephone number. Details of credit card would also be stored.

This hand drawn version has been drawn simpler as guest details consist of much more.

Figure 17.1 Sample document: accommodation booking

Room Details

Room Number	Double/ Single	En Suite	Small/ Large	Television	Wireless Connection	Decoration/Style	Extra.
Example	Double	Yes	S	Yes	No	4 poster bed, traditional	Garden view.
1	Single	Yes	S	Yes	Yes	Brass Bed	Garden View
2	Double	Yes	Standard	Yes	Yes	4 Poster	Jacuzzi Bath
3	Small Double	Yes	Small	Yes	Yes	Canopied	" "
4	Single	Yes	Standard	Yes	Yes	Brass Bed	" "
5	Single	Yes	S	Yes	Yes	Brass Bed	" "
6	Double	Yes	Standard	Yes	Yes	Canopied Brass Bed	Garden View Spa Bath.
7	Small Double	Yes	S	Yes	Yes	" " "	Garden View
8	Single	Yes	Standard	Yes	Yes	Wooden Cot Beds	" "
9	Single	Yes	Standard	Yes	Yes	" "	" "
10	Single	Yes	Standard	Yes	Yes	" "	" "
11	Double	Yes	Standard	Yes	Yes	Four Poster	Courtyard View
12	Double	Yes	Large	Yes	Yes	Canopied	" "
14	Twin	Yes	Standard	Yes	Yes	Matching Cot Beds	Garden View
15	Single	Yes	Large	Yes	Yes	Brass Bed	Courtyard View
16	Double	Yes	Standard	Yes	Yes	Canopied Half Tester	" "
17	Double	Yes	Large	Yes	Yes	7ft Canopied Bed	High ceilings fully beamed Honeymoon's beans & Garden Vi.
18	Double	Yes	Large	Yes	Yes	Canopied Half Tester	Spa Bath

(eg redecorating) such as room 2   Details of credit card would also be stored.   of much more.

Figure 17.2 Sample document: room details

Example interview transcript

Transcript of an interview with my client, Mr David Fairbrother, Managing Director of Makepeace plc. held at Makepeace offices, Station Street on 14 October.

Me: Hi. Thank you for agreeing to be my client.

DF: I'm happy to help.

Me: Now, over the phone you said that you'd like an environmental ICT policy for your company.

DF: Yes.

Me: So why do you want this policy?

DF: Well I guess we're all worried about climate change and I think we should all do our bit to reduce carbon emissions. We have just over 100 employees, all of whom have a PC. If we all reduce our energy consumption, we can make a difference. Not only will that cut CO_2 emissions but energy prices have gone up a lot recently and this would cut our electricity bills. I am sure that there are other things we can do to reduce our carbon footprint. I know that some computers use more energy than others so I was looking for advice.

Me: Do you have any environmental policies at present, such as staff turning off computers and other appliances when not in use, or using recycled paper?

DF: No. And they're not very good at it! That is why I want a company-wide policy so that all my employees follow it and take the environment seriously. We need to raise awareness of environmental issues with staff. We all want a better quality of life for future generations.

Me: Do you want to have a procurement policy that means that when you buy any item, the environment is considered? For example, you might only buy recycled paper.

DF: I think that would be a good idea.

Me: So will you have procedures and codes of practice to ensure that these policies are followed by your employees?

DF: There is no point in having policies unless they are followed.

Me: And waste-minimisation is important to you?

DF: Absolutely.

Me: And do you want to measure your environmental performance?

DF: Oh yes. We want to know how well we are doing.

Me: And do you want performance targets, such as reducing energy use by 10 per cent year-on-year?

DF: Yes.

Me: Are you interested in social issues such as donating old PCs to the third world?

DF: Oh yes. It is important for us to be good neighbours. Our policies should be ethical at all times.

Me: Will you integrate environmental and social factors in your decision making?

DF: Yes.

Me: And will you regularly review the policy?

DF: Of course.

Me: Do you want your suppliers to adopt similar policies?

DF: Certainly.

Me: Well thank you. I will start to put some rough designs together and get back to you.

DF: Sure.

Me: Bye.

DF: Bye.

Activity 1

From the Makepeace interview transcript:

1. Write down **two** conclusions about the environmental performance of the company's staff.
2. List **eight** other things that David Fairbrother wants to achieve through having an environmental ICT policy.

Your report should include:

- transcripts of any interviews
- the results of a questionnaire (you do not need to hand in the questionnaire sheets; it is sufficient to hand in the combined results)
- any sample documents that you have collected
- the results of any observation of the system in action
- your conclusions drawn from your investigation
- a list of the client's requirements.

Example interview analysis

Analysis of an interview with the manager of the Gladstone Arms Hotel, Mrs Karen Anslow:

From the interview, I could clearly see the advantages and disadvantages of the current system. I have put the advantages and disadvantages into a table; it clearly shows that the disadvantages outweigh the advantages. This shows that a new system needs to be created in order to make the hotel booking system more efficient.

Advantages of the current system	Disadvantages of the current system
The system is easy to use. Little staff training is required.	Bookings aren't backed up so they could get lost, damaged or into the wrong hands. Staff have to enter data over again when the same customer comes back. This wastes time. Entering data repeatedly could lead to errors in the system and dissatisfied customers. Writing down data is slow and inefficient. It's harder to find information that is stored in two places (the hotel and the restaurant). Double-bookings have occurred.

Example client requirements

Booking system for the Gladstone Arms Hotel:

1. Book meeting rooms
2. Book tables in the restaurant
3. Book hotel rooms
4. Prevent double-booking of rooms or tables
5. Keep a record of all bookings
6. Store names and addresses of customers
7. Search for customers
8. Provide a list of all rooms or tables free on a specific day or evening
9. Easily delete or cancel bookings
10. Easily edit bookings
11. Easy to use by someone who is not technical
12. 100 per cent accurate and reliable
13. User documentation appropriate to the skill levels of the staff

18

Analysis and deliverables

In this chapter, we look at how to analyse the client's requirements and outline what the proposed system will do. The analysis and deliverables section of your final report is worth up to 15 marks. It should comprise:

- a statement of scope – what is the system going to do and what constraints are there?
- a description of the proposed system
- documentation of processes – a full description of the process, such as making a booking
- a description of the users of the proposed system – who will use the new system? What skills do they have?
- evaluation criteria – criteria to evaluate the success of your system
- deliverables – what exactly will be provided to the client and when?
- evidence of checking the findings with the client – transcripts of interviews, emails, etc. as evidence of discussing the project with the client.

Statement of scope

The statement of scope of the proposed system will document what the system will do, what the system can't do and its constraints (internal or external), such as hardware and software constraints, data transfer and communication constraints, staffing and environmental constraints.

Example system scope

Environmental policy, Makepeace plc

The environmental policy that I shall produce is restricted to the use of ICT equipment at Makepeace plc.

It does not include items that are not related to ICT use, such as heating or transport. It only covers the company Makepeace plc, although Makepeace would like their suppliers to have similar policies.

Possible constraints on the policy include:

■ New hardware is being produced all the time. The policy must be flexible enough to cater for new hardware being developed.
■ The policy must include guidelines on the purchase and upgrading of equipment and how this will be monitored.
■ Makepeace plc must always follow legal restrictions such as on the disposal of electronic equipment.
■ Employees of the company may not follow the guidelines. Spot checks, codes of conduct and sanctions for not following the guidelines may be necessary.

Description of proposed system ◀

You should describe the proposed system, including the benefits and likely impacts on the organisation.

Documentation of processes ◀

What processes does the system support? What exactly happens in these processes? What inputs and outputs are involved? The box shows a sample process for the Gladstone Arms Hotel. Of course, there would be many processes involved in the system.

Example process

Gladstone Arms Hotel: Booking a table at the restaurant:

1. When someone phones to book a table at the restaurant, they will be asked for the date, time, the number of people and any special dietary requirements. These details will be input into the computer using a special on-screen form.
2. The day of the week will appear on the screen automatically. This is a great help in ensuring that staff don't get the date wrong, as they can say, "That's a Thursday". If the customer was interested in say a Friday, it is clear that a mistake has been made and the correct date can be entered.

3. Details of all the bookings at the restaurant on that date will appear on the screen. The user can then see if a table is free. Normally if a table is booked in the evening, it cannot be booked again that evening unless the reservation is very early or very late.

4. If a table is free, the booking form reappears. The customer is asked for their name and phone number, which are entered onto the booking form and stored in the database.

5. If a table is not available, the customer is informed and asked if another date might be suitable.

Description of the users of the proposed system

Include details of all the users of the proposed system and their roles within the organisation.

Document their ICT skills as this will affect the design of the system.

Evaluation criteria

Evaluation criteria are designed to help evaluate objectively whether the new system is successful or not. They are usually presented as a list of questions to ask about the new system.

Evaluation criteria should be derived from the requirements of the client. For example, if one of the client's needs was that there should be continually improving environmental targets, one evaluation criterion might be: are there targets for continually improving environmental performance?

You must include both qualitative and quantitative evaluation criteria. Tests should be linked to the evaluation criteria – see the test plan in Chapter 19.

► Quantitative criteria

Quantitative criteria are based on a quantity – often a numerical value. The result is entirely objective.

- Does the document print in less than five seconds?
- Is there a start-up screen?
- Will it work on my PC?
- Is it 100 per cent accurate?
- Is there different user documentation to reflect the different skill levels of the users?
- Does the on-screen plan of the restaurant show every table?
- Can you select a table or room with a pointing device such as a mouse?

- Are rooms that are booked shown in a different colour?
- Are there targets for continually improving environmental performance?
- Will the policy be reviewed annually?

The last four criteria above must have an answer that is either yes or no, but they are objective.

▶ Qualitative criteria

Qualitative criteria are based on a quality. They are subjective, i.e. one person's view is not necessarily the same as someone else's. For example:

- Is it easy to book a table?
- Are the input screens clear?
- Is the booking of rooms intuitive?
- Is the text clear and free of jargon?
- Is it easy to cancel a booked room or change to another date?
- Are the policies ethical?

The criteria above must have an answer that is either yes or no, but are subjective.

Example evaluation criteria

Environmental ICT policy, Makepeace plc.

1. Does the policy set out how to reduce CO_2 emissions?
2. By how much will the policy reduce electricity bills and the carbon footprint?
3. Does the policy include an environmental procurement policy?
4. Does the policy include procedures and codes of practice to ensure policies are followed?
5. Does the policy include steps to minimise waste?
6. Does the policy describe how environmental performance will be monitored?
7. Are there targets in the policy for continually improving environmental performance?
8. Does the policy explain how old equipment should be disposed of?
9. Are the policies ethical?
10. Does the policy include having environmental and social factors integrated in decision making?
11. Will the policy be reviewed annually?
12. Is the wording of the policy clear and free of jargon?
13. Is the wording of the policy easy to understand?
14. Does the policy include steps for employees to follow to reduce their carbon footprint?
15. Is the policy in a format that can be easily displayed and read at the company offices?

Deliverables ◄

What is to be produced and handed over to the client? Will it be a prototype system, a partial system or the complete system? When will it be finished by? The database must be in an agreed form. Will there be a technical manual? In what format will the user manual be and what will it contain? What documentation will be included?

Professional developers producing a system for a client would normally agree a contract with the client stating exactly what the deliverables are.

Evidence of checking the findings with the client ◄

Your client may make changes in their requirements at this stage, for example because they forgot something earlier. They might disagree with some of your findings. You may need to make some amendments. It is vital that your analysis is checked with the client and you must provide evidence of this taking place. It could be in the form of transcripts of interviews, emails, etc.

Activity

1. Which of the criteria in the sample evaluation criteria above are qualitative criteria?
2. Which of the criteria in the sample evaluation criteria above are quantitative criteria?
3. Identify **five** deliverables for the booking system at the Gladstone Arms Hotel.

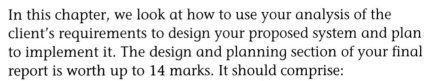

Design and planning for implementation

AQA Unit 4 Section 3

In this chapter, we look at how to use your analysis of the client's requirements to design your proposed system and plan to implement it. The design and planning section of your final report is worth up to 14 marks. It should comprise:

- evidence of investigating alternative solutions
- draft design work
- final design work
- plans for implementation, testing and installation, including proposed time scales
- training requirements for the new system
- the testing strategy
- a test plan.

Evidence of investigating alternative design solutions

You should describe possible alternative solutions.

For a software solution project, you should consider different applications packages and possibly different software types.

For a report project, you will need to consider the best way of presenting the project to the audience.

Each possible solution should be evaluated objectively against the client needs. You should justify your chosen solution.

Example alternative software solutions

There are many possible solutions that need to be considered when creating a new system for the Gladstone Arms Hotel.

Below I have highlighted the common software that could be used and for each I have given the advantages and disadvantages of using it.

HTML solution

The system could be web-based. Orders could be made over the Internet and, because technology is always improving and more people have the Internet, the Gladstone Arms Hotel can reach a wide market.

The advantages of using a web solution are:

- It reaches a wider market as more people have access to the Internet.
- The web pages could be designed to look exactly like the current system and so be easy to use.
- The web pages could be linked to a database system which stores the booking details.

The disadvantages of using a web design are:

- A lot of knowledge and complicated technological functions are needed to create web pages and link them to a database.
- Codes are used for colour schemes, etc. and so you would need to know different codes in order to make the system more efficient.
- It may be difficult to reach the Gladstone Arms Hotel's intended market as having the system only on the Internet means that they may limit customers.
- With a web page, the Gladstone Arms Hotel staff don't need to communicate with their customers.

Microsoft Excel solution

Excel is a commonly used spreadsheet program that is part of the Microsoft Office package. Booking details could be stored in a spreadsheet.

The advantages of using Microsoft Excel are:

- It is simple to use.
- Many of the users will have used it before and won't need a lot of training to know how to use the system.
- Microsoft Excel uses a common interface so it makes it easier for users to use the software.
- Macros could be used to make the system easier to operate.
- The software comes as standard with Microsoft Office.

The disadvantages of using Microsoft Excel are:

- Data is not saved automatically so data needs to be saved regularly.
- The software has not been designed to be used for storing data but more for carrying out calculations.
- Dialogue boxes to enter data would need to be individually designed, which would be time-consuming as there is no wizard to perform this operation.
- Search functions are more complex than if using a database solution.

Paper solution

A paper solution is still worth considering. The Gladstone Arms Hotel's current system is working, although it does not have a search facility.

The advantages of using a paper solution are:

- The system is easy to use; there is no need for a computer, so everyone can use it.
- It is cheap; there is no need to purchase equipment or software.
- There is no need to train staff as they are already using the system.
- It is reliable – it won't break down.

The disadvantages of using a paper solution are:

- It uses more staff so it is not efficient.
- It can lead to human errors occurring – data cannot be checked automatically as it is entered.
- Paper solutions can take up a lot of physical space.
- There is no backup system.
- There is no real search facility.
- The system can get lost if the diaries are moved from their normal location for any reason.

Relational database management system (RDBMS) solution

A relational database is designed to store data efficiently. Two examples of RDBMS software are evaluated over the page.

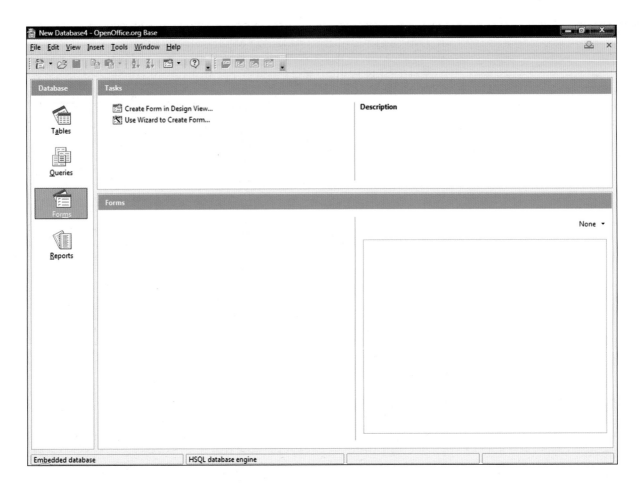

Figure 19.1 OpenOffice.org Base

OpenOffice.org base

OpenOffice.org Base is an open-source program that can be downloaded for free from the Internet (see http://www.openoffice.org). Just because it is free, doesn't mean it is no good. It is widely used and, as relational database software, it avoids redundant (repeated) and inconsistent data.

The advantages of using OpenOffice.org Base are:

- It is free. It can be downloaded and used by any business free of charge.
- It is simple to use.
- It is compatible with most other business software.

The disadvantages of using OpenOffice.org Base are:

- It can be very slow in benchmark tests with other similar software.
- Some people think that the user interface is not intuitive.
- There are not nearly as many users as for Microsoft Access.
- There are not as many support materials as for Microsoft Access.

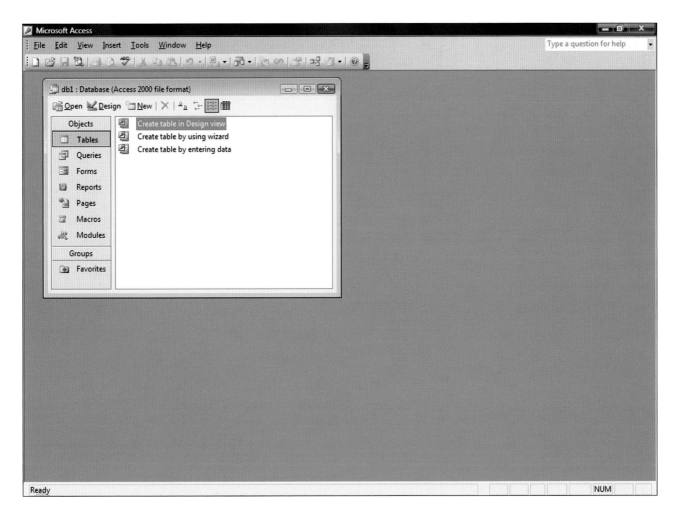

Figure 19.2 Microsoft Access

Microsoft Access

Microsoft Access is also relational database software and so avoids redundant (repeated) and inconsistent data. It is part of the Microsoft Office suite and so is the most widely used database software.

The advantages of using Microsoft Access are:

- It is used worldwide with millions of users.
- It has a common user interface so is easy to understand.
- It is fast and reliable.
- Searching is easy.
- It is simple software to use and can make any system efficient.
- It is designed to be used alongside software such as Microsoft Excel and Microsoft Word.
- There are excellent wizards to help in setting up tables, queries, forms and reports.
- Visual Basic programming can be used to enhance the RDBMS.

- The software is fully customisable, so forms and reports can be made to look like the forms and reports in the current system.
- There are lots of support materials: books, manuals, websites, discussion forums, etc.

The disadvantages of using Microsoft Access are:

- It is not easy to use the software and it is not always intuitive.
- The software is not free, unlike OpenOffice.org Base.
- Versions of Microsoft Access are not compatible with later versions. If the client has an older version of Access, they might not be able to use the system.

Conclusion

The possible solutions that I have analysed all have advantages and disadvantages. The HTML solution is similar to the database system as it has similar features. However, I would need to know a lot of HTML in order to produce a system. This would take a lot of time and so an HTML solution wouldn't be the best solution.

OpenOffice.org Base is free, so this is a huge advantage as no initial costs go into making the system and so will benefit the Gladstone Arms Hotel. However, the disadvantages outweigh the advantages. Compatibility could be an issue and the lack of interface and poor performance could adversely affect the efficiency of the system.

Microsoft Excel comes as standard with the Microsoft Office package and many people know how to use the software. This makes it so much easier for staff to get to know the system. However, Microsoft Excel has problems with redundant data and inconsistent data which would not help the Gladstone Arms Hotel.

An improved paper system could benefit the Gladstone Arms Hotel, as it would be easy to set up and use. However, it takes up a lot of physical space that the Gladstone Arms Hotel can ill afford. Some human errors have occurred in the system and although it is possible to check the day of the week in the diary to prevent errors, it is not as good as getting a response from the computer. There is also no backup and data loss could occur.

Therefore, the relational database system seems to be the best possible solution. It has features that allow relationships to take place between different tables and data to link the whole system together, so avoiding redundant and inconsistent data. Search facilities are excellent, so it is easy to search for tonight's reservations. This is only one advantage of using a relational database as the proposed system for the Gladstone Arms Hotel. I have looked at two relational databases, Microsoft Access and OpenOffice.org Base.

Reasons for chosen solution

I have chosen Microsoft Access as the software to use. The reasons for choosing a relational database system are that the system can link different tables together and make relationships between data, which avoids redundant data and inconsistent data.

I have chosen Microsoft Access as the software to use because it is very well used. There are lots of books, manuals and training course in Access. It has been thoroughly tried and tested and so is unlikely to have errors. It comes as standard with many versions of Microsoft Office and so can be easily accessible.

The software is fully customisable to suit the client. Therefore, this software is the best suited to the Gladstone Arms Hotel.

Draft design work ◀

These are the first designs that you will show to your client for their comments and approval. The nature of the designs will depend on your project, but they should be clear and detailed enough for somebody else to implement.

Although at this stage designs are rough, they should not be scruffy. Use a pencil and ruler. Make sure that any writing is clear. Use colour if appropriate.

▶ Database designs

Designs for a relational database would include:

- a data dictionary containing the names of tables, primary keys, names of fields in each table and field types, e.g. text, numeric, date/time, etc.
- relationships between tables in an entity–relationship diagram (see Figure 19.3)
- rough designs of forms and reports
- designs for queries and macros
- designs for a switchboard.

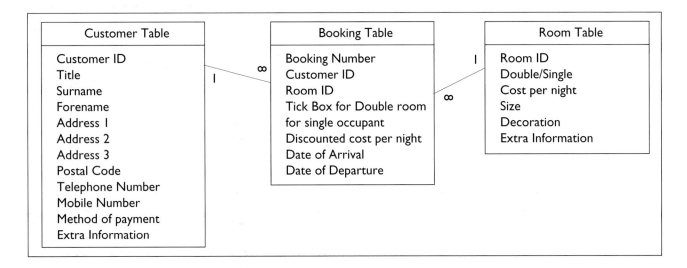

Customer Table	Booking Table	Room Table
Customer ID	Booking Number	Room ID
Title	Customer ID	Double/Single
Surname	Room ID	Cost per night
Forename	Tick Box for Double room	Size
Address 1	for single occupant	Decoration
Address 2	Discounted cost per night	Extra Information
Address 3	Date of Arrival	
Postal Code	Date of Departure	
Telephone Number		
Mobile Number		
Method of payment		
Extra Information		

Figure 19.3 Entity–relationship diagram

▶ Animations

Designs for an animation would include:

- storyboards
- screen designs
- timings
- colour schemes.

► Web pages

Designs for web pages would include:

- page designs
- hyperlinks
- images
- interactivity.

► Spreadsheets

Designs for a spreadsheet would include:

- sheet designs
- functions and formulas to be used
- colour schemes.

► ICT report

Designs for an ICT report would include:

- titles of sections of the report
- contents of each section.

Final design work ◄

The draft designs must be shown to the client for comments, suggestions, etc. You must provide evidence of client feedback, which you will then use to correct and improve your designs.

Your final designs should be annotated to show changes made to the draft designs. Final designs should be shown to the client for them to "sign off", i.e. agree.

Plans for implementation, testing and installation ◄

You must break the work down into small sub-tasks and then produce an implementation timetable for all the tasks that includes proposed timescales. It is a good idea to break the whole project down into weekly stages so that you can easily monitor progress. This is not possible if tasks are so large that they take several weeks.

Example implementation plan

Gladstone Arms Hotel

Task	Time needed	Deadline
Create a table to store Customer details.	One day to enter data	02/02/2010
Create a table to store Room details.	30 minutes	09/02/2010
Create a table to store Bookings.	30 minutes	09/02/2010
Set up a relationship between the Room table and the Booking table using the Room ID.	10 minutes	09/02/2010
Set up a relationship between the Customer table and the Booking table using the Customer ID.	10 minutes	09/02/2010
Create a form to add new customer, edit customer records and delete old customers. Call this Customer Form.	1 hour	09/02/2010
Create macros to move around the records, print and go back to main menu.	2 hours	16/02/2010
Create a form to add new rooms and edit room details. Call this Room Form.	1 hour	16/02/2010
Create macros to move around the records, print and go back to main menu.	2 hours	23/02/2010
Create a form to produce bookings and cancel bookings, call it Booking Form.	1 hour	23/02/2010
Create macros to move around the records, print and go back to main menu.	2 hours	02/03/2010
Set up a query to search for booked rooms.	1 hour	02/03/2010
…		
Installation of new system at the hotel	1 week	06/04/2010
Training of hotel staff	2 days	13/04/2010
…		

Training requirements for the new system ◀

What training will be required for the new system? Training should be included in the implementation timetable plan as it is essential that users are trained ready for the introduction of the new system. How will training be delivered? One-to-one? To all the users at the same time? Who will deliver the training?

Testing strategy ◀

It is vital that your solution is thoroughly tested before it is used. The testing strategy defines what needs to be tested. It is likely that the test strategy will involve:

- using known test data to check that the actual results are the same as the expected results
- checking that all the evaluation criteria have been met

- checking that all the client needs have been met
- using erroneous and extreme data to provoke failure
- getting users to carry out a walk-through test, that is to use the solution from beginning to end to check that it works as expected.

Test plan ◀

The test plan normally:

- is set out in a table
- has a column of numbered tests
- includes the purpose of the test
- includes test data, such as date of arrival = 8 March 2010
- includes the expected answer, such as 3 nights or £270
- includes a blank column where the actual answers will be entered once the test has been carried out
- includes tests that client needs have been met
- includes tests that evaluation criteria have been satisfied.

The test plan should concentrate on testing complete processes and the system as a whole. For example, the excerpt from a test plan below tests a complete process – the calculation of the amount on the bill, including number of nights and any discount. Real test data is used to check that the outcome is as expected.

Example test plan: process

Gladstone Arms Hotel

Test	Purpose	Test Data	Expected Outcome	Actual Outcome
To test the bill calculation.	To ensure that the calculation of the bill is correct.	Date of arrival: 8 March 2010. Date of departure: 11 March 2010 Room 9.	The stay is for 3 nights. 3 nights @ £82 per night = £246.	
To test the bill calculation.	To ensure that the calculation of the bill is correct.	Date of arrival: 8 March 2010. Date of departure: 3 April 2010 Room 11. Double room single occupant.	This stay is 26 nights. Normally £115 per night. 20 per cent discount = £23 per night. Price per night = £115 – £23 = £92. 26 nights @ £92 per night = £2392.	

The second excerpt from a test plan tests the solution as a whole, looking at what is included and whether it meets the needs of the client. The test plan is linked with the evaluation criteria described in Chapter 18.

▼

Example test plan: system

Makepeace plc

Test	Purpose	Test Data	Expected Outcome	Actual Outcome
Does the policy include measurement of environmental performance?	Client requirement Evaluation criterion #6.	Check policy for environmental performance information.	Environmental performance information included.	
Does the policy lead to reduced electricity bills and a reduced carbon footprint?	Client requirement Evaluation criterion #2.	Compare old bills with recent bills over a period of time.	Reduced electricity bills.	
Is the wording of the policy easy to understand?	Client requirement Evaluation criterion #13.	Show policy to five members of staff and ask them if there are any parts that are not clear.	Some unclear parts may be recognised. (Policy may need changing in line with comments.)	
Will the policy be regularly reviewed?	Client requirement Evaluation criterion #11.	Check policy for next review date.	Next review date is at the end of the year.	
...				

Evidence of isolated unit tests that don't test a complete process or system is not required.

20

Testing and documentation of the implementation

AQA Unit 4 Section 4

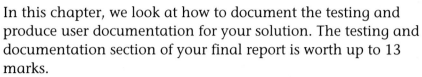

In this chapter, we look at how to document the testing and produce user documentation for your solution. The testing and documentation section of your final report is worth up to 13 marks.

You will need to include screenshots and other output from your solution, to show exactly how you have implemented your solution.

You do not need to produce:

- a step-by-step guide to how you implemented the solution
- instructions on how to set up the solution
- a guide to any software you have used.

The testing and documentation section of your report should comprise:

- evidence of testing
- evidence of client or end-user testing
- comprehensive documentation of the solution.

Evidence of testing

◄

Your testing should follow your test plan (see Chapter 19). Testing should test that the user requirements (Chapter 17) and the qualitative and quantitative evaluation criteria (Chapter 18) have been met.

For every item in the test plan, you should give the result of your test with evidence. The evidence would normally be a screenshot but it may be a witness statement – a statement signed by your teacher or your client to say that something has worked or not. For example, you could get your client to test a particular part of the system, record the results and compare them with the expected results.

Example test evidence

Gladstone Arms Hotel

This test tests several components of the solution:

- the number of nights calculation
- the cost per night for a particular room look-up
- the discount calculation.

It also tests the complete process of working out the bill. Client requirement #12 was 100 per cent accuracy. Tests must test individual parts of the solution but the tests should also test the whole system – in this case the total cost is accurate.

Test	Purpose	Test Data	Expected Outcome	Actual Outcome
To test the bill calculation.	To ensure that the calculation of the bill is correct.	Date of arrival: 8 March 2010. Date of departure: 3 April 2010 Room 11. Double room single occupant.	This stay is 26 nights. Normally £115 per night. 20 per cent discount = £23 per night. Price per night = £115 – £23 =£92. 26 nights @ £92 per night = £2392.	The cost was £2392 as shown in Figure 20.1.

Figure 20.1 Booking form

Evidence of client and user testing ◀

The client and the users should be involved in the testing process and you should provide evidence of this. For example, you should give a user some tasks to complete using the system, such as:

- taking a booking
- registering a new customer
- printing today's bookings in the restaurant
- seeing if room 11 is booked for next Saturday.

Include screenshots and any printouts. If you have evidence, such as any user comments whether handwritten or in emails or letters or photographs of the client testing the system, you should include them.

User documentation ◀

Your user documentation should include whatever has been agreed to be included with the client (see Deliverables in Chapter 18). This could be one or more of:

- installation instructions
- maintenance instructions
- a full user guide
- "getting started" notes for people who don't want to read a full manual.

The user guide should contain everything that a user of the solution would need to know, including:

- how to start the system
- start-up screens, buttons and menus
- error messages
- how to enter data
- what outputs are available (e.g. on-screen or printed) and how to obtain each of these.

It should also contain examples of:

- data entry forms
- output screens
- printed outputs.

Different users may need different user documentation. We know that the skill levels of staff at the Gladstone Arms Hotel vary from highly literate to no experience at all. It may be necessary to produce more than one version of the user guide.

Documentation for ICT novices should avoid using jargon. It should be clear and well-illustrated.

Technical documentation ◀

Your technical documentation should explain everything that a technical expert would need to know to maintain or develop the solution, including:

- specification of required hardware, software and other resources
- any programming or HTML coding used
- original designs
- details of any calculations, formulae, animations and functions used
- details of any verification and validation procedures.

21

Evaluation of the implemented solution

AQA Unit 4 Section 5 ◀

In this chapter, we look at how you should evaluate your solution. The evaluation section of your final report is worth up to 7 marks. In particular, we are looking at:

- Have you met the original needs of the client?
- How well have you done it?

Your evaluation must be logical and based on evidence, such as:

- the original client needs drawn up (see Chapter 17)
- the evaluation criteria created (see Chapter 18)
- the testing (see Chapter 20).

Evaluation against the client's needs and evaluation criteria ◀

You should list the original client's needs and for each one state whether or not the need has been met. You must include evidence and you will probably want to include some screenshots.

You should list the original evaluation criteria and for each one state whether or not the need has been met. Again you must include evidence and you will probably want to include some screenshots.

Example evaluation

Environmental ICT policy, Makepeace plc

Evaluation criterion	Has it been met and why?
Are there targets in the policy for continually improving environmental performance?	Yes. Targets have been set for the next three years. 10 per cent reduction in one year. 15 per cent in two years, 20 per cent in three years (see page 6).
Does the policy explain how old equipment should be disposed of?	Yes. Disposal of old equipment must follow the WEEE directive. This is explained in the policy (see page 7).
Are the policies ethical?	I believe the policies are ethical. The company will try to be sustainable in everything it does.
Does the policy include having environmental and social factors integrated in decision making?	All major decisions of the company board will be based on a report covering environmental and social factors.
Will the policy be reviewed annually?	The policy will be reviewed every year in January (see page 11).
...	

You should also include:

- strengths and weaknesses of your solution
- ease of use – is it intuitive?
- possible improvements to your solution
- comments from your client.

Example evaluation

Gladstone Arms Hotel

Strengths

- Karen wanted a system that reduced human error. When the user enters details for a new customer, the system has appropriate validation that allows the user only to enter sensible data, thus reducing errors.
- The final system avoids duplicate information. By allowing the user to store information, such as customer's details, the user doesn't need to re-enter details. This saves time and is more efficient.
- As the system automatically calculates the total cost of bookings, this makes it easier for the user as well as making sure it is accurate.
- The system looks professional. The reports are designed to look professional but also to match the diaries in the old system.
- The system that I created has more features to help the user, for example the "Rooms Booked" report shows all the rooms that are booked.

Weaknesses

- The new system does display some weakness. In the analysis, Karen wanted to have passwords to make sure that data is secure. However, I have not added this to the system.
- Another problem with the system is that it doesn't eliminate the problem of double booking as I have not prevented overlapping appointments, i.e. you can book Room 6 from 1st March to the 8th March and also book the same room from 6th March till 12th March.
- Although it is possible to search by room or by date, I have not added a search by surname facility as this was not required by Karen.
- Another limitation is the build-up of old data. As the system is used more and more, the amount of data increases. I have not created an archive file to store old data. This means that, in time, the system will run more slowly.

Client Comments

After viewing the system I wanted to see what Karen Anslow's overall comments were and whether she would be willing to use the system for the Gladstone Arms Hotel. Below are her comments:

Overall the system has exceeded my expectations. The fact that the system can store information such as customer details means that duplicating is reduced and so this saves time. Also, I'm impressed with the reports. In the current system, the bookings can only be used for taking orders, however in this system the bookings are used to show reports such as the history of the customer, and to tell my staff which customers are arriving on what date. I think this is really clever, as the system is using information to help make the Gladstone Arms more efficient and also it is easier to make decisions.

However, my main concern is that if I did use this system, there is still a chance that double booking could occur. As I have said in previous comments having double booking in the system could lead to dissatisfied customers and a loss of business. If I were to change to a new system, I would want this problem to be eliminated.

Future Development

By looking at the strengths and weaknesses of the system as well as looking at Karen's comments about not introducing this system unless some of the limitations have been developed, it shows that future development needs to be taken into account if this system is to be used in the Gladstone Arms Hotel.

- Having passwords in the system would be necessary to secure data.
- A future development needs to find a solution to prevent double booking occurring in the system, therefore meeting Karen's requirements.
- There is nowhere in the system that the user can search for a surname. I would like to add this feature.

Developing these three areas in the system could lead to Karen reviewing whether the system is suitable and therefore could mean that the system would be used by the Gladstone Arms.

Evaluation of your own performance

You should also include an evaluation of your own performance in creating a solution for your client. In particular you should look at:

- strengths and weaknesses in the approach you have taken to your work
- how you could improve your performance on similar work in the future.

Examples of areas that you may wish to consider for strengths and weaknesses are:

- Time planning – were the times allowed achievable?
- Timekeeping – have you stuck to your deadlines? Did you leave too much to the last minute?
- Knowledge of the software (where appropriate) – have you a good working knowledge of the software or did you have to keep referring back to manuals which can waste time?
- Quality of written English, e.g. in the documentation. Is it easy to read, concise and complete?
- Contact with your client – have you regularly contacted your client for feedback?

22 The project report

AQA Unit 4 Section 6

In this chapter, we look at what you have to hand in. The structure and presentation of your final report is worth up to seven marks.

You will hand in a word-processed report that comprises all the following sections:

- Background and investigation (see Chapter 17)
- Analysis and deliverables (see Chapter 18)
- Design and planning for implementation (see Chapter 19)
- Testing and documentation of implementation (see Chapter 20)
- Evaluation of the implemented solution (see Chapter 21).

Up to seven marks are awarded for the quality of written communication, such as use of language and word-processing features and inclusion of images. Your report should:

- be well-structured – that is, in a logical order with all sections having clear titles
- be produced to a professional standard making good use of word-processing features such as headers or footers, spelling and grammar checks, page breaks
- include numbered pages
- include your name, candidate number, centre name and centre number in the page footer of each page
- be written using suitable language (including technical terms where appropriate, such as form, report, archive, switchboard, macro, etc.)
- be illustrated appropriately with screenshots evidencing your work
- be firmly attached, for example, using treasury tags
- include a Candidate Record Form (CRF) signed by you to confirm that the work submitted is your own and giving details of any sources that you have used to help you, such as this textbook.

You will not lose marks for stating sources but if you use any sources without crediting them, this may be considered malpractice. It is a good idea to include a bibliography noting websites, magazines and books used.

Example bibliography

Environment Agency. *Waste electrical and electronic equipment (WEEE)* *http://www.environment-agency.gov.uk/business/topics/waste/32084.aspx*.

Personal Computer World, *http://www.pcw.co.uk/*.

Rendell and Mott (2008). *Database Projects in Access,* Edition 3. Hodder Education.

Index